IMAGES AND IDEAS IN LITERATURE OF THE ENGLISH RENAISSANCE

Images and Ideas in Literature of the English Renaissance

Patrick Grant

The University of Massachusetts Press

© Patrick Grant 1979

Published in the United States of America by
THE UNIVERSITY OF MASSACHUSETTS PRESS
Amherst, Massachusetts

First published 1979 by
THE MACMILLAN PRESS LTD
London and Basingstoke
Associated companies in Delhi
Dublin Hong Kong Johannesburg Lagos
Melbourne New York Singapore Tokyo

Typeset in Great Britain by
SANTYPE INTERNATIONAL LTD, SALISBURY
and printed in Great Britain by
UNWIN BROTHERS LIMITED
The Gresham Press
Old Woking, Surrey

Library of Congress Cataloging in Publication Data

Grant, Patrick
　Images and ideas in literature of the English
Renaissance.
　Includes bibliographical references and index.
　1. English literature—Early modern, 1500–1700—
History and criticism.
　I. Title
PR431.G67　　821'.008'015　　78–53176

ISBN 0–87023–163–4

To Laurence Lerner

Contents

List of Plates

Preface

During the early Renaissance in England, poets like Spenser 'believed in' their images. They established by second nature a correspondence between the meaning of images and the material substance of things they depicted. Such correspondences grew out of an Augustinian tradition in which the continuity of matter, image and transcendent Idea was assumed, and in which the images of rhetoric were a means of directing us through everyday experience to contemplation of eternal truth.

With the rise of science, and especially during the seventeenth century, the widespread acceptance of a quantitative view of matter caused a crisis for this older theory by encouraging a conflict between the traditional view of corporeal nature and a Cartesian, deistic observation of the world of objects. One consequence was that the new philosophy opened a breach between mental images and the divine Ideas which, traditionally, God had used as a blueprint in creating the world.

Whether or not they knew the philosophers in detail, poets of the period dwelt in a world of linguistic discourse profoundly in process of change, and throughout the seventeenth century, literary men as never before came to suspect the usefulness of images for depicting the true nature of the material world. As early as Shakespeare in *The Tempest* the old habits were subject to a contrary movement, and Milton and the later Metaphysicals show a direct response to the challenge offered to poets wishing to serve traditional piety in an intellectual environment increasingly bent on abandoning Augustine for Locke.

My attempt to discuss the eclipse of a mediaeval, poetic vision of things by the disintegration of matter from symbol to atom depends to some extent on a clear distinction between the argument about ideas and literary history. I therefore make the case independently that during the seventeenth century a mediaeval view of images did yield to that of the empiricists. My authors then are examples of some ways in which literature took up the challenge posed by such a development. But in each case I felt also that I had something to say which would be of service to the poetry and of interest to a specialist in the subject. My suggestions on *Muiopotmos* and the *effectus passionis* for Book I of Spenser's *Faerie Queene*, the iconography of *caritas* for *The Tempest*, the influence of the French Capucins on Crashaw, the structural relationship of time to temptation in *Paradise Regained*, and the effects of the Oratorians on John Norris are, I believe, new. I have tried thus to have the practice of criticism complement the analysis of ideas by adopting methods appropriate to the nature of my material in the particular cases. The reader who wishes to test further how the rise of materialism affected the course of literary history, must attend to a wider range of examples. The present study may be of some assistance in the task.

I would especially like to acknowledge the help of Charles Doyle, Laurence Lerner, and Tony Nuttall, who read the manuscript and made invaluable suggestions for improvement. The Canada Council provided a research grant for the summer of 1974, and a leave fellowship which enabled me to complete the book while on sabbatical in 1975–6. Permission to reproduce materials printed earlier have been received from *The University of Toronto Quarterly* for my article 'Time and Temptation in Paradise Regained', XLIII, 1 (Fall, 1973), 32–47, and from *Review of English Studies*, for 'The Magic of Charity: a Background of Prospero', N.S. XVII, 2 (March, 1976), 1–16. Permissions to reproduce the plates have been received from the following: The Archiwum Archidiecezjalne, Poland, for a woodcut, dated 1558. The Basilica di San Petronio, Bologna, for Giovanni Modena's Fresco. The Art Institute of Chicago for a wood panel 'The Crucifixion'. The British Museum for BM Arundel

44, ff. 28v, 29r, Kings 7, ff. 45r, 54r, Royal 2A xviii, f. 5v, F. Gafurius, *Practica Musice* (1496), K1, G3. The Scuola Dalmata Dei SS. Giorgio E Trifone, Venice, for Vittore Carpaccio, 'St. George Slaying the Dragon'. The Galleria Borghese, Rome, for Titian, 'Sacred and Profane Love'. The Galleria Palatina, Florence, for Giovanni Rost, 'The Vindication of Innocence'.

April 1978

PATRICK GRANT

1 The Matter of Roots: Belief, Images, and Bodies

Some of the oldest, most basic concerns of poetry and theology have to do with impermanence among things and nostalgia for beauty that endures. 'Nostalgia' itself derives from two Greek words, *nostos* (return home) and *algos* (pain); it indicates home-sickness, a kind of melancholia caused by prolonged absence from where one belongs. It is a central theme of the second Homeric epic, and although the staying-power of a work like the *Odyssey* resists simple explanation, one of the book's most enduring effects is an extraordinary and powerful evocation of the hero's separation from what he loves, and his longing to return home. Odysseus' persistence towards a goal, even through his weaknesses and dallying, gives value to the strength of the intuition that draws him back.

The same theme underlies Genesis 3, but the story of Adam and Eve has a different emphasis. Genesis gives us first a glimpse of paradise, an affirmation of the order and harmony of nature as God intended it, before showing us our ejected first parents. The story contrasts what we are now in our death-ridden selves with what we really are in our full natures, could we be restored to our true habitat, paradise, where there is no suffering, and where beauty endures. By showing us what Odysseus suffers among impermanent things to get there, the *Odyssey* thus evokes the meaning of home. Genesis 3 does it by showing us a quality of beauty we have lost, and although the exclusion-pain of Genesis is in a way the opposite of the return-pain of the *Odyssey*, both produce in the reader or listener the same feeling, nostalgia.

Whether or not the authors themselves could have thought of these two stories in anything like such abstract terms is a vexed question. On the one hand, the actual feelings of an author can only be guessed at, often remotely if at all from autobiographical evidence or similar kinds of testimony. On the other, the images (by which I mean not the actual *phantasmata* in his mind, but the appeal in his art to sense experience to convey his meaning)[1] continue powerfully to elicit our recognition that the person who made this story or thing did basically feel like us, even if his ideas were quite different from ours. Thus, although the author of Genesis 3 did not think in the conceptual or metaphysical terms of a doctrine of Original Sin,[2] it is much less certain that he was not stung by a pang of remorse and a sense of loss, when he considered the elements of his story, rather like those experienced by large numbers of his readers through history to the present time. Despite his lack of an abstract vocabulary, the images he has chosen still seem to express for us something of how it was to be human in the conditions under which he lived.

The poles of abstract theory and personal emotion which I am suggesting here interact in complex ways, and are separable only in imagination. But it is easy to conceive how significant alterations to the theory could reflect sharply in images which embody it, and that the images may be in turn barometers for the kinds of pressures imposed by the theory on complex emotions. Certainly, in the course of modern European civilisation there has been no more radical alteration to prevailing theory than occurred during the Renaissance and Reformation period; and, in particular, a profound re-estimation of the meaning and constitution of the physical world itself precipitated changes which were to alter the entire external structure of society as well as cause a crisis in religious faith. During this period the poets in a variety of ways sought images to embody the new ideas, and the Renaissance transformation of the material world became also a powerful concern of literature. Yet those poets who did respond to the challenge continued to bear witness that despite the vast re-organisations men still lived in a world where impermanence was a painful fact and intuitions of enduring beauty had not given over their hauntings. Patiently questioned, their images can provide some insight into the problems involved in reconciling the material world of a new science to the old matter of religious faith: a new empirical atomism to the spirituality which Christians had traditionally affirmed as the ground of their best intuitions and highest values, and for which, in the seventeenth century, the poets still held themselves spokesmen.

Clearly, we must be wary of passing in such a manner too simply from intellectual history to literature, and I am concerned in this study to do two different, or at least two distinguishable, things. First, to describe a certain development of the matter-of-Odysseus and the matter-of-Genesis into a theory of images generally accepted during the Middle Ages, then taking a radical change of direction in the seventeenth century. Second, to show that the work of some seventeenth-century poets was affected by this development, and to suggest that their writings could offer educative insight for sensibilities bound on the hazardous enterprise of re-channelling old emotions into the moulds of new ideas, brilliantly designed but often uncertainly calculated to receive them. My approach to the poetry of seventeenth-century England therefore takes as its starting point some formative thoughts from the earlier times, and to these I now turn.

AUGUSTINE AND THE MEDIAEVAL THEORY

The most influential of early Christian writers striving to provide a coherent foundation of ideas for a young and fast-growing Western Church was especially absorbed by the facts of mutability and the lure of the absolute. The formulations he offered to relate these facts of experience to his Christian faith remained enormously important for moulding the sensibility of the makers of images in the Christian civilisation which followed him. Though St Augustine of Hippo worked with a limited technical vocabulary, especially for describing large concepts such as God and the nature of matter,[3] he managed to be highly suggestive on these questions precisely because he was also something of a poet who combined the central motif of the *Odyssey* (which he knew through the *Aeneid*)[4] and the paradisal theme of Genesis 3. The *Confessions*, his central and best-known book, is the story of a soul wandering, Odysseus-like, in time, and seeking its only home, the lost Eden (now, in Augustine, an immutable world of Platonic Forms) wherein after death and the trials of mutability it may be restored to enduring bliss. The themes of impermanence and lasting beauty thus become means for Augustine of exploring the important theological difference between God the transcendent object of faith, and an imperfect material world with which the Christian writer has to deal as somehow manifesting the divine source.

Augustine's main distinction is that God alone is not mutable ('He truly Is, because He is unchangeable'),[5] while the created spirit of man does suffer change, being subject to time:[6] 'their heart fluttereth between the motions of things past and to come, and is still unstable' until 'the whole is present'.[7] Because man also has a body, he must undergo physical or spatial change to some degree as well, and his restlessness on both counts is painful because it is a condition of fallenness. Yet, although 'severed amid times'[8] man may, by a flash of intuition, 'awhile catch the glory of that ever-fixed Eternity',[9] and such poignant recollection by contrast with his present state causes both joy and pain.

Augustine warns us, however, that the fallen time of human experience 'cannot be compared'[10] with the higher realm of eternity, and to explain how we can intuit a timeless reality at all from our time-bound perspective, he adapts the Platonist hypothesis that our capacity to make judgements implies an intelligible realm of absolute standards which somehow actively inform our particular evaluations. On the general principle he is quite straightforward:

> For my present purpose, it is sufficient that Plato held the following theories: that there are two worlds—an intelligible world in which the truth itself resides, and this sensible world which it is manifest that we perceive by sight and touch.[11]

The complexity with which this blunt avowal is developed is as significant as the assertion of principle itself, for Platonism has rarely been persuasive when reduced flatly to propositions, and the best book for illustrating Augustine's capacity to embody precept in moving image remains the *Confessions*. There he deploys the Platonists' abstract vocabulary to describe his philosophic principles, but joins it also to a Pauline sense of lived experience true to the perplexities of human nature seeking permanence in a kaleidoscopic shifting of space and time. Our experience of pain ('I know not whence I came into this dying life [shall I call it?] or living death'),[12] and of longing ('groaning *with groanings unutterable*, in my wayfaring, and remembering Jerusalem, with heart lifted up towards it, Jerusalem my country, Jerusalem my mother'),[13] is exploited throughout, while a carefully gauged dramatic voice contrives to present such basic human concerns in light of a theory which contains but does not oversimplify the reader's own involvement. Nothing is more important to Augustine's technique or more fundamental to the way in which he thinks about the relationship between God and the material world than the process of leading the reader through shifting images which evoke restlessness and yearning, and towards the apprehension of a transcendent Truth which the author believes these images cryptically manifest.

The *Confessions* begins with a series of seemingly random and unconnected recollections of Augustine's infancy and boyhood. Of his very earliest years he can remember nothing, but reconstructs them from observation of other infants, noting that selfish greed and envy afflict even babies (I, vii, 11). He tells of his boyhood and early schooling at Thagaste and the neighbouring town of Madauros, and how he found sinful delight in 'vain shows' (I, xvii, 30), how he thieved food out of pure greed from the cellar of his parents' house, and how he lorded it over his companions through vanity and 'by vain desire of pre-eminence' (I, xvii, 30). When he turned sixteen, 'the madness of lust . . . took the rule over me' (II, ii, 3) and he fell into bad ways with girls. Then, the event everyone remembers, he recalls robbing an orchard of pears and flinging the unripe fruit to hogs (II, iv, 9). The story continues by recounting Augustine's wanderings as a student and teacher through the Middle East and Italy, telling of his eventual conversion and reconciliation with his mother before her death at Ostia, and ending with Book IX. Book X then provides a treatise on memory, which develops into an extended examination by the author of his own conscience under the threefold heading of '*the lust of the flesh, the lust of the eyes, and the ambition of the world*' (X, xxx, 41). Books XI and XII are an elaborate examination of the first chapter of Genesis and contain an equally elaborate meditation on the nature of time. Book XIII, the last, contains a further examination of Genesis and develops into a prophetic statement on the church in the world.

On first reading it is difficult to see how the opening personal recollections fit with the concluding books. There are a number of ingenious theories,[14] but the main point seems to be closely connected to Augustine's constant awareness of writing after the event. His details are carefully selected as much to demonstrate a total view of man in history as to provide the nuts and bolts of an actual autobiography. The significance of those early recollections is intended, for instance, not to become clear until Book X, when Augustine examines his conscience in terms of the three cardinal sins of lust, curiosity, and pride, which, he tells us elsewhere, 'comprise all sins'.[15] In light of this we see, in retrospect, the pattern implicit in the gluttony of little babies, the vain shows of the adolescent, and the pride of the schoolboy, which exemplify the three main types of sin. Unbeknown to himself, and partly obscured from the reader, Augustine's early life had really been an exemplar of human error and sinfulness, a fact which we discover only from the vantage point of the clearer vision, subsequent to conversion, in Book X. The theft of pears, which to some readers has seemed disproportionately emphasised, now warrants that emphasis because this sin, if properly understood, represents the mystery of iniquity in general, thus encompassing the other three types of transgression: it is the archetype of all sin, a theft of fruit from a garden.

Augustine's aim has been twofold: first to convince us that God's guiding hand was there from the beginning; second, to recreate the problems as he encountered them so that they also will be problems or puzzles for us, the readers, and we will be drawn into the work, and Augustine's pilgrimage in a sense will become our pilgrimage too. The very first words of the *Confessions* are therefore a prayer which puts God definitely at the centre: '*Great art thou, O Lord, and greatly to be praised; great is Thy power, and Thy wisdom infinite*' (I, i, 1). But God is described soon after in terms which show that the presence Augustine praises is a paradoxical one: 'most merciful, yet most just; most hidden, yet most present; most beautiful, yet most strong; stable, yet incomprehensible; unchangeable, yet all-changing' (I, iv, 4). We are both assured and baffled as we share the author's knowledge that God is present, yet also the point of view of the sinner who did not at all see God's presence in the events as they occurred in time. God is the transcendent object of the author's devotion and prayer; an elusively immanent principle *now* in all his words as an author, as well as having been, *then*, present (though ignored) in Augustine's actions as a young man.

Only to the regenerate mind does this paradox of immanence and transcendence become increasingly meaningful, and the long examination of memory in Book X acts as a preface to Augustine's threefold examination of conscience because through memory the meaning of time is best discovered. In light of the importance Augustine thus gives to memory, it becomes increasingly clear that the overall structure of the *Confessions* itself is intended to correspond to the divisions of time. Time past is dealt with in Books I–IX, the memory of Augustine's past life. The present is the subject of Book X, with its present examination of conscience. The final books, which are concerned with the history of the church, and which stress Augustine's intuitions of eternity and the promise of rest, are most concerned with the future. The story is not only of one man, but of all men who have fallen into 'changeableness of times' (XII, x, 13) and seek a return to the immutable joy they have forfeited with their loss of Eden.

The reader, like the author, therefore comes to discover himself not free from suffering and intellectual blindness consequent on the fall. But clear knowledge is hard-won, and Augustine is fond of comparing the condition of human existence in time to the process of a spoken sentence, meaningful only in the silence which fulfills it and in light of which it becomes retrospectively complete. He is, moreover, ready to identify such syntactical process with ontological structure, for the meaning of creation he believes is also revealed through Logos, the Word made incarnate in time, and, like the divine immanence of God, needing to be recognised in the creation and through the deeds and words of men. For the angels, problems of recognition do not exist, because angels are in eternity. They gaze directly on God and therefore have no need 'by reading to know of Thy Word': they '*always behold* Thy *face*, and there read without any syllables in time, what willeth Thy eternal will; they read, they choose, they love' (XIII, xv, 18). With us it is different. Although we may guess the end of a sentence through the incompleted pattern of words, the meaning is not fully revealed to us during the time taken to speak. Because of our incapacity to grasp the sense fully while we dwell in its unfolding we must endure in faith that meaning at last will come clear. Faith, therefore, like words in a sentence, seeks completion, and is fulfilled in the immutable vision of God.[16]

Augustine does not give to the word 'faith' a univocal sense,[17] and his favourite appeal to Isaias 7:9, *nisi credideritis, non intelligitis* ('unless you will have believed, you will not understand') serves his multivalent theory particularly well. He takes the verse to mean in general that we live in a world where 'we must very earnestly consider the force of time and place' and where faith is necessary to knowledge 'because we cannot see the whole with which the part harmonises'.[18] But this can be interpreted in two senses: first that under the conditions of space and time we have to make prior commitments[19] that something can be learned, and when we discover what it is, our faith has found completion in understanding. Thus faith is necessary for man in an everyday secular sense in order just to get along in the world. But Augustine nowhere allows this wider and proleptic interpretation to usurp the second, more important, sense that faith is directed at an unrepresentable God. Accordingly we might expect to chart different qualities of faith according to our different degrees or kinds of knowledge, and Augustine proposes something of the sort in his important distinction between *sapientia* and *scientia*. The first describes the mind illuminated by Ideas; the second, a workaday knowledge necessary to action in the world. The higher knowledge Augustine also equates with 'intellectual vision' to distinguish it from the 'spiritual' and 'corporeal' visions which he associates with *scientia*.[20] Intellectual vision at its most sublime is imageless as well as silent[21]—a mysterious and unmediated splendour of Form in which we cannot rest during our earthly lives, though Augustine claims we may experience it briefly in exceptional circumstances.[22] It belongs in eternity, to which in this world we address ourselves primarily in faith. Yet intellectual vision is implied in all the contents of *scientia*, and is necessary if we are to make sense of the lower realms where our knowledge is imperfect and mixed.[23]

On the lowest, corporeal, level Augustine claims simply an interaction between the body and the object from which the mind then creates an image representing the object, and commits it to memory.[24] But because human thought responds immediately to the perception of bodies by this formation and collation of "spiritual" images, corporeal vision is never experienced by itself, without some intellectual component.[25] Presumably the fact that Augustine never seemed to doubt the existence of bodies encouraged him to posit corporeal vision on logical grounds, though it seems we cannot ever verify it in experience.[26] But the main point is that spiritual vision involves a mixture of mutability (derived from the corporeal) and immutability (derived from the intellectual), and the hallmark of spiritual vision is the image.[27] Thus the meaning of images, like that of a man's life in time and history or the unfolding words of a sentence, becomes clear by reference to the imageless source of intelligibility, the final object of faith. It follows that images are subject to the same imperfection as man in time, and must be accepted in the same trust that the pattern of their meaning will be revealed in light of the vision they signify. On the one hand the object of faith is therefore transcendent and imageless (intellectual vision), but on the other the eternal species of temporal things is really if imperfectly represented by the images in our minds (spiritual vision). From this point Augustine is free to stress how rich may be the analogies between our images and transcendent Ideas. The free range of the analogy-making faculty is therefore encouraged because we can discover by this uniquely human means (animals and angels do not have 'spiritual vision') something of how spirit moves in the world of bodies.

IMAGES AND RHETORIC

The images under discussion so far have been mainly those in the mind and not in literature. Yet the literary practice of the *Confessions* vindicates Augustine's epistemology, and the enduring human emotions to which we respond in the autobiography find expression in images which offer us also an explanation of man's place in nature. The point is clear from a reading of *De doctrina Christiana*, which combines Augustine's theory of images in the mind with his theory of rhetoric. The *De doctrina* first of all states clearly that images both in the mind and in literature are a function of man's spiritual interpretation of corporeal nature by which the physical objects of the world become signs of God's purpose and creative power.[28] The human mind does not so much invent signs and images as discover their significance. The creation is itself a divine poem and we are part of its imagery and rhythm as it moves towards completness of meaning;[29] so the poet may assist God's crafts-manship by disposing his own images to help the reader pene-trate to some extent the truth of things. The poem therefore makes no pretence to autonomous existence, but extends itself into the reader's life for completion, so that 'his way of living may be, as it were, an eloquent speech'.[30] Again Augustine assumes real likenesses between the forms of material nature, the image-ideas of the artist, and the principles by which God shapes his creation. Our discovery of such likenesses in literature, however, must be laboured after, and by the light of *De doctrina* we can see that Augustine's obscure use of images in the *Confes-sions* serves a carefully calculated theological purpose, for poetry we learn is obscure (as parts of scripture are obscure) to remind us of our darkened reason[31] and thus stimulate us to work out the significant meanings for ourselves.[32]

From such a theory the techniques of mediaeval allegory and mythography develop quite naturally, for the sentence beneath the fable, the kernel within the husk, the exemplum under the enigma, have a psychological justification in the pleasure of discovery[33] as Augustine describes it, and a theologi-cal justification in the belief that temporal obscurity is illu-minated by the light of eternal value. Allegory, on this model, is not simply the depiction of a preconceived set of abstractions by a parallel set of images. It is a mimesis of the way in which images participate in the mysterious and imageless fullness of intellectual vision.

Boccaccio, whose *Genealogy of the Pagan Gods* became for the late Middle Ages and Renaissance a veritable handbook of allegorical convention on the Augustinian model, is clear about how the actual expression and pagan colour of the old stories are really obscure manifestations of the Christian mysteries in which poets believe, as Augustine says. Boccaccio argues that poetry (and here he includes mythology) 'proceeds from the bosom of God',[34] and encloses 'the high mysteries of things divine'.[35] He talks of Moses' 'poetic longing'[36] and claims that the myths of the gentile poets share in a garbled and impure fashion the original secrets imparted on Sinai. He confirms

Aristotle's precept that the first poets were theologians,[37] and sees the original meaning of poetry as inspired song which 'streamed forth',[38] revealing God's wisdom to the souls of his prophets.

In collapsing together the inspiration of prophets and poets, Boccaccio clearly continues to approach the rhetoric of scripture in the manner outlined in *De doctrina*: the words of the Bible, like those of the orators, are signs to bring us to God. In both cases the signs are accepted in faith and interpreted by allegorical exegesis which refers them to the higher mystery. Allegory, according to this theory, is peculiarly a poetry of faith, depending for completion on the evidence of things not seen but disclosed to the illuminated reader. It could be defined as an attempt to see faithfully through images, and as rhetoric its effect depends on believing that these images can penetrate to some extent the true constitution of reality.[39]

So far we have been examining mainly the connection upwards, in Augustine's theory, towards intellectual vision. We should now look briefly at the connection downwards towards the corporeal, and again Augustine's desire to combine Plato and St Paul can help us to understand the principal design of his thought.

In St Paul, first of all, the injunction to discover the invisible things of God by things that are made (Romans 1:20), and the sense of 'revelation of the mystery which was kept secret since the world began' (Romans 6:25–6), already duplicate something of Plato's hypothesis on Ideas as exemplars. But Augustine's emphasis on faith as a precondition of understanding is essentially Pauline, and at the dramatic centre of the *Confessions* Augustine's conversion entails his reading of Romans in a spirit of child-like acceptance and simplicity.[40] Again following Biblical example, Augustine does not assume, like Plato, a superior or arrogant attitude to things of creation, either to the corporeal world or the images which it partly engenders. 'It would be ridiculous', he writes, to condemn the defects of 'beasts, trees, and other mutable and mortal creatures', for all 'are good simply because they exist'.[41] Still, in his exegesis of the Biblical story of creation, Augustine can resort enthusiastically to the Platonist theory which describes the natural world as a distinctly inferior copy of the Ideas (Plato's Forms) in God's mind.[42] The world is structured in a three-tiered hierarchy with God

at the top, the human soul in the middle, and the world
of bodies at the bottom.[43] Just as God is immutable, so the
world of bodies is subject to continual change, being, on the
Platonic model, the farthest removed thing in creation from
the divine source. Like the author of the *Timaeus*, Augustine
is forced to a kind of 'spurious reasoning'[44] as imagination
attempts to approach the original corporeal stuff of the universe
which exists on the very verge of identifiable reality. 'So that
when thought seeketh what the sense may conceive under this
. . . it may endeavour either to know it, by being ignorant
of it; or to be ignorant, by knowing it.'[45] Augustine engages
in a good deal of such verbal juggling to show that basic
matter has less identity than words can say. In his own attempts
to grasp it, he tells us, he eventually stopped questioning his
imaginative 'spirit' altogether, 'it being filled with the images
of formed bodies'.[46] The formless matter created from nothing[47]
by God's act is, he concludes, itself 'almost nothing'[48]—a fluid,
mutable, invisible and unorganised realm which can scarcely
even be said to exist. In it the image of God can be but
faintly traced by a difficult exercise of reductive imagination.

The interest Augustine demonstrates here in the elusive relationship between images and matter shows, as I have said,
his usual desire to preserve both Biblical conviction and Platonist
theory, and one result is that matter, being good, becomes
primarily useful in explaining the formation of images. It is
then easy to see how the knowledge of material things, according
to this theory, should be used to elucidate signs, just as signs,
properly interpreted, lead towards the vision of eternal realities.
Though Augustine does not use the language of causality in
the Aristotelian sense,[49] God, as the end of all growth and
development, the end of all signs, words and images, and as
the final cause of creation, is identical with the Reality before
which images, like faith, will pass away. But equally, as a
condition of the earthly pilgrimage, we must believe that the
signs of spiritual vision point towards enduring beauty through
the material impermanence which likewise plays a significant
part in our phantasms. The formation of images, according
to Augustine, is thus closely allied to a theory of matter as
fluid and impermanent. Indeed, a commitment to images on
the Augustinian model seems to entail a theory in which matter
has relatively little identity or reality, for the fact that matter

is indeterminate and fluid until it receives form from above
guarantees the continuity between material substance and mental image which Augustine everywhere assumes. If the images
of spiritual vision really represent the 'ideas' in objects, the
human mind can then truly refer the meaning of the lower
creation, in praise, to God. One consequence of such a view
is that a proper understanding of the material world inevitably
turns the gaze of the beholder heavenwards in contemplation,
and not towards the object as an end worthy of detailed examination in itself.

Throughout the Middle Ages, the principles of Christian
humanism, whether in Biblical exegesis, education, literary practice, or devotional discipline, owe a great deal to this Augustinian
theory. Even the influence of Aristotle in the thirteenth century,
however much more empirical, did not radically change the
Augustinian principles on images,[50] belief, and bodies, because
on the essential questions Aristotle remains much closer to Plato
than is often supposed.[51] Accordingly, St Thomas Aquinas can
remain the chief representative of Aristotle in the thirteenth
century without departing radically from Augustine's kind of
Platonism; as a recent critic concludes, St Thomas 'agrees
with the basic Augustinian theory of signs on all the important
points'.[52]

Admittedly, there are real differences in spirit between Aristotle and Plato which should not be disregarded. It is conventional
to notice that Plato is interested in being and Aristotle in
becoming, and that in consequence Aristotle is sceptical about
Plato's world of Ideas. By writing in the *Metaphysics* that forms
are immanent in individuals instead of transcendent, Aristotle
seems, moreover, by a stroke of genius to dispense altogether
with the unwieldy apparatus of Plato's duplicate higher world.[53]
The subject of philosophical enquiry, says Aristotle, is what
exists, 'that which is primarily',[54] namely substance. A hard-
boiled respect for plain bodies ('this here thing')[55] characterises
his entire philosophical procedure. Yet in the *Metaphysics*, particularly chapter Z, the extended analysis of substance becomes
difficult, for although Aristotle is concerned with particular
things he also tries to retain the basic Platonist insight that
we have real knowledge of intelligible structures. In the *Categories*
(5, 2a, 11–16) Aristotle had distinguished 'primary substance'
(the thing-in-itself) from 'secondary substance' (the abstracted

essence in the mind), and even though he abandons this classification in the *Metaphysics* it still denotes his main intuition that substance is somehow the thing-in-itself, and yet can be known.[56] Thus in the *Ethics*, which for a good part expresses the point of view of a common-sense observer of human behaviour, Aristotle ends by reverting to the contemplation of transcendent divine splendour as the real condition of human happiness, and as an ultimate foundation of order in the world.[57] Consistently he assumes that form is more real than matter, which is a mere passive capacity, a pure potentiality brought into act by the influence of form.[58] Aristotle pursues this distinction towards a first and most real principle of pure activity, an informing energy, not admittedly conceived as a Platonic Idea, but which he calls nonetheless, in language suspiciously Platonic, the Thought of Thought.[59] So, despite the differences between them, Aristotle remains at one with his mentor Plato in suggesting that the ideas of things are abstracted by the mind which truly apprehends essences. His empiricism is a good deal less radical than it may at first appear.

True, by developing one side of Aristotle's theory it is possible to arrive at a highly naturalistic and determinist philosophy and to reach conclusions which orthodox believers imbued with Augustinian premises might deem dangerous. Thus Averroes was condemned for deducing from Aristotle that men shared a common soul,[60] and Pomponazzi for arguing that philosophy could not prove the soul's immortality.[61] St Bonaventure's hardy attempt to show that the world must have had a beginning originates in Aquinas's demonstration on Aristotelian grounds that it is impossible to arrive at such a conclusion by natural reason.[62] Bonaventure, working in the direct line of Augustinian tradition, sought to confirm that the highest function of human reason is to demonstrate that truths known to the faith-illumined intellect are necessary; the most threatening thing about Aquinas's embracement of Aristotle was the very division it encouraged between the processes of natural reason and knowledge that comes by faith. Aristotle, says Bonaventure, made the basic error by criticising Plato's Ideas, and from this have sprung all the other faults which have led inevitably to a tyrannic and fatalist philosophy.[63] Yet, as we have seen, Aristotle does not reject Plato's ideas as clearly as Bonaventure seems to think, and neither does Aquinas.

For St Thomas the creation remains hierarchically structured with God the *fons et origo* forming the lower natures according to divine Ideas,[64] and matter, as in Aristotle, is indeterminate and unimaginable by the human mind. It is a mere potency determinable by form which confers identity and intelligibility upon it.[65] Between God and the realm of bodies is therefore a hierarchy of substances and causes which reach through corporeal, vegetable, animal, human, and angelic forms towards the creator on whom all depends.[66] Aquinas shares with his favourite Augustine the basic sense of a fluid, impermanent realm of matter and of the divine Ideas as exemplars of the created world. Here the two men belong to a universe of discourse more fully divorced from the empirical nominalism which was to follow them than they are from each other. As Gilson says, although Aquinas's' adaptation of Aristotle imparts an existential cast to his theory of knowledge, Thomistic realism remains 'heir of everything sound in the Greek realist philosophies'.[67] For Aquinas, just as for Augustine, 'if a physics of bodies exists, it is because there exists first a mystical theology of the divine life'.[68] Admittedly, Aquinas does allow a good deal less to human knowledge than Augustine who claims that in this life we can sometimes have the imageless experience of intellectual vision. For Aquinas, the mind must rather infer the forms indirectly from the effects of sensible bodies[69] and be content with only a 'tiny . . . connatural' light which is 'enough for our knowing',[70] but which leaves us with an arduous responsibility of building certain knowledge by slow degrees. By insisting on the imperfection of our minds, Aquinas underlines and does not at all diminish the Augustinian precept that our knowledge must be founded on faith which will pass away only when final happiness is enjoyed in the vision of God.[71]

As a result of such similarities, and despite the different emphases, Aquinas's theory of art and beauty is not conceptually far removed, either, from the basic teaching of the *De doctrina* on signs as representations of mysteries. Art, Aquinas explains, is a human act which brings to us a sense of the hidden beauty of form which we never apprehend directly.[72] In the beautiful object we apprehend something of Beauty itself, which shines out from the ordered matter which the artist has arranged according to his conception and in terms of his images (25). The artifact, like every form, 'participates' in the divine splendour (31), and like every fair imitation, it mediates something of the real Beauty of God, even though such partial beauties are evanescent, for they can give no perfect joy (36). Yet the theoretical closeness of this to Augustine might seem serviceable only to shout aloud the real differences in practice between the *Confessions* and the *Summa Theologica*. The *Summa* indeed may seem doggedly bent on confirming that there is but little joy in the processes of human learning, and the laborious precisions appear unfortunately far removed from the passionate self-expression of Augustine's autobiography.

Curiously, however, the *Summa* does constitute a vindication of Augustinian rhetoric. The famous five proofs for the existence of God, for example, appear on a single page[73] and may at first seem disappointing, unengaging, even simple-minded. Respect for what they entail, and for the mind which has affirmed them so directly, grows only by slow degrees as the vast complexities and unerring refinements of the larger argument develop, and as the simple assertions accrue to themselves an enormous rhetorical power from the sheer weight and intricacy of the edifice of language and insight in which they are engrafted. We may not be persuaded by the five proofs any more than by Augustine's blunt avowal of the Platonist precepts, but we may be persuaded by the *Summa* which itself becomes a vast symbol of the human mind reaching towards God through the multiplicity of the world's images.[74] When Aquinas said, near his death, that it all seemed to him as straw,[75] he was not merely voicing a disappointed admission that his life's work was a waste. Like Augustine, he knew that the images pass before the mystery, and to confirm this truth at the end was simply to confirm what he knew all along about the relationship between language and the vision of God. The experience again is that of a man who believes in his images so that they may be absorbed, like his faith, in the silence of vision. Aquinas may not have had a great deal of influence on the literature of his times,[76] but I am suggesting that he *is* literature of a sort that his times would understand in terms of Augustinian thought. Theology, as Petrarch later observed, is really a kind of poetry about God,[77] and by assuming a conformity between material substance and Idea mediated by the analogy-making of the imagination, Aquinas like Augustine concludes that language, whatever the mode of discourse, should be a vehicle for revealing God's purposes to man. The force of the preposition 'in', therefore, as part of my phrase that Aquinas like Augustine 'believes *in* his images', is to describe such a sense of the speaker's direct participation in the meaning of things. In such a theory (and in the experience it partly expresses and partly engenders) the question has not yet seriously arisen whether or not the images are a special interpretation of material substance: if this were the case, they could of course no longer stand *prima facie* as evidence of a God-ordained design in the world of bodies, and in consequence the latitude granted to a free-ranging imagination would be a great deal checked and curtailed.

NEW EXPLANATIONS

The widespread attack on the Scholastic systems during the Renaissance involved not only a discussion about the conventions of language but a repudiation of a whole way of looking at and thinking about the world.[78] As we have seen, for Augustine and Aquinas, images are signs to be clarified in the light of intellectual vision and such a view of the world suggests that salvation is an ascent through the mutability of time to the enduring beauty of eternity. But the theories of Descartes and Bacon and Locke alike excluded the possibility of a higher reality being mediated so readily by images as Augustine and Aquinas had thought. The new men were basically antisacramental, and they denied the usefulness of final causality for advancing human knowledge.[79] Descartes' attitude, and technique, are typical. He first piously draws attention to God's transcendence and so to His incomprehensible nature ('Knowing already that my nature is extremely weak and limited, while the nature of God is, on the contrary, immeasurable, incomprehensible, and infinite') and then draws a perfunctory conclusion: 'this is enough by itself to show that what are called final causes are of no use at all in Natural Philosophy'.[80] The consequences of refocussing the mediaeval view to the one represented here are momentous for explaining the place and function of images in human knowledge; and in this context the intense debate on iconoclasm during the Renaissance and Reformation is especially significant. It highlights the main lines of attack on the sacramental view of images in a world increasingly coming to accept a Cartesian theory of matter and the concomitant belief that images do not mediate higher realities as the old theory had assumed. In denouncing idolatry and arguing for severe verisimilitude, the iconclasts not surprisingly courted also a highly literalistic view of images, and the results for art were extremely complex.[81] But by insisting on the non-divine or natural quality of our mental representations of things they were also helping to prepare the way for a scientific view of nature as a realm of extended substance, and in this new view matter was to have a reality more firm, definite, and measurable, even if a good deal less enchanted, than mediaeval man had imagined. Thomas Hobbes is an important example of the new thinking. Though his trenchant argument was often more than his contemporaries could comfortably assimilate,[82] his stamp remains upon them all.

The scorn Hobbes heaped on his scholastic forebears is matched only by the power of his demonstration that their substances and essences and quiddities were the inventions of deranged imaginations, 'there being nothing in the world universal but names'.[83] More seriously, he claims, such abstract mental projections as forms and substances are dangerous because they so easily become the means for a corrupt priestcraft to claim authority based on mediating, through these unreal universals, between time and eternity.[84] Looking to his admired Galileo,[85] Hobbes argues instead that the structure of matter is atomic, adding that the ideas and images and thoughts with which the human mind is blessed are explainable in terms of the motions of corporeal bodies. Consequently, if universals are always in the end images and images always corporeal (the residual impressions of '*decaying sense*', as Hobbes says),[86] there can be no independent reality for essences or universals as we conceive them. This is true even for our idea of God, which is just a name for the conclusion we reach when thinking about the first cause: 'by the visible things in this world, and their admirable order, a man may conceive there is a cause of them, which men call God; and yet not have an idea, or image of him in his mind.'[87]

On these grounds Hobbes advises Christian sovereigns to break down images which their subjects have been accustomed to worship.[88] Since an image is merely 'the resemblance of something visible' it follows 'that there can be, no image of a thing infinite' (648), and to worship God as somehow 'inanimating' (652) the finite matter of such representations is idolatrous. Hobbes points out that our use of Scriptural images is not sinful unless we take them as mediators of some real higher nature (658). There is, in short, no means by which corporeally determined mental configurations can ontologically shadow forth transcendent reality. Nor does Hobbes even allow an eternity in the scholastic (and Augustinian) definition of *nunc stans* wherein time as we know it may be annihilated and in which, traditionally, the mystery resided. Instead, he describes eternity as an infinitely prolonged time.[89] Thus, if our images cannot mediate real universals, and if there is no eternal realm distinct from this world, the Church with its sacraments must appear the device of power-hungry or deluded clerics. Instead, says Hobbes, we must look to salvation, not vertically, but horizontally in a future time, the millennium which will take place under material conditions not substantially different from those we experience in our lives now.[90]

After reading Hobbes it becomes clear that the real enemy of Plato is not so much Aristotle as Democritus, who identified the material world with reality and allowed to the atoms, as the basic components of material nature, the attributes of true substance and motion which can account for the evolution of form. In antiquity the Democritean premises were adopted by the Epicureans, and especially at the hands of Lucretius were used, in a proto-Hobbesian fashion, to dispense with the transcendental machinery of Gods and spirits which, Lucretius argued, were responsible merely for a good deal of human misery and provided a ready tool for the manipulation of the masses by alert politicians.[91] Although Lucretius did preserve a place in his philosophy for the Gods, it stressed their indifference, and especially during the Renaissance, Lucretius became synonymous in most men's minds with atheism. It is therefore striking that so many of the men of scientific genius during the sixteenth and seventeenth centuries should have reverted to some form of atomism, threatening as its implications seemed to orthodoxy,[92] as best adequate to promote their new investigations of the physical world. For Bacon, the system of Democritus seems plainly the best, and Gassendi straightforwardly championed Lucretius and the atomic theory in the name of the new physics as did Giordano Bruno, while Lorenzo Valla's *Dialogue on Pleasure* espoused Epicurus. Even Descartes, though he rejected a full-blown atomic theory (claiming that no matter how small an atom was, God could divide it) settled for something very like it.[93] He substituted corpuscles for atoms, and, positing God as the first mover, argued by way of the famous theory of vortices that the particular movement of bodies is due to the laws of impact and conduction. The theory extends eventually to Newton's and Boyle's picturably mechanical universe,[94] until at last De La Mettrie,[95] working from both Descartes and Newton, pronounced man himself to be a machine.

As I have described it so far, the difference between the old position and the new can reduce readily enough to a single point: *The new men were finding not likeness but discontinuity between images and substance.* Repeatedly, the scorn of Descartes, Bacon, and Hobbes for mediaeval philosophy is directed at the fact that there is no basis in objects for the 'essences' which the older thinkers imagined and then labelled with words and took to be real things. Yet the gradual and complex emergence of the new point of view is also important, for I am not suggesting that Lucretian atomism suddenly freed men somehow from belief in transcendent realities, or even that many paid lip-service to orthodoxy while secretly pursuing other courses. Indeed I am suggesting the opposite, for the impetus of 1,500 years of religious awareness and idealism does not suddenly evaporate, and by and large the men of the Renaissance sought ways to adapt the traditional teachings of Christianity to their new theories of the physical world and consequent new social and intellectual conditions. The result was a turmoil of partial and confused solutions, such as Descartes' notorious attempt to bridge the gap between the material and spiritual via the pineal gland and the animal spirits, or Malebranche's effort to reconcile Cartesian extension with St Augustine by the elaborate theories of occasionalism. In England, the Cambridge Platonist Henry More shows a typically uncertain attitude to the new method: at first, for More, Descartes seemed to save the reality of the spirit, but then seemed for all practical purposes only to yield the world entirely to the mechanists by relegating the spirit to a subjective realm, and More ended up accusing Descartes of sowing the seeds of atheism.[96] These kinds of solution of course no one could find happy, though they addressed an unavoidable problem, for scientists and spiritual writers alike did continue to believe by and large that their images *could* show forth the wisdom of an almighty Creator. Yet with the critical wedge now driven between image and object, the analogies suggested by imagination must be questioned carefully if they are truly to serve belief. For men of letters in the seventeenth century, whether poets or philosophers, some new principles of critical procedure had come to stay, and there could be no turning back. From being fluid, matter had become hard: the 'pure potentiality' and 'prime matter' of the scholastics which had guaranteed conformity between substance and Idea are now merely the butts of endless arrows of abuse as matter is assumed to be a real, definite, and eminently measurable thing. Further, the procedures of scientific investigation are now effectively divorced from the concept of final causality. So, if matter is real in itself and not a formless cryptic embryo existing on the edges of intelligibility, it does not require the 'spiritual vision' of St Augustine to invest it with significance, or the divine Ideas to endow it with meaning. Finally, it becomes impossible to explain the images themselves simply as Augustine had taught: the heart of the nominalist attack on Scholasticism is that words are conventional and do not indicate essential properties of things; we should therefore beware of the deceptive potential of images, especially those which deal with secondary qualities like colour and sound, which clearly cannot exist in the object in anything like the subjective manner in which we experience them. For Augustine, as we have seen, the study of bodies was useful to vivify the truths revealed to faith. For Locke, we must instead clarify our images in order to grasp the structure of objects. Thus, for Augustine the knowledge of things has served to clarify signs; for Locke the knowledge of signs serves to clarify things.

As St. Augustine's thought has represented for this discussion the main intellectual positions of the mediaeval period, so can Locke's stand for the new spirit of Enlightenment. But despite his gifts for exposition, Locke's thought is far from simple. The complexity arises because he wants to explain the new materialism clearly, but tries to be less uncompromising than Hobbes and to accommodate the best of traditional custom and religious convention. His attempt, however, in the name of common sense to have the best of both worlds leads to

problems and quandaries in Locke's theory, and these are typical
of many similar efforts by his contemporaries to relate images
to physical nature on the one hand while maintaining belief
in spiritual realities on the other.[97]

Locke begins by assuming the actuality of material substance,
which he then distinguishes from our mental representation
of it. Primary qualities such as solidity and figure, he argues,
have more reality in the object than, say, colour. Yet there
is no good account in Locke of why this should be so, and
it does not seem to have occurred to him that if secondary
qualities are subjective, so primary qualities may be also. Undaunted, Locke is content to postulate a real substance underlying the material world, even while conceding that we cannot
know it directly. 'Sensation convinces us that there are solid
extended substances', but the substance of body itself is 'unknown to us'[98] and we should not attempt to pry into it.
Here Locke leaves himself open to Bishop Berkeley's attack
charging that we cannot then be sure of any such underlying
substance at all. Yet the main point, despite this kind of logical
problem, is that Locke did manage to promote very successfully
his prevailing optimistic certainty that the world *is* constituted
basically of some definite thing subject to its own laws and
identity. At the same time he confirmed the important principle
of discontinuity between substance, image, and Idea. On the
one hand, final causes are not relevant to our empirical investigations of nature, and, on the other, material substance does
not conform simply to our images. Still, as a convinced Christian,
Locke believed in a transcendent God and contrived, in good
faith, to go on finding analogies like his mediaeval forebears
between the order of the universe and the wisdom of its creator.
But he could not do so by a theory uncritically maintaining
the principle of real likenesses. Instead, the aim of language
is to codify in a disciplined fashion the workings of a universe
that runs like clock, from which we may reasonably infer a
clockmaker God.[99] Like others who employed the clock analogy,
Locke used it as a way of reconciling his God to mechanistic
physics: in a world where final causality is unimportant, the
deity conveniently becomes the watchmaker himself—the
engineer who has wound the machine up before letting it go.

Locke's watchmaker remains the Christian God, but the shift
of emphasis from the crucified redeemer of the old devotional

poets to the new transcendent artifex of the eighteenth century[100] marks also an important shift in the interpretation of how images may relate to the objects of faith. From participating in the mystery through images (for example the cross) we now stand back to appreciate a divine ingenuity in objectively clear design. Not surprisingly, Locke has no love at all for the subjective impressionism of the fictive image, and persistently denounces the vanities of poetry as subversive of the clear and proper ends of human thought.[101] Certainly he does not 'believe in the images' in the old sense, though this does not mean either that he refuses to take them seriously.[102] Rather we might say that Locke believes his images will reveal most when they are most critically examined. The experience of discontinuity itself, paradoxically, now becomes the ground of piety by challenging the mind to discover, through it, God's purposes.

I have stressed that, although the empiricists found themselves making assumptions about material nature which engendered a theory of images in many ways incompatible with the one that had sustained their mediaeval ancestors, there is no clear break with the past. The poets especially may be expected to give evidence of this kind of continuity, for their witness is mainly to such complexities of human adjustment as go ignored in opposed theories: although John Milton was a man of his times, his central *topos* as a poet harks back to Genesis 3. The age-old nostalgia for paradise amidst our experience of impermanence remains for him among the most significant of human emotions. Still, philosophers as well as poets felt the importance of acknowledging an informing past, even if they often did so less directly, and the point is evident, once more, in Locke, whose curiously perplexed illusions of clarity can so often reveal the nature of problems his society faced at large. For example, at the last moment in his 'Letter Concerning Toleration', Locke almost inconsistently hangs back and refuses to allow atheists a place in his otherwise totally secular state.[103] He refuses, it seems, to cut the thread finally between the religious and secular, even though he had just been making a most eloquent case for the clear necessity of doing so. In terms of Locke's main argument, there is no reason why a well-run secular society should not be self-sustaining, and if it adopts an empirical, nominalist, and kinetic view of the world, there is no cause for it to be religious. A person who has no sense of the material world rooted in divine mystery is indeed an atheist, a pure kineticist, and there is no reason according to Locke why he should be anything else except on the evidence of a faith and dogmas which are, by definition, not the concern of the state. Yet Locke balks, giving the barely creditable reason that you cannot trust a man to keep his oath if he does not believe in God, and therefore you should not tolerate atheism. Plainly, something more weighty than this equivocation is at work to deflect the author from his logical conclusion, and perhaps we can find it in the obscure but real sense Locke had that man is profoundly a product of his cultural inheritance, of the 'custom' which Locke sees at different times as an impediment to clear thought and a guarantee of stability.

Certainly we may suggest that the importance of custom to social organisation does help to confirm that a man is in a sense all that he has been, in cultural as well as physiological terms. Religious passions and energies together with the images which express them do not go away simply because they are ignored.[104] The messianic hopes of Christianity—for instance the desire for a new Eden in a perfect world of Forms—do not cease to inspire because the world of Forms is discounted by new explanations of words and the material world. So, through modern history from the seventeenth century we watch the emergence of a purely secular kind of idealism which attempts to ignore the importance for secular affairs of traditional religious passions and energies. But, untrammelled by the restraining doctrine of Original Sin, the old messianic fervour of Christianity has more recently re-declared itself in the secular realm with unexpected violence. It is as if a wily and sceptical Odysseus had decided to go his own way after having kept company for so long with the first parents of Genesis 3. For the kind of civilisation fostered by Western Europeans, their alliance had been extremely important because the story of the Fall provided some explanation of why our experience of mutability and death is a fact of human nature. Such knowledge, institutionalised, served on a large scale to temper over-reaching desires for complete happiness now in the temporal conditions of human society. Locke's strictures against atheists, so barely explained by him, are perhaps based on some such intuition. Even though his development of the new ideas outran his sure sense of how the necessary continuities with the past could best be preserved, he remained sensitive, sometimes against the drift of his logic, that they should be.

In helping to educate such sensitivities, poetry especially comes into its own, and throughout the seventeenth century the question of how traditional values could remain the objects of faith, and at the same time be reconciled to the claims of materialism, presents for poetry a special challenge. I have attempted in this chapter to describe some aspects of this problem and to introduce some terms for further discussion. In doing so I have described a mediaeval, Augustinian experience of 'believing in' images, and I have taken 'belief' to imply a transcendent object, rather than in the more flexible sense as a kind of trust that enables us to acquire ordinary knowledge and regulate our everyday lives. All the thinkers with whom this book deals believe in transcendent Truth, and they also assume that material things exist and are instrumental to the process of thinking. Consequently, by 'image' I mean the mental representation of a material substance as well as the appeal made to such an experience in literature. Thus, as we have seen from Augustine and his mediaeval followers, a writer 'believes in his images' by presuming real likenesses between material substance (the form of the object), the image-idea (which the human mind configurates), and the Idea (the eternal species). Such a man is not concerned with whether or not his mind may be making an interpretation of the object and not abstracting the real form, and his writing mirrors his assumptions. For him, a qualitative theory of matter guarantees the kind of indwelling and continuity which constitutes his most important explanation of how the universe is meaningful. In literature, he thinks of himself as celebrating the world through real analogies which he apprehends and then expresses truly in his images.

For the writer who rejects the old theory, the image-idea in the mind no longer mediates so obviously between idea-in-the-object and Idea in God. The new man is aware instead of a discontinuity: the fact that his images do not entirely conform to things. He may wish still to find the analogies between physical and spiritual facts, and throughout the seventeenth century he certainly contrived to do so, though he does not now uncritically presume the likeness principles. Still, as an orthodox believer he trusts that his images if properly questioned and shaped will reveal the design of a transcendent God. But the way is through dislocation, for the uncritical participation assumed by 'in' is no longer possible. For the poet under such conditions the job is to explore how this dislocation can serve the ends of faith, but in face of an uneasy intuition, of which he apprises his readers while warning them against it, that discontinuity may develop merely into separation.

Clearly, not all the poets reacted equally to the challenge posed by such developments, and my authors, from the philosophically uncritical Spenser who wrote just before the beginning of the seventeenth century, to the highly critical John Norris who wrote at the end, provide examples of how some works of literature engaged problems posed about images by the new thinking about material nature. We can surmise, however, that to some extent such writings contributed also to that larger, changing climate of opinion which led gradually to the demise of the mediaeval vision of the world. But first, to Spenser, whose poetry records a tremor of the new movement, although his way of using images still stands solidly on the old theory.

2 The Arms of the Red Cross: Believing in the Images

MUIOPOTMOS

The Faerie Queene was published in two volumes, each of three books, in the years 1590 and 1596. It is well enough known that Spenser sought to win preferment at court by his poetry, and that his hopes were largely disappointed. If, as is likely, the strange and beautiful poem *Muiopotmos, or The Fate of the Butterfly* was written between the two volumes of Spenser's masterpiece, it may well reflect something of its author's disillusionment with poetry as a means of making a living.[1] The story tells of Clarion, the brilliant silver-winged butterfly who is 'Painted with thousand colours' (90) and spends his days among lavender and marigolds until he flies into the web of the spider Aragnoll and gets eaten—a fate which nicely suggests the poet attempting to make his way at court by flashing his colours but being devoured by those practised spiders, the politicians.[2] The poet's grudge seems most explicit when the ladies secretly envy 'the gorgeous Flie' (109) but are unwilling openly to acknowledge their delight in him or accept him as a member of their high society. Elsewhere, the significance of the butterfly as a symbol of art is also clear. I refer not only to Clarion's brilliant colours and nimble flights, but to the account of the genesis of Aragnoll the spider from Arachne, the maid who challenged Minerva to a weaving competition and, on losing it, turned into a spider for envy. An important detail, which Spenser did not derive from any of his sources, is that Minerva wins by embroidering a butterfly into her tapestry (329), and when Arachne sees the glory of Minerva's art crowned by these wonderful wings, she falls in defeat. In going out of his way to make the butterfly the distinguishing achievement of the tapestry, Spenser is telling us something about the relation between butterflies and art in the poem in general.

At this point I should mention the standard observation that the butterfly is usually a symbol for psyche. Spenser, though he would not have known the early Christian funerary art which concentrates on this meaning, still would have found it to hand in any lexicon (for instance the 1580 edition of Scapula)[3] and it is no strain to suggest that he knew the Greeks used the same word for 'soul' and 'butterfly'. By completing the equation it is easy to conclude that *Muiopotmos* is primarily about Clarion, the soul (Psyche), and Aragnoll the Satanic tempter who seeks to destroy it. But I introduce this suggestion really in order to modify it, for Spenser makes it quite clear that the butterfly is *not* Psyche. The first of all butterflies was Venus's maid, Astree, who was transformed because Cupid was attracted to her. Venus's reaction to the intrigue was stimulated by the memory of an earlier affair not unlike it:

Whereof the Goddesse gathering iealous feare,
Not yet vnmindfull, how not long agoe
Her sonne to *Psyche* secrete loue did beare,   (129—31)

Venus, in short, was once angered by Cupid's love for Psyche, and now to prevent his further infatuation with Astree, Venus turns her into a butterfly. Astree is *like* Psyche, but that is all. And so is Clarion, and so is the butterfly on Minerva's embroidery. And with all of them Spenser demonstrates a theory of art familiar to his contemporaries, and based on the Augustinian kind of epistemology examined in the first chapter, namely that it participates in and bodies forth the mysterious hidden energy of the soul (psyche) and represents it by clothing it in images but does not thereby disclose its innermost nature.[4]

Admittedly, the butterflies in *Muiopotmos* also fulfill the more obvious though still subtle organisational function of providing motivation for the antagonism between Aragnoll and Clarion: the spider remembers his mother's defeat by Minerva, and the butterfly is a symbol to him of his own hateful condition. But this only raises the further question—what has the spider who eats the butterfly to do with poetry, and what is indicated by their relationship, besides antagonism? It will not do here simply to say that Aragnoll is a court politician (though he may be *like* one), and that Clarion is the poet. Nor can the relationship be explained in terms of sexual allegory on the usual Spenserian model of *discordia concors*, for both Clarion and Aragnoll are male. Yet an answer may be found, indirectly, by looking at the most elaborate allegory of sexual love in *The Faerie Queene*, in the episode of Amoret and Scudamour, the separated lovers whose story is most fully related but not concluded in Books III and IV.

At the deadly house of Busyrane, Amoret is chained and tormented and her captivity, I take it, symbolises the sufferings involved in the married love in which she is being educated throughout her story.[5] The chaste Britomart, coming to rescue Amoret, keeps watch in the first chamber and views there a rich and sinister tapestry depicting Cupid's wars (III, xi, 28). Spenser's chief source for the tapestry is Ovid's *Metamorphoses* VI, 103–28,[6] the same description of the contest between Minerva and Arachne as is used in *Muiopotmos*. Clearly, in this case *Busyrane* is a type of the spider, and his web is made up of the seductive but dangerous artistry of the tapestry, 'Wouen with gold and silke so close and nere,/That the rich metall lurked priuily,/As faining to be hid from enuious eye;/Yet here, and there, and euery where vnawares/It shewd it selfe, and shone vnwillingly' (III, xi, 28). Likewise, in the specious art of the Bower of Bliss, again we are asked to consider the wiles of a spider as the temptress Acrasia hangs over a prostrate Verdant caught up in her 'vele of silke and siluer thin':

More subtile web *Arachne* can not spin,
Nor the fine nets, which oft we wouen see
Of scorched deaw, do not in th' aire more lightly flee.
(II, xii, 77)

Acrasia's bower, like Busyrane's tapestry, is a masterpiece of seductive entrapment; both suggest, in the figure of the spider's web, the power of art used for destructive ends. Nor is Verdant too unlike the young Clarion (or the young Red Cross Knight, though I will come to this later); both are described as jolly knights, inattentive to the meaning of their armour, and their forgetful self-indulgence is symbolised by Verdant who hangs his shield upon a tree (II, xii, 80).

With these equivalences in mind, I can now suggest that *Muiopotmos* is (in part at least) a poem about the spiritual consequences of good and bad art. That the spirit itself is a mystery Spenser does not ever deny, and his treatment of spiritual secrets is always circumspect though never simplistically agnostic, which is part of the reason his art remains genuinely complex. Yet he does seem convinced that for men in a fallen, mutable world of half-lights, true poetry provides a glimpse of the paradisal centre, the unfallen nature to which we may be restored. Just as the fleeting glory of Mount Acidale in Book VI of *The Faerie Queene* offers us a moment of joy which the poet knows his highest aim is to express, so in *Muiopotmos* the central mystery is Psyche, who conspicuously does not appear except under a veil, like the hermaphrodite representing the central mystery encountered by Amoret in the temple of Venus before the escape from Busyrane's house. By encountering the veiled mystery, Amoret comes to understand the meaning of her commitment to Scudamour, and Spenser thereby shows us that poems can direct our slow attentions also to intuitions of enduring value, even if not finally revealing the mysteries.[7] Images, in short, can mediate the imageless reality of intellectual vision, but not encompass it. Thus, in *Muiopotmos* Psyche is not presented but rather represented, and not only by Clarion but also by Aragnoll, not only by the butterfly wings but by the silky web, for these together represent the mysterious energies or powers of the soul in art, constructive and destructive. Just as Busyrane's phantasmagoria represents the destructive force of specious art upon Amoret's imagination, so in *Muiopotmos* the treacherous spider Aragnoll for envy devours the substance of the butterfly and turns it into something poisonous. The glorious colour and movement of Clarion, on the other hand, evoke the aspiration of the soul through images towards its source, and here the traditional allegory of Psyche may again have a bearing.

Reading the story from Apuleius, the Christian mythographers generally agree that Psyche is the soul, and her long and arduous pursuit of Cupid (occasioned by her transgressing the injunction not to look on his face when he visits her by night) is a result of the soul having attempted to see the divine mysteries by the light of reason.[8] After many wanderings and much suffering, Psyche and Cupid are reunited, and this suggests the journey of the soul through the world and its flight heavenward in contemplation. For Fulgentius, the story thus interpreted turns easily into an allegory of the Fall,[9] and the obviously Platonist component in the contemplative interpretation received further re-enforcement during the Renaissance from Plotinus's suggestion that the pictures and fables of Amor and Psyche indicate the soul's flight to her father's house.[10]

In Spenser, the images of labouring yet aspiring psyche combine notably in *An Hymne of Heavenly Love*, where love's 'golden wings' lift the soul heavenward to view 'those admirable things' which are 'Farre aboue feeble reach of earthly sight' (II, 1–5). The imagery of *Muiopotmos* is similarly suggestive, but with one slight and interesting difference. Though Clarion's wings are like those of the aspiring soul in the hymn, they lack purposeful direction. Clarion does not know with any certainty where he is going. Though he acknowledges the 'renowmed sire' whose 'wide rule' (40) he hopes one day to inherit, Clarion simply 'casts his glutton sense to satisfie' (179) his passion for variety as he roams through the garden. So it will not do to interpret Clarion directly through the mythographers in terms of contemplation. He lives too immediately in a fallen world, in the 'gay gardins' where we learn that 'Arte' contends with 'lauish Nature' (161 ff.), a sure indication in Spenser of the seductive garden of the post-lapsarian state.[11] In this setting he does not even know that his enemy Aragnoll lies in wait for him. He is careless, in short, of the state of affairs that makes his armour necessary, and in such blithe insouciance he tempts providence.

I take it then that Clarion would resemble Psyche after she had lost Cupid by looking illicitly at his face, and if this were an allegory of the Fall, the transgression is already committed. Yet in Spenser's poem there is no evidence of Psyche's subsequent dedicated search or painful eros-longing. So I repeat that Clarion is *like* Psyche in certain ways, but *not* Psyche, for Psyche remains mysterious in *Muiopotmos*, and Clarion represents merely the glorious imaginative power of the soul which must find directions out through the labyrinths of the fallen garden. In such a predicament Clarion's substance may well be devoured by the spider as a consequence of finding the

wrong direction, and the poem's 'tragicall effect' (9) is to
show this happening. In tragedy, however, you need at least
a sense of potential value, if only to see it destroyed, and
in Clarion we find it simply in the brilliance he manifests
and the promise he shows of making himself worthy to inherit
the 'wide rule' (40). But in Clarion, alas, we see also an
unhappy version of Amoret. She escapes from Busyrane, the
spider armed with specious art, the imagination gone awry
and devouring the substance of the person who embodies it,
and there are two havens which help to protect her from
his worst designs. The first I have already mentioned—the
temple of Venus, where she encounters the veiled hermaphrodite—and the second is the garden of Adonis where, significantly,
we are told that Psyche and Cupid play, having found each
other. By contrast, the butterfly Clarion is destroyed, and the
mystery of Psyche will never be discovered by him.

Muiopotmos, therefore, despite an obvious mock-heroism and
delicate tone has, at the centre, a thread of bitterness. The
tragedy of Psyche in a fallen world seems to be that her potential
for good made manifest by the imagination must be weighed
against the equivalent potential triumph of Aragnoll, the same
power corrupted by envy and malice. The subtle relationships
between Clarion and Aragnoll do not become finally clear
by this distinction, but it is part of my point that they should
not. Spenser, relying on the inherent power of his traditional
images, leads us by way of an increasingly intricate web of
analogies (which we soon feel are endlessly pursuable) towards
the realm of the ontological for a validation of his meaning.
Like all true (as distinct from frigid) allegory, Spenser's challenges us with intuitions of the metaphysical which have a
claim on us equivalent to the haunting power of the images
in which they find expression.[12] *Muiopotmos*, then, besides being
a beautiful poem, can be a valuable guide to Spenser's method,
and to his sense of how the imagination—the world of fantasy
with which he was currently preoccupied in *The Faerie Queene*—
can manifest in images the soul's potential for good or ill.

THE SIGN OF THE RED CROSS

These remarks on *Muiopotmos* are a preface to my discussion
of Book I of *The Faerie Queene*, the story of Red Cross Knight,

who like Clarion[13] the butterfly is well-armed but naïve, and
suffers also from over confidence before the wily ways of the
world's tempters. Yet the knight of holiness[14] has something
important to say to the 'tragicall' author of *Muiopotmos*, for
although his red cross indicates the suffering of a typical 'man
of earth'[15] the story of St George suggests also that the tragedy
of fallen human nature may be transcended. Interestingly, Book
I is the only book of *The Faerie Queene* to give a direct glimpse
of what the rewards of faithful endurance may be like in the
next world. Red Cross Knight in the House of Holiness looks
momentarily on the New Jerusalem, the true end of his journey
on earth, and a sight far surpassing his best imaginings. Significant here is Spenser's insistence on the transcendent quality
of the vision, and that it goes beyond his images. There are,
initially, 'wals and towres' and 'precious stone', but the poet
interrupts this account to say that art really cannot describe
what the knight sees: 'that earthly tong/Cannot describe, nor
wit of man can tell;/Too high a ditty for my simple song'
(I, x, 55). Red Cross Knight is instead under the guidance
of Contemplation, whose eyes have lost their sight as, in a
way, has the image-making faculty of the poet before the heavenly city which exists where 'eternall peace and happinesse
doth dwell' (I, x, 55), outside the realm of time. The account
recalls Augustine's eternal city and his similar teaching on
the imageless 'intellectual vision' by which we may sometimes
experience transcendent beauty.

As Kathleen Williams points out, the victory of Red Cross
Knight in winning this vision is very important to all the
quests that follow. Without some sense of a relationship between
our terrestrial world and the New Jerusalem beyond, there
would be no feeling of the order which *The Faerie Queene* strives
to imitate.[16] There is some powerful intuition of transcendent
value in the other books too, but the contrast between image
and mystery is most specific in Book I. In this context it is
easy to suggest that the red cross itself signifies the struggle
to which human nature is committed within the conditions
of space and time as a prologue to such joy as may await
the journey's end. As the way of the cross leads to New Jerusalem, so by analogy, on an Augustinian model, does the way
of images lead to contemplative vision. Yet, despite the explicitness of Spenser's title for Book I, not much attention has been

paid to his use of the cross in it, and I would like now to suggest some ways in which a reading of the poem is enriched by attention to this central Christian icon.

Here arises an important issue of critical principle, for how does one interpret a text iconographically? Iconography *adds* meaning to meaning; it allows us to take one element and then join it to all the further elements in the tradition that it recalls. What then is to stop us taking any detail from a long and complex text, and by building on it to say that it is the central detail, and that from it everything can be illuminated? Meanwhile another reader takes a different detail and relates it to another tradition and erects a different structure and a different interpretation. Each (and there could be a vast number) may be a genuine way of enriching our reading, but we cannot easily claim any of them is central.

I am concerned to tread carefully here, and so acknowledge myself at the outset attempting to show in terms of my particular theme, not Spenser's single structural device, but how his images characteristically work: that is, according to the principles suggested by my discussion of *Muiopotmos*. At the same time I resist the conclusion that any iconographic point would be equally germane. It is too easy, moving from Spenser's broadly Augustinian attitude to images as multivalent signs of transcendent truths, just to feel that everything in his poem can, with equal appropriateness, become just anything else. Spenser himself may give us some basis for such a feeling, for he is peculiarly able to let traditional images stand in his work for themselves: he does not, for instance, very often care to help us determine how an iconographic tableau in, say, Book VI can complement another which in some ways it may recall in Book I. We may often doubt, in consequence, that he intended any given relationship specifically, yet the whole method of discourse in *The Faerie Queene* assumes that edifying lines of relationship can always be found between parts. An iconographic approach to the text is therefore in keeping with the spirit of Spenser's own iconographic practice, for it is a means of showing how the images work by doing the kind of thing they also do, and a particular discussion on such lines is especially pertinent if it illuminates the poem's obvious, declared subject. Thus the hero of Book I bears clearly in his name, on his breast and his shield the sign of the cross, and we might suspect

Spenser of deliberately exploiting this symbol. At the same time Spenser would doubtless be wary because of the widespread suspicion of idolatry in the early English Church.

The reformers of course did not completely eradicate ecclesiastical artifacts, and Anglican worship managed to streamline rather than destroy the old uses. Still, the road towards compromise was not smooth, and a hard-line position, espoused by bishops such as Jewel and Hooper, is reflected for example in the sour directives of the 28th Article of the Royal Injunction of 1547:

> that they shall take away utterly exinct and destroy all shrines, covering of shrines, all tables, candlesticks, trindles or rolls of wax, pictures, paintings, and all other monuments of feigned miracles, pilgrimages, idolatry, and superstition: so that there remain no memory of the same in walls, glass-windows, or elsewhere within their churches or houses. And they shall exhort all their parishioners to do the like within their several houses.[17]

By contrast, *The King's Book*[18] (as it was commonly called) expresses the moderate argument and draws a well-worn distinction between images worshipped for their own sake and those conceived simply as aids to devotion. The crucifix is taken as a key example. It does not offend against the second commandment forbidding graven images because Christ assumed human flesh, and this is what the crucifix shows. Such an image can therefore help us to recall the 'paynefull and cruel passion' of our Savior and thereby discourage us from the sins which helped to cause such suffering. The moderates, when abjuring Catholic images, did so because of an extravagance which encouraged veneration of the image itself, and not because of the basic devotional practices of Catholicism. Indeed to attempt the eradication of traditional practices would mean in the end sacrificing too much that was hallowed and valued in national life, as those divines well knew who cautiously attempted to negotiate a compromise. That their way forward was obscured by practical uncertainties is nicely summarised in the almost comic dispute between Bishops Parker, Cox, Grindal, and Jewel concerning a crucifix, 'That little silver cross' which Queen Elizabeth maintained in her chapel and which, over a period of eleven years, managed to be several times removed and replaced.[19] By being a useful aid for meditation, and by bringing God and man so dramatically together, the cross had become a fruitful ground for argument about the use of images at all in Christian worship. The crucifix was therefore not just one among many devotional aids to be deplored or defended; it was a peculiarly sensitive divining rod for revealing where you stood on the entire debate on ecclesiastical ornament.

With little extrapolation we can see how such controversy raises questions on the relationship between image and historical event, between inner spiritual reality and the world of objects, and we can move easily from here to the peculiar ethos of *The Faerie Queene* which notoriously demonstrates the perplexing fluidity of a mind at once aware of critical questions on these issues, but at the same time careless of the rigours of consistency which they imply. Certainly it seems clear, as Vergil Whitaker[20] argues, that the initial description of Red Cross Knight's armour is a pointed declaration of disagreement with the Puritan iconoclasts:

> But on his brest a bloudie Crosse he bore,
> The deare remembrance of his dying Lord,
> For whose sweete sake that glorious badge he wore,
> And dead as liuing ever him ador'd:
> Vpon his shield the like was also scor'd,
> For soueraine hope, which in his helpe he had.   (I, i. 2)

These two crosses are bold enough, and the one on the shield invokes the protection of Christ, a use of imagery repudiated by the Puritans. Moreover, Whitaker suggests, there may be an allusion to the function of the cross in the Anglican baptism rite, and if this is the case Spenser again declares allegiance with the iconophiles rather than the iconoclasts in that recurringly heated controversy. Nevertheless, there is a heartfelt despisal of Catholic ornateness throughout Book I, which emerges chiefly through the satire upon Lucifera, Duessa, and the rest. The knight's 'faire companion', Fidessa, who is clad in scarlet, 'Purfled with gold and pearle of rich assay', wearing a Persian mitre and garnished with 'crownes and owches' (I, ii. 13), tinsel trappings, bells and bosses, soon reveals, through her descent from the Emperor of the West, that she is the Catholic Church. Her ornateness is a sign of decadence. So if Spenser is no iconoclast neither is his Protestant suspicion of Catholic ornament in doubt, and because he works in such an intellectual climate it is feasible that traditional icons of the cross may remain present in Book I even though they are not exploited in a Catholic manner. Spenser's images will not occasion offense, but in this, the most clearly theological part of *The Faerie Queene*, they can illuminate one of the poem's most important themes, namely the pursuit of Christian holiness in a fallen world.

THE EFFECTUS PASSIONIS

Though it is difficult to determine the specific provenance of Spenser's images, a certain pattern of allusions to the cross in Book I shows striking affinity to a widespread iconographic programme for depicting the centrality of the cross to human history. There is no question here of demonstrating that Spenser had seen particular examples, but I will assume, as Rosemond Tuve[21] argues, that pictures especially helped to form his conceptions and that he had available to him in the rich stores of illuminated books and manuscripts which formed part of the great and thriving collections of his day,[22] a repository of source material fraught with traditional significance and visual appeal.

With this in mind, let me describe briefly a remarkable iconographic programme for depicting the crucifixion which has at its centre the animated arms of a red cross.[23] The series shows centrally the suffering redeemer, and from the extremities of his cross, both vertical and horizontal, grow hands which minister to figures situated above and below, on the left and on the right. (See plates 1–3.) The arm extending from the top holds a key, signifying the unlocking of the gates of heaven. The hand at the bottom reaches down through the earth at the foot of the cross and assaults hell-mouth with a weapon, signifying the harrowing of hell. The hand reaching out to the right (Christ's left side, *sinistra*) holds a sword which pierces a woman riding an ass or goat. She is sometimes blindfold, often lavishly ornamented, and bears behind her sacrificial lambs. Sometimes she carries a standard which falls in pieces, and she is sometimes accompanied by a depiction of Eve eating the forbidden fruit, holding a skull in her hand, or otherwise indicating that she introduces death to the world. Though the woman appears most frequently, she is sometimes replaced by the prophets, and again the blindfold, the descending sword, the sacrifice and the forbidden fruit are featured. All this suggests the old law, the *aera sub lege*, abrogated by the sacrifice of Christ which breaks the bondage of death, frees man from the blind error of legalism, and introduces the *aera sub gratia*. The woman is the traditional *synagoga* and, as we shall see, is offset by *ecclesia*. She is associated with the transgressing Eve, the tree of death, the fruitless sacrifice, and below her on the same side lies hellmouth.

On the left (Christ's right side, *dextra*) the arm of the cross is held in a gesture of blessing, or reaches a crown towards the head of a woman who is the counterpart of *synagoga*. This woman sometimes rides a beast with the head and body of a lion, but modified to indicate the emblems of the four evangelists (lion, ox, eagle, and man). She holds a chalice to the wound in Christ's side, and in her other hand a resurrection cross. (This is the *crux longa* or *hasta longa*, which features a long shaft crossed at the top, from which floats a white banner often with a red cross). She is surrounded by figures who represent the church, and beside her sometimes is the tree of life, the fruit of which is living, not dead. Those examples which substitute the prophets for the blindfold woman also show male figures on the *ecclesia* side, who represent ministers of the church and offer the host or otherwise signify their celebration of the new dispensation. But the woman is more usual, and below her, also holding a triumphal cross with the floating red-crossed banner,[24] Christ breaks the bars of hell. *Ecclesia* is thus associated with clear sight instead of error, the fruitful sacrifice of blood, the living tree, and the new Eve.

In all the examples, we see, as one version dated 1558 announces in its title, the *Effectus Passionis Ihesu Christi*,[25] a compact yet schematic depiction of the meaning of the cross. The suffering image is boldly in the centre, showing the historical event of Christ's death; yet the trans-historical significance of the event is indicated by the directions in which the arms reach both across history and through history. These pictures deliver a message compellingly personal and apocalyptic, showing the purposes of eternity sacramentally mediated into time. We see the church militant (the armed 'arms'), the church triumphant (the crowning hand and the unlocking of heaven), the cross as *lignum vitae* the fruit of which restores to health as the fruit of Eve's tree had poisoned to death. And we see, centrally, the suffering which is the key to transformation from old to new. Christ's pain is thus exemplary, whether we interpret it as an encouragement to bear our own physical suffering, as proof against temptations which torment our spirit, or as witness to the trials of faith.[26] A caption on the 1558 engraving to which I have already referred makes this last, and most important, meaning clear by citing Hosea 2:20 on the *ecclesia* side: 'sponsabo te mihi in fide'.[27]

St Paul, the special apostle of faith, who saw the cross as a stumbling block and a scandal to faithless wisdom, appropriately provides the key text for an extensive series of patristic and mediaeval commentaries on these 'arms' of the cross. In Ephesians 3:17–18 Paul desires that 'Christ may dwell in your hearts through faith' for if we are, through faith, 'rooted and grounded in charity' we 'may be able to comprehend, with all the saints, what is the breadth, and length, and height, and depth'. St Paul does not say of what, but St Augustine takes him to mean the cross, and in several passages goes on in some detail to describe the parts to which the dimensions apply, concluding that the cross thus interpreted describes the 'whole action'[28] of a Christian. In Letter 140 Augustine stresses first the necessity of Christ's dwelling by faith in our hearts, for 'in this our pilgrimage, "faith worketh by charity"'. Only in the life to come will charity be 'full and perfect' in contemplative knowledge of God when faith, like the cross, will pass away. Then, referring to the Ephesians passage, Augustine says Christ chose an ignominious death because 'in it He stood out as the master of his breadth and length and height and depth':

> For, there is breadth in that crossbeam which is fastened above; this refers to good works because the hands are stretched there. There is length in the visible part of the beam which stretches from that one down to the earth; for there, so to speak, He stands, that is, He remains and perseveres, which is the attribute of long-suffering. The height is in that part of the cross which extends above the transverse beam, and is left to point upward, that is, at the head of the Crucified, because the expection of those who hope

rightly is above. And now, indeed, that part of the beam which does not appear, which is buried and hidden, from which the whole rises upward, signifies the depth of that freely given grace; there the minds of many are crushed as they try to fathom it . . . .[29]

In a subsequent letter (no. 147), Augustine again points out how the arms of the cross signify works, how the height inspires us to reach for heavenly rewards, and the depth suggests the mystery from which grace emerges for our deliverance. He again stresses the difference between earthly knowledge and contemplation, warning that we should not persevere in good works for fruitless temporal rewards. We should seek rather the eternal good, binding ourselves meanwhile by 'the rule of faith'. The cross thus shows 'our present knowledge by faith' and not 'our future knowledge by contemplation'.[30]

These passages, subjected to continual re-working through the Middle Ages,[31] help to confirm a clear equivalence between the traditions of iconography and verbal formulations of the theologians: Augustine sees the crucifixion as historical event and yet as symbolically mediating trans-temporal truth. The living cross shows the way through history to eternity, from old to new law, from fruitless works to charity, from dead letter to living church,[32] from the conditions of our pilgrimage-to-be-endured to the contemplative, imageless knowledge of heaven, and from the depths of iniquity to the heights of glory through grace of redemption. Nor are other elements of the *effectus passionis* iconography absent from the written tradition, though these passages from Augustine do not mention them. One can read repeatedly in commonplace and patristic sources of the typology of the cross of Christ and the tree of life,[33] of the cross as the key to heaven,[34] as reproof of blind error and banner of the true church,[35] as restorer of Eden and provider of fruit from the true vine as distinct from the death-giving fruit of the tree from which Eve first ate.[36]

But it would clutter these pages and not further my argument to confirm with examples what is accessible in other studies.[37] I isolate Augustine's passage because of his powerful influence on subsequent tradition, and because his treatment of the cross so clearly affirms the mediaeval theory of images described in my previous chapter. Also, from Augustine I can highlight a point less easy to make in visual terms, namely that the cross signifies the challenge of faith which marks our earthly pilgrimage, as the above passages proclaim. This point receives special attention in the age of Spenser, as, for instance, the 'Homilie for Good Friday' makes clear:

> So the death of Christ shall stand us in no force, unless wee apply it to our selves in such sort as GOD hath appoynted. . . . whereby we may take fruit and profite to our soules health.
>
> What meane is that? forsooth it is faith. Not an unconstant or wavering faith: but a sure, stedfast, grounded, and unfained faith.[38]

As I have suggested, it is hard to show that Spenser had looked at a specific example of the *effectus passionis* iconography mainly because the imagination is likely to synthesise various elements to make a particular (though typical) picture, which may clearly enough derive from the traditional icons, and yet be stylistically individual. Still, the *effectus passionis* programme was widespread throughout Europe, including Spenser's England, and even a brief, selective look through one of the great collections of illustrated manuscripts will show how widely represented in primers, books of hours, saints' lives, illustrated bibles and specula are all the main elements. While examples of the complete programme are comparatively rare, Spenser may well have seen one, and certainly he had seen sections of the programme among the wide variety of sources available to him.[39] If we remember that in many illustrated books the materials on separate pages should be read, like a slow moving-picture, as a continuum, it is easy to see how an imagination attuned to such conventions would collate separate pieces into a single composite picture. Approached in this way, illustrated books soon show that the *effectus passionis* was a commonplace conception, and it is fascinating to see how frequently visual allusions to the passion gain in suggestiveness if we are aware of the larger pattern from which they derive (see plates 4–7). The method of loosely arranging parts around a coherently imagined but not always fully represented centre accords well with Spenser's practice in *The Faerie Queene* itself.

To look at Red Cross Knight's career from this perspective is therefore helpful, for, while Spenser subordinates the icons of Book I to a carefully 'interior', Protestant, emphasis, the structure of his poem suggests also his familiarity with the *effectus passionis.* On the one hand the 'mystery' of Book I, like Psyche in *Muiopotmos*, remains hidden, for it is the mystery of faith which is unrepresentable. On the other hand it can be mediated truly though partially through a body of images long associated with the sign of the cross. In Book I this mystery of the holy cross is present in two main ways. The first has to do with Spenser's interpretation of the St George legend itself, and the second involves a series of *exempla* of the crucifixion, offset by a series of parodies.

THE PASSION OF ST GEORGE

The legend of St George the martyr clearly alludes, in its main versions, to the passion of Christ. In general outline, the story recounts how St George, riding through the province of Lybya, comes to the city of Sylene which is stricken by pestilence caused by a dragon. To allay the dragon's malignant breath (it spreads the plague) there is a daily sacrifice of two sheep. But the dragon requires the more savoury meat of human sacrifice. The King's daughter, dressed as a bride, is about to offer herself when St George intervenes. He spears the dragon, binds it with the maiden's girdle and has her lead it back to the city. George promises to kill the dragon if the King and his people convert to Christianity. They do, and George fulfills his promise, after which the King offers him great treasures. George refuses, and re-directs the money to relief of the poor and to the building of churches. The King then offers his daughter in marriage but George again declines, saying he cannot rest but must continue on his way. The concluding and less well-known phase of the story then describes the end of the saint's life, and his defiance of the emperor Diocletian for persecuting Christians. George cries out first against injustice and then denounces the Roman gods as devils. He is apprehended by the provost Dacian, and there are protracted accounts of hideous torments, all of which George miraculously survives. Dacian then brings him to a temple where George once more denounces the idols, which instantly fall to pieces. After further torment (during which Datian's wife is converted and promptly executed) the saint is finally suffered to die by decapitation.

The fantastic stories connected with the martyrdom came

under sceptical review even from the fifth century when Pope Gelasius declared George to be one of those saints 'whose names are justly reverenced among men, but whose acts are known only to God'.[40] During the Renaissance, in the spirit of Pope Gelasius, a good deal of energy was expended trying to distinguish between a 'symbolical' meaning for the tale and the supposed 'events' behind it.[41] Yet one thing all the interpreters agreed to was an equivalence between George's death and the passion of Christ. This theme indeed became the most important means of linking the dragon story to the martyrdom, for each is concerned with the faith and perseverence which are especially signified by the cross. The maiden's faith in the first part is 'dead' and will not defeat the dragon until her city casts its allegiance with Christianity. In the second part George's faith, by sustaining him in his far journey, is the means of his eventual glorification.

Mantuan's *Life of St George* (1509) which Spenser had probably read, whether in the original or in Alexander Barclay's translation (1515),[42] clarifies the associations between faith, martyrdom, and the passion. Mantuan begins by calling attention to his main subject matter, which he describes simply as George's 'mortall passyon' (*Prologue*, 58). As the saint encounters the dragon he makes the sign of the cross on his breast (853), and when he addresses the citizens of Sylene he tells them roundly that they live in 'blynde errour' (1039) for which Christ has already suffered 'dedely payne' (1056). He asks them to unlock their gates (996) as Christ has unlocked heaven by his death on the cross, and their freedom from bondage will be accompanied by the burning of the old dragon (1144). Their error will then be replaced by faith (1179), and the maiden whose hand George refuses is directed to persevere in virtue and to give her attentions to the church (1198 ff.).

Here the cross as separator of blind error from *ecclesia*, as key to heaven, confounder of the devil, and example of a living faith 'armed' in the world, is clear, and as Mantuan continues, he makes the crucifixion theme even more plain. When George leaves Sylene he makes a pilgrimage to Mount Calvary, visiting the very scene of Christ's passion (1360). The visit comes immediately after the repeated exhortations to the King and citizens of Sylene on the life of faith, and prefaces the martyrdom section. It thus forms a link between the two

main parts of the legend, and in choosing to interpolate this
journey to the site of the crucifixion Mantuan seeks to underline
the motif which he thought the two sections of the story had
in common. Finally, faced with persecution by Diocletian,
George resolves once more to fight in Christ's name and to
oppose 'error blynde' (1736) by following the example of
Christ's fighting for all of us on the cross (1774 ff.). Throughout
the ensuing suffering at the hands of Dacian, Christ's passion
is repeatedly invoked. We are told of George's own 'passyon'
(2621) and of how his pain is sustained by the memory of
Christ's blood (1932). The breaking of the idols drives the
fiends deep into hell (2232) and becomes a kind of harrowing
wherein 'blyndnes' (2432) and 'errours' (2436) and the 'olde
serpent' (2681) are defeated, while a strengthening angel (1919
ff.) ministers from above as George, a 'stedfast pyller of fayth'
(2669), bears the cross of martyrdom to glory.

The story of St George in this account consists therefore
of a body of fanciful and disparate materials made coherent
through the traditional *effectus passionis* iconography. Mantuan's
treatment is not unusual. The same emphases appear in the
Legenda Aurea,[43] where George repeatedly signs himself with
the cross (114; 115; 117), is the pilgrim of faith (112) and
a 'holy wrastler' (112) like Christ crucified. Aelfric's *Life* contrasts the 'unbelieving men' whose handiwork constructs idols
with George's dedication to the cross.[44] Mirk provides similar
emphases,[45] and Tristram White's *The Martyrdome of St. George
of the Cross* (1614) offers an example which, coming a little
later than Spenser, demonstrates the survival of such traditions
through the period when *The Faerie Queene* was written. White's
poem begins by comparing Christ, the 'crowned Conquerour
of Hell' (A3) who teaches us about suffering, to St George,
our 'owne true Knight' (A3). During his martyrdom, George
hangs between the powers of heaven and hell. Above, angels
encourage him with 'balmie breath' (B3), and below, hell
receives the sins expunged by the martyr's example. George
is sustained by faith and by recollection of the cross:

None other Charme had hee, but which in vaine
Was never us'd, *Faith in God on high,*
Who by the crosse taught us both ignomie,
And friends, and fortunes, and Deaths selfe to slight.
(B3)

The final death blow is 'The key which let thee out from things below' (C4), and the allusion is to redemption by the key of the cross. Consequently George's fame extends from sunrise to sunset, and from one pole to another because he has, like a soldier, shed his blood '*which spread the Christian Faith so much*' (D2). Thus the 'arms' of the holy cross, the imagery of keys, and the cosmic trans-historical dimensions of the tree provide once more a structural principle for retelling the legend. Significantly, the Protestant White also describes Diocletian's idolatry in terms suggesting worship in the Roman Catholic Church. The 'gorgeous throne', 'Roman ensigns', and crowned emperor satirise, much like Duessa, the use of ornament in the Church of Rome. Such adaptation of traditional mediaeval and Catholic materials to anti-Catholic satire was familiar practice among Protestant apologists, and not least Spenser.

Finally Peter Heylyn, writing in 1631, confirms how widespread during his day was the St George legend: the saint's picture is everywhere, he says, even on 'our common Signeposts',[46] and for evidence of the sanctification of the legend by tradition, Heylyn alludes to its occurrence in such familiar devotional aids and liturgical materials as the *Horae B. Mariae* (92), the Roman Breviary, the Sarum missal, and the *Diurnum* (206). For instance, after the reading from John 15, 'I am the true vine', the mass has a post-communion prayer to the saint (205), and the Sarum use has a collect to recall 'the death and passion of St *George* thy martyr' (206). Thus the materials which provided popular visual accounts of the *effectus passionis* contained also interpretations of the St George story, and the habits of mind which found links between the two in literature, no doubt did so in the visual traditions as well. The point is confirmed by a brief look at Carpaccio's (*c.* 1465–*c.* 1522) celebrated fresco, 'St George Slaying the Dragon'.

On the right of Carpaccio's painting, George on his charger lances the dragon which rears at him from the left. Behind the saint on the right stands the maiden, and behind her, on a steep hill, is a domed church. (See plate 7.) On the sea, also at the right, are two sailing ships. On the left surrounding the dragon are the bones and half-devoured flesh of its victims, and behind, on a plain, is an ornate city with a tower from which a group of spectators watches the struggle. Dividing the painting, almost at mid-section, stands a single tree. On the right it produces green leaves and on the left it is withered and fruitless. Clearly, it typifies the cross, and the withered and fruitful branches suggest the traditional relationship between the tree of death which issued in the old law and the tree of life which redeemed humanity from it. Thus the dragon is surrounded by victims, the fruitless sacrifices offered by the city on the plain, which is a type of the synagogue in our earlier examples, and of the *aera sub lege*[47] in general. On the fruitful side the lady (*ecclesia*) stands like a madonna, and behind her is the church, the *aera sub gratia*, with a narrow and steep pathway winding up to it. The sailing ships suggest man's earthly pilgrimage, like the 'weary vessel' of the final stanza of Spenser's Book I in which the 'jolly mariners', or readers, are advised to set sail after the refreshment of the poem. The ship may therefore suggest the potentially fruitful journey undertaken in faith, and the iconographic relationship between cross and ship is conventional.[48]

In adducing this range of material on the legend I can see that Spenser's departures from it are important for the critic set on determining the special quality of the poetry. But my main point has to do with Spenser's icons, and my conclusion is that the author of a poem as concerned as Book I with the trials of faith, having as its hero a knight called Redcrosse who is also St George, would scarcely be unapprised of the use of the cross as an emblem of faith in all the best-known versions of the St George legend itself. This group of motifs, should the poem now sustain our discovery of them in the text, we might conclude is in some sense validly 'there' rather than arbitrarily read in.

THE RED CROSS KNIGHT

I have suggested that the habit of looking at the St George legend by way of visual images of the crucifixion would be familar to Spenser. One result of this is to add a dimension of pathos to Spenser's treatment of the Red Cross Knight. When St George in canto xii leaves Una, the informed reader knows he returns to the world to face the untold suffering of immolation. The saint's love, remaining in the world, is *amor cruciatus*, and his task is perseverance in faith. Yet the pathos comes not merely from the reader's recognition of what lies in store for the saint, but from the recognition that the saint himself does not know. Then in the last stanza on the 'weary bark', the reader is directed to a voyage of his own—'And then againe abroad,/On the long voyage whereto she is bent' (I, xii, 42). Between the suffering which St George must endure (upon which the reader, knowing the legend, enjoys a privileged perspective) and the unknown conditions of the reader's own voyage (upon which the only privileged perspective is God's) is an edifying analogy. As in Augustine's *Confessions*, Spenser's imagery extends into the reader's own life for completion. By realising a continuity between the poem and traditional source material which interprets St George in terms of the passion, the reader is led to consider for himself the challenge of faith which is at the heart of the mystery of the holy cross as it had been described from Augustine to Calvin, and now also through the signs, or images, of Spenser's poem.[49] *The Faerie Queene* repeatedly gains poignancy, as C. S. Lewis says, from this kind of double vision in which our understanding of a character differs from his own confused ideas of himself.[50] So, a simple encounter for the Red Cross Knight will often bear an allegorical meaning for us: for instance, as George observes the pageant of seven deadly sins he is unaware of their significance, but it is clear to the reader. Or consider the knight's hurt self-esteem and yet, perhaps, glimmering recognition of his predicament as he meets Lucifera. The key stanza occurs just after he meets the queen but before the pageant of deadly sins:

> Goodly they all that knight do entertaine,
> Right glad with him to haue increast their crew:
> But to *Duess'* each one himselfe did paine
> All kindnesse and faire courtesie to shew;
> For in that court whylome her well they knew:
> Yet the stout Faerie mongst the middest crowd
> Thought all their glorie vaine in knightly vew,
> And that great Princesse too exceeding prowd,
> That to strange knight no better countenance
>   allowd.   (I, iv, 15)

Does George think 'all their glorie vaine' because Lucifera is discourteous to strangers, and does he therefore begin to

see through the pride and pomp of her self-adulation? Or
does his feeling that 'no better countenance' has been allowed
him indicate his hurt self-esteem and thus the very overweening
quality which has caused him to be in the house of pride
in the first place? The ambivalence here depends partly on
our transcendent position: we know what Lucifera means and
so appreciate the first interpretation. But we also know the
mistake Red Cross Knight has made in allowing himself to
be deceived by Archimago and separated from Una, and so
we can appreciate the second. For Red Cross Knight, however,
the entire journey towards Jerusalem (which he does not even
glimpse until near the end of Book I) is conducted through
half-lights, and Spenser prepares us to notice this from the
beginning by having the knight meet Error in that gloomy
cave of canto i. There, Red Cross is 'fearefull more of shame,/Then of the certaine perill he stood in' (I, i, 24). The
disparity, amidst the actual dimness of the setting, between
the knight's perspective (bounded by his feelings of shame)
and the reader's (appreciative of the allegory and the real
danger of Error) shows the uncertainty of self-knowledge in
a mutable world, a theme which reaches fulfilment in the
reader's own acceptance of uncertainty at the end. The episode
with Error thus prepares for many further, similar effects in
the poem which follows. These can be broad or subtle, bold
or ambiguous, but they seem to penetrate all levels of Spenser's
retelling of the tale, and his concern in all this, I have suggested,
is to bring the reader to the mystery of faith by having him
appreciate real analogies between the conditions under which
St George bears the emblem of the red cross through the world
of the poem and the conditions which pertain to the 'weary
voyage' on which the reader is in turn engaged. Arthur voices
this lesson most succinctly just before lamenting the 'fresh bleeding wound' caused by his separation from the Faerie Queene:

Full hard it is (quoth he) to read aright
The course of heauenly cause, or vnderstand
The secret meaning of th' eternall might,
That rules mens wayes, and rules the thoughts of liuing
      wight.   (I, ix, 6)

Not surprisingly, within this general technique of using the
legend as allegory to help express the mystery of faith, we
discover a further series of allusions to the *effectus passionis* icono-

graphy itself. The familiar motifs are all present—the cross as a means of redemption through the vicarious shedding of blood, the distinction between fruitful and fruitless blood, the cross with its 'arms' as symbols of the church militant, the iconography of trees, the representation of blind error as distinct from *ecclesia*, the motifs of the keys, the harrowing of hell by the triumphal cross, and the association of the cross with faithful endurance in the world. Moreover, many episodes in which these elements occur can be imagined visually as tableaux wherein the parts are symmetrically arranged.

Red Cross Knight, when we first meet him, not only bears his cross before him on shield and breast, but his arms retain the cruel marks of 'many'a bloudy fielde' (I, i, 1) and his 'glorious badge' is 'bloudie' (I, i, 2). Throughout an unusually blood-drenched book, Spenser wants us continually to associate the bloodletting with this opening association to the cross, and there are many clues for enabling us to do so. For instance, when Una is attacked by Sansloy, nature's reaction to the assault evokes the crucifixion when sun and moon were darkened at the ninth hour:

That molten starres do drop like weeping eyes;
And *Phoebus* flying so most shamefull sight,
His blushing face in foggy cloud implyes,
And hides for shame.   (I, vi, 6)

This passage closely parallels what happens when Arthur uncovers his shield:

For so exceeding shone his glistring ray,
That *Phoebus* golden face it did attaint,
As when a cloud his beames doth ouer-lay;
And siluer *Cynthia* wexed pale and faint.   (I, vii, 34)

In both cases the crucifixion is implied: in the first, we are asked to respond to the suffering of the church militant (here deprived of her 'arms' in the form of the Red Cross Knight's protection) and in the second to the church triumphant and the mystery of grace which redeems Red Cross from Orgoglio's dungeon. The story of St George is of course closely connected to both, for he owes allegiance to Una whom he must protect, and is redeemed by Arthur, who protects him. Una and Arthur are thus linked to each other through Spenser's emphasising their conjoint relationship to the cross. Again, when Arthur rescues Red Cross Knight, the fight with Orgoglio evokes Christ crucified as the 'holy wrestler', and again the ninth-hour scene occurs:

> The sad earth wounded with so sore assay,
> Did grone full grieuous vnderneath the blow,
> And trembling with strange feare, did like an earthquake
>   show.   (I, viii, 8)

To confirm the allusion Spenser makes a remarkable (though for him typical) category shift within the image itself whereby the narrative action is suspended for several stanzas so that the cross symbolism may emerge clearly. During the battle, as critics of the allegory have shown, Orgoglio ceases to be an objective enemy and becomes a component of Arthur's own person—perhaps fleshly pride—which must be defeated if Red Cross Knight is to be released. This meaning highlights both the redemptive power of the cross (in releasing the Red Cross Knight) and the fact that the passion also tests Christ's flesh. The cross is therefore implicit, but basic to the entire episode. For instance, when the maimed Orgoglio from his 'truncked stocke' bleeds streams of blood 'like fresh water . . . from riuen rocke' (I, viii, 10), we read an allusion to the wounds of Christ and to the typology of the water from Christ's side and the water struck from the rock by Moses.[51] The description of Orgoglio's wounds and Arthur's endurance consequently becomes an allegory for Christ suffering the wounds in his own flesh. As Orgoglio wallows further in blood and nears defeat, the veil falls off Arthur's shield and its 'flashing beames' pour out. As they do, Orgoglio tumbles down 'as an aged tree'. The earth trembles, and Duessa, who stands by as a spectator, is wounded to the heart while the 'royall Virgin', Una, greets Arthur's victory, asking 'How shall I quite the paines, ye suffer for my sake?' (I, viii, 20ff.).

It is hard to resist that this scene evokes the *effectus passionis* programme: the central bloody drama of the cross militant and triumphant involves destruction of the withered tree and wounding the evil woman while the maiden rejoices in victory and is sustained through the suffering by grace which pours forth to enable Arthur to enter Orgoglio's dungeon and harrow that hell for the redemption of George, the 'man of earth'. We can imagine these women positioned on either side, with a left arm wounding Duessa and a right arm blessing Una while the fiend falls beneath and the Knight revives, though lying captive in hellmouth. A transcendental element to complete the picture by providing for the 'height' of the cross, the 'hope for celestial things' as Augustine says,[52] is introduced when Arthur, just after the battle, recounts the dream of Gloriana. In it he glimpses the higher realm to which he believes his long journey will restore him, and in so doing heal his wounds.

Arthur's dream also parallels Red Cross Knight's vision of Jerusalem, which the text instructs us to read in terms of the cross. After his 'labours long' George is led up a mountain resembling Mount Sinai where Moses, the 'mighty man of God', received 'writ in stone/With bloudy letters' the pronouncement of the law, and with it the 'bitter doome of death and balefull mone' (I, x, 52 ff.). The mountain is also compared to the Mount of Olives where Christ suffered torments of mental anguish prior to crucifixion.[53] From this eminence Red Cross Knight has his vision, and the poem makes clear the importance of the setting. Jerusalem is the destination of those

> purg'd from sinfull guilt,
> With pretious bloud, which cruelly was spilt
> On cursed tree, of that vnspotted lam,
> That for the sinnes of all the world was kilt.
>
> (I, x, 57)

The way towards vision is clearly the way of the cross, and St George is advised that all who attain glory have 'liu'd in like paine' (I, x, 62). So he is encouraged to continue his 'painefull pilgrimage' (I, x, 61) and to 'proue thy puissaunt armes' (I, x, 66). Significantly, Fidelia (faith), who instructs Red Cross Knight prior to his ascent of the mountain of Contemplation, holds in her hand the emblem of St John[54]—a golden cup with a serpent. The cup is filled also with wine and water, symbols of Christ's wounds, and the raised serpent is a common type of Christ crucified. The point is confirmed when Fidelia finally offers the knight as her testament—the testament of faith—a book 'that was both signd and seald with blood' (I, x, 13). Red Cross Knight accepts her instruction and at the behest of Contemplation returns to his journey.

At the end of Book I St George at last encounters the dragon and becomes himself a type of the suffering Christ. Canto xi describes the battle and features elements usually associated with the dragon fight in the legend: the maiden stands by and the king (in this case Adam) watches from his locked city. Spenser, like Carpaccio and Mantuan before him, seems naturally drawn to explicate this scene in terms of the cross, and the Knight endures a type of passion. He is 'Faint, wearie, sore, emboyled, grieued, brent/With heat, toyle, wounds, armes, smart, and inward fire' (I, xi, 28). He is wounded in the side but sustained by the fruit of the 'goodly tree' which he has come to restore. Once, before the reign of the dragon, this tree 'freely sprong out of the fruitfull ground' (I, xi, 46–47) and will now do so again as a result of the battle being fought. But although St George is at this point Christlike, he does not cease to be the mere man dependent on benefits won by Christ's suffering. The sacraments of baptism and eucharist strengthen him and are indicated by the revivifying power of the well of life and tree of life of stanzas 29 and 46. While George receives them he is not Christ but the weak man-of-earth, and we see again how easily Spenser's imagery can offend logical consistency to intensify the central icons, in this case the locked town which suggests the *aera sub lege*, and the tree of death and life which suggests the cross. But, as we read of the wounds and passion, at moments we feel, and especially on the third day, that the narrative is suspended as with the Orgoglio episode, and we meditate again the crucifixion.[55] As one level of meaning seems to become transparent to another and higher one the images seem likewise to approach the central mystery from which the poem, according to this view of how images work, derives its most moving power.[56]

Throughout Book I, and over against these allusions to the cross, yet by way of intensifying them, is a series of parodies of the *effectus passionis* which reveals the spiritual dereliction of the villains rather than the fruitful sacrifices of the heroes. Here Spenser avoids creating the impression that only the good suffer, and confirms the general insight that nobody in a fallen world can avoid carrying his cross. As Thomas à Kempis says:

> You cannot escape it, withersoever you run. For wheresoever you go you carry yourself with you, and shall always find yourself. Turn upwards or turn downwards, turn inwards or turn outwards: everywhere you shall find the cross.[57]

Spenser I think agrees, and in so doing implies that the difference between hero and villain is in the end what they make of their crosses. So in Book I the villains like the heroes are often described through images which relate to the passion, but the suffering and bloodletting of the villains is a consequence of their own vengefulness and is fruitless and wasteful. Spenser even uses the phrase 'fruitles bloud' (I, vi, 45) to describe the fray between Sansloy and Satyrane during which Una manages to slip away undetected as the two futile warriors spread their blood far and wide in order to keep her captive. Indeed the entire section of the poem which deals with the exploits of the 'paynims' Sansfoy, Sansjoy, and Sansloy seems to represent the spiritual condition of man under pre-Christian (or non-Christian) dispensations in the era, roughly speaking, *sub lege*.[58] Sansfoy attacks the cross on sight—'Curse on that Crosse (quoth then the *Sarazin*)' (I, ii, 18)—for it is the antidote to what he stands for, namely lack of faith. His brother Sansjoy is motivated entirely by lust for vengeance, a sentiment especially characteristic of an old law mentality. He is moved, in a parody of the crucifixion, to 'redeem' the wandering ghost of the dead Sansfoy. He longs for 'bloud and vengeance' (I, v, 7) but does not realise that redemption does not come from shedding somebody else's blood. Sansloy, the ultimate in futility, sheds the most fruitless blood of all and manages not only to lose Una, but in his eagerness to attack the 'Red crosse' (I, iii, 34) wounds his old friend Archimago by mistake. In each case the temper of the Sans brothers is most clearly revealed as they face the shield and react to the emblem on it. Each in his own way is defeated by the cross and each sheds his own blood fruitlessly in an attempt to repudiate it. In the brothers we thus see a range of reactions generally pertaining to the *aera sub lege*, and the poem implies (though again we see what Red Cross Knight does not) a series of diminishments of insight as we pass from Sansfoy to Sansjoy and Sansloy.

Strictly speaking, Sansjoy is the only one who corresponds to the Mosaic law as Spenser probably understood it in its negative aspect. He is the most legalistic of the brothers, demanding revenge, and living, as his name implies, without the hope and happiness that come with Christ: he has law without benefit of grace. Sansloy, as *his* name indicates, is without benefit of law at all, and so represents the merely chaotic and primitive condition from which the Israelites found partial but incomplete deliverance in the law. Finally Sansfoy represents those who have had the benefits of faith but who backslide or otherwise reject it. This explains why Sansfoy accompanies Fidessa (Duessa in disguise) and why the story of Fidessa's descent from the Emperor of the West identifies her as the Roman Catholic Church. Sansfoy's faithlessness, it seems, is the result of his allegiance to a decadent and misdirected Church, a perversion rather than a simple deficiency. His condition is more iniquitous than that of his two brothers.

After the death of Sansfoy, when Fidessa recounts her history for Red Cross Knight, she makes an important allusion to the crucifixion which helps to clarify her allegiance to the Sans brothers, and also relate them as a group to the main action through the symbol of the cross as the sign of faith. Fidessa tells of her beloved prince who 'cruelly was slain':

His blessed body spoild of liuely breath,
Was afterward, I know not how, conuaid
And fro me hid: of whose most innocent death
When tidings came to me vnhappy maid,
O how great sorrow my sad soule assaid.
Then forth I went his woefull corse to find,
And many yeares throughout the world I straid,
A virgin widow, whose deepe wounded mind
With loue, long time did languish as the striken
    hind.

(I, ii, 24)

The ironies are manifold: Red Cross Knight sees simply an adventure, a chance encounter. He does not appreciate the disguised allegory of Fidessa's story which tells of Christ's death and the early history of the Catholic Church. We have an advantage both on Red Cross Knight and on her, for she seeks only a 'woefull corse', seemingly unaware of what we (appreciators of the allegory) all know, that Christ arose on the third day and his risen spirit continues to inform the true church in the world. Fidessa unwittingly has described herself in terms that show her as the false church. But Spenser has an advantage over all of us, for there is something we do not know either—that Fidessa is really Duessa. So evcryone has something to learn, and the regressive exploitations of awareness operate here, as throughout the poem, to represent the perplexed conditions of faith which, through the allegory of the church in the world, Spenser merges with the motif of the cross.

With the entire group of Sans brothers and Fidessa, Spenser therefore examines what the *effectus passionis* programme shows *sinistra*. By including Sansfoy he conforms to Protestant practice which did not hesitate to use Catholic satire on the blindness of the old law to satirise Catholicism itself.[59] The inclusion of Sansloy deepens our understanding of the old law by helping us to see Sansjoy's advance on paganism as well as his limitations in relation to the new dispensation.

Among other important examples of scenes structured around the symbols of fruitless blood and parodying the true cross is the episode at the cave of Despair in canto ix. Despair has much in common with Sansjoy in particular, and argues consistently in legalistic terms. He demands that Red Cross Knight, now an acknowledged sinner, justify himself. What legal claim can he make, Despair asks, 'For life must life, and bloud must bloud repay' (I, ix, 43)? What can such a sinner merit in God's eyes, for does he not acknowledge the 'righteous sentence of th' Almighties law' (I, ix, 50)? God's law, in short, leads inevitably to despair because postlapsarian man can never successfully observe it, only come to know his own sinfulness through it.

This way of describing bondage to the law is of course commonplace in Christian tradition, but Despair's speech contains also an implicit parody of the cross, which provides a perspective on his legalistic argument and helps to integrate it with the main body of the poem. When we first approach his cave we see it surrounded by fruitless trees: 'old stockes and stubs of trees,/Whereon nor fruit nor leafe was euer seene' (I, ix, 34). Close by lies the body of Sir Terwin, 'All wallowd in his owne yet luke-warme blood' (I, ix, 36), a fruitless sacrifice to the kind of arguments Despair adduces. Despair then attempts to dissuade Red Cross Knight from his pilgrimage, his 'wearie, wandring way' (I, ix, 39), and advises,

> Thou wretched man, of death hast greatest need,
> If in true ballance thou wilt weigh thy state.

> (I, ix, 45)

The irony is delicate, as in Fidessa's story, for the perspectives of Despair, Red Cross Knight, and the reader are all different, a fact which gains significance when we see the allusion here to the cross which is often pictured as a balance.[60] Again, Red Cross Knight is simply confused, and in the throes of Despair's insidious and languorous appeal just to give up. Despair argues what seems to himself to be logical—that if Red Cross Knight weighs his sins in a just balance, he will find he deserves death. But the reader takes 'wretched man', 'greatest need', and 'true ballance' in a different sense, for what the wretched man as sinner really needs is a death indeed, but one that occurs in the balance of the cross which alone cancels the bondage upon which Despair's argument depends. The superb arrangement of syntax and vocabulary manages to preserve Despair's perspective, and yet have us cry out, as if in answer, 'Yes, but don't you *see* the meaning of your own condition: why you are rebuked by your very own words?'[61] Once more the cross shows us succinctly the values with which the poem is most concerned. The fruitless trees, the fruitless blood, the ambiguous lines on the balance, and also the phantasms of death conjured by Despair in stanza 49 to provide a kind of negative example of a meditation on the passion, are parodies of the cross and provide structural coherency for the episode.

Somewhere between the barren trees of Despair and the fruitful ones in canto xii lie the two trees of the doubting and doting lovers, Fradubio and Fraelissa. Their significance in relation to the other trees is plain enough in general terms[62] and I will not say much about them. Like Red Cross Knight, Fradubio and Fraelissa are, if my text can bear the pun, in a state of suspension: not only because they are still on the way of the cross in a fallen world but because, literally, they are paralysed. Their condition has come about by a combination of weakness (Fraelissa—frailty) and failure of faith (Fradubio—brother doubt). Yet, though paralysed, they acknowledge their sins and hope for restoration through eventual immersion in 'a liuing well' (I, ii, 43). They are subjected to suffering consequent on sin, but the 'wretched tree' (I, ii, 33) which each of them has become flourishes nonetheless, sending forth shoots of hope and bleeding painfully as they wait on grace. Their predicament intensifies our sense of the similar, human situation of Red Cross Knight. He, as *homo viator*, is also subjected to the challenge implied by the cross in which hope lies, despite his limited knowledge of this fact. Again Spenser preserves the cross symbolism by choosing a story[63] which enables him to highlight trees, blood, redemptive water, and the problem of good faith.

The theme of fruitless blood leads readily to the allied iconographical motif of blind error. The cave of Error herself in canto i is a 'darksome hole' because she hates light and prefers, blindly, 'in desert darknesse to remaine' (I, i, 14–16). The central action in this encounter is the wounding in which, as Error falls, her hideous offspring rush to suck her blood:

> They flocked all about her bleeding wound,
> And sucked vp their dying mothers blood,
> Making her death their life, and eke her hurt their
> good.   (I, i, 25)

They drink till they swell and burst: 'well worthy end/Of such as drunke her life, the which them nurst' (I, i, 26), and the fruitless blood of Error becomes both a monstrous parody of *mater ecclesia*[64] whose breasts traditionally nourish her children with milk not blood, and of Christ whose blood sustains rather than slays the faithful.[65] But the point I wish to isolate is the implied contrast between *ecclesia* and blind error in context of the blood, for we must not forget that, again, Una stands by and observes the scene. Our visual recreation of the encounter thus confirms a tableau-like structure which matches strikingly the schematic, pictorial oppositions of the *effectus passionis* convention.

There is a good deal elsewhere in Book I to suggest that Spenser was paying particular attention to blind error. Corcecca, who represents blind devotion in the Catholic Church, is one example. As we have seen, anti-Catholic satire blends in Spenser with traditional satire directed against the *aera sub lege*. This is made iconographically clear in Book I by the opposition between Corcecca and Una who represents the true Church. Corcecca, the 'blind old woman', runs mad 'through malice, and reuenging will' (I, iii, 22) and abuses Una with violent words, wishing that she might stray 'in endlesse error' (I, iii, 23) which is ironically Corcecca's own condition. Una at this point is accompanied by her lion, and the opposition between the blind woman associated with error and revenge, and the fair lady with her lion again evokes the pictorial conventions of the *effectus passionis*. The lion (which in Malory defends a young lady who is explicitly the 'new law of holy church')[66] is also most prominent among the beasts[67] associated with the lady opposed to blind error in the iconographic tradition.

The word 'error' is used repeatedly[68] also to describe the headlong career of Sansloy, and by association with his fruitless bloodletting and vengefulness helps to confirm his allegiance to the other *sub lege* figures. Again, Despair, like Error, inhabits a dark cave where he sits with 'griesie lockes' so hanging that they 'hid his face' (I, ix, 35). This is a parody of Una's veil, and also a blindfold, and the association between Despair's dedication to the old law and his being blindfold in a dark cave shows pictorially how he belongs to the *aera sub lege*. Once again Una is present and stands opposed to Despair with Red Cross Knight in the middle, and the arrangement helps to suggest that Spenser is working from a consistently recalled visual tradition.

I can conclude this survey of 'blindfold' iconography with the figure of Ignaro, who will serve also to introduce the theme of keys. In Orgoglio's dungeon, Ignaro the 'old old man' (I, viii, 30) is gatekeeper, but his life and its meaning are a puzzle to him. He cannot open any of the doors, and to all Arthur's questions he answers only that 'he could not tell' (I, viii, 32 ff). By his age and inability to free the souls locked in Orgoglio's dungeon, he seems to represent the futility of the old law.[69] This is reinforced by the fact that 'his eye sight him failed long ygo' (I, viii, 30): he is another type of blind error. In addition, Ignaro is grotesque. Everything about him is turned backwards and his feet and face point in opposite directions—'very vncouth sight' (I, viii, 31). In this context his keys are significant, and Spenser focuses upon the fact that they hang on his arm. As Arthur makes his way to the dungeon he plucks the keys away but finds they cannot unlock the innermost door, which yields only to 'furious force, and indignation fell' (I, viii, 39). On the other side lies the prison holding St George 'deepe' and 'darke as hell', and only after 'long paines and labours manifold' (I, viii, 40) does Arthur manage to raise up and free the Knight from it.

The account stresses the uselessness of Ignaro's keys. Like everything else about him they arc the wrong way round, but the irony is evident only if we recall the icon which the keys evoke. On the 'arms' of the cross the upper one unlocks heaven's gate, but hell has to be forced by Christ's power.

Spenser draws attention clearly to 'arms' as he describes the keys, which he associates in turn with Ignaro's perverse allegiance to the old law. So the poetry highlights the harrowing of hell theme in Arthur's assault on the dragon, and also relates the whole episode to an *effectio passionis* structure. The description of Ignaro, read in this light, ceases to be a fanciful embellishment and becomes firmly rooted in the poem. Spenser's intention here is confirmed if we turn to the part of Book I most concerned with the 'height' of the cross, namely the section of canto x where Heavenly Contemplation directs Red Cross Knight towards Jerusalem. The old man's eyes, we learn, are dim because his heavenward gaze, dark with excessive bright, has blunted his ability to see the lower world clearly. He reminds us immediately of Ignaro, except that Contemplation is an exemplar of wisdom, not blind error. Again there are keys, but Contemplation does not carry them himself. They are provided, significantly, by faith: 'Whereof the keyes are to thy hand behight/By wise *Fidelia*' (I, x, 50). Armed with them, and 'after labours long, and sad delay' (I, x, 52) wherein he imitates the sacrifice of Christ 'On cursed tree' (I, x, 57), Red Cross Knight is able at last to climb the mount of Contemplation and glimpse the City of Jerusalem. The symmetry between this account and the Ignaro episode is striking, and it gains depth and coherence if we see the iconography of the cross as a co-ordinating principle. Ignaro, associated with the old law, is using his keys wrongly, for hell is harrowed by Christ's force. The keys rather open the heavenly city of contemplative vision, and they do so through a gift of faith whereby Red Cross Knight, though still on the royal road of the cross, can glimpse the transcendent world which will sustain him on his 'painefull pilgrimage' (I, x, 61).

I have tried to show in this account that Spenser had his title for Book I very much in mind as he wrote and that the arms of the red cross, particularly as understood by way of the *effectus passionis* iconography, provide a structural principle which helped him to write a poem of great richness and subtlety, and yet with the quality of tightness which has always been recognised as a special characteristic of Book I. The treatments of the St George legend upon which Spenser drew had already established a precedent for dealing with the saint's life as a type of the passion of Christ. In adapting the iconography of the cross to the account of his Knight's adventures, Spenser rather fulfils than departs from the spirit of his sources. Further, by consistently exploiting the gap in awareness between St George and the reader, the Protestant poet is able to show that the red cross pertains especially to the fallen conditions of knowledge in this world and that the challenge of faith is the key to salvation. But Spenser, a pictorial artist above all, draws on a variety of iconographic conventions to help body forth this meaning. The contrasts between trees, between blood shed for redemption and blood shed fruitlessly, the presentation of 'arms' of the cross, both militant and triumphant, the motifs of blind error, of *ecclesia* and of the keys of Contemplation, of the harrowing of hell and the contrast of the *aera sub lege* and the *aera sub gratia*, and the elaborate interplay between type and antitype, exemplar and parody, present the reader with a diversity which then gathers to coherence around the *effectus passionis* convention. As we move through a variety of images with a sense of discovering their hidden meaning, we experience something of what Augustine describes in his theory of signs in *De doctrina*. This use of images is iconographic, and is Spenser's basic mode in *The Faerie Queene*.

CONCLUSION: THE BUTTERFLY AND THE CROSS

At this point I should try to bring the beginning of my argument on *Muiopotmos* into some relation with my conclusions on Book I. We have seen that as he encounters the adventures of Red Cross Knight, the reader is asked increasingly to acknowledge the imponderables of his own life under conditions of a limited knowledge analogous to that of St George within the poem. In doing so, the reader ends up facing the same sort of problem he was left with in *Muiopotmos*. On one level this is the quandary of the 'dark conceit' itself, of the peculiarly piercing but elusive power of allegory which can deploy images with such seeming inconsistency and yet such moving effect. It is the problem in another guise of the symbiosis between butterfly and spider in a fallen world where images are inconstant and fragmentary, but can make compelling claims on reality. *Muiopotmos*, a poem about poetry, provides some insight to Spenser's method and preconceptions.

Psyche, I have argued, is the central and veiled mystery. She does not appear, and the poem suggests that she can be partially represented in images but not finally described by them. 'Intellectual vision' is not amenable to human discourse in a fallen world, yet the intuited mysteries, the tacit but powerful value centres of the poem, are either served by imagination or distorted by it, as the brilliant butterfly and envious spider signify. Here I am claiming that Spenser's imagery leads us to metaphysics for its validation, though as we encounter the poem the images come first[70] and our sense of the metaphysical component is only as strong as the power of the images to move us to it. In *Muiopotmos* Spenser seems to acknowledge this function of image as sign, and his poetry, here as elsewhere, depends on a profound experience of the world and of language in terms of real analogies centering on transcendent mysteries which cannot be proven by poems except insofar as the mysteries provide meaning for the signs which poems deploy.

Equivalent to veiled Psyche in *Muiopotmos*, is the central mystery in Book I, the imponderable relation of faith to redemption, signified by the cross. A lively sense of the inner dimensions of this mystery encouraged Protestants to deplore what seemed an idolatrous Catholic worship of pictorial images, and Spenser, as *Muiopotmos* and the allied passages on art in Books II and III of *The Faerie Queene* suggest, must himself have been asking some critical questions about images and values, spurred on no doubt by the contemporary climate of theological and polemical debate. But Spenser was no theorist, and though careful not to offend against a prevailing orthodoxy, he remains rooted in the older mediaeval ways of knowing things. He still believes in his images in a typically mediaeval manner. So in Book I we are brought to the mystery of faith by means analogous to those deployed in *Muiopotmos*. The icons and their rich patternings present a series of increasingly complex and interrelated signs through which we are moved to a sense of the mystery which may haunt us like Arthur's dream simply because he, like us, desires the images to have meaning. If we do not desire such a completion or feel the need for it then, simply, the poem fails and Spenserian allegory will not be for us. Either way, ironically, the poem challenges us, like Augustine's *Confessions*, with our own capacity for faith.

Although Spenser therefore shows some sense of the challenge presented to 'spiritual vision' by the new critical interest in images, this concern is not seriously taken up in his poetry; certainly it does not undermine his felt sense of correspondence between the meaning of images, the things they depict, and the transcendental truths to which they direct us. This is much less the case with Shakespeare in *The Tempest*, to which I will now turn.

3 The Tempest and the Magic of Charity: Believing the Images

MASQUE AND DRAMA: INTELLECTUAL AND CORPOREAL VISION

The Tempest is a highly complex and subtle play. After *Macbeth* it is the shortest in the Shakespeare canon, with the fewest scenes and most music, and often it seems to belong more to the precise, delicate realm of masque than the dynamic world of drama. Like the island on which it is set, *The Tempest* has a peculiar, hermetically sealed quality,[1] and one consequence is that the play has especially invited allegorical interpretation as critical ingenuity attempts to chart correspondences between the self-contained island and the 'real' or 'outside' world which it depicts. We are told such things as, Shakespeare (Prospero) is handing over his art (Miranda) to John Fletcher (Ferdinand); God (Prospero) is guiding everyman (the shipwrecked party) through the world (the island) towards salvation (Milan),[2] and so on.

Clearly, the play is more elusive than such flat readings allow, even if we do continue to feel Shakespeare *is* in a sense saying something about art and providence, grace and forgiveness. Suggestions of such higher meanings are beautifully enough rendered that we cannot dismiss them without moving too close for comfort to the play's own cynics, Sebastian and Antonio. As a recent critic says, Shakespeare is equally successful at resisting allegory and cynicism,[3] and certainly an audience is challenged continually to preserve a just sense of the play's

power to represent intuitions of transcendent values while
dramatising the perplex of particular human interpretations
of a world where no two experiences of reality are quite the
same.

A complex structure contributes much to Shakespeare's success in sustaining this challenge, and *The Tempest* carefully
combines a series of careful parallels with a subtle tone to
provide always wry or ironical perspectives on the hard-nosed
usurping wiseacres and the wonder-struck lovers alike, so that
simple cynicism and simple wish-fulfilling idealism are equally
disarmed. For instance, when Miranda speaks her famous lines
on the assortment of humanity which has visited the island,
'O, wonder!/How many goodly creatures are there here!' (V,
i, 182–3), her father replies in a half-line slyly engineered by
Shakespeare to complete her speech which had ended a half-line
short: ''Tis new to thee'. Prospero's remark, neither indulgent
nor bitter, reminds us that Miranda's gracious capacity to see
things new is naïve, and Shakespeare's use of the meter makes
clear in terms of structure what the verse implies in tone.
Shakespeare, we are aware here, is also aware of the difference
in perspective between his two characters, and in the resultant
gentle irony lies one important contrast to Spenser. Although
The Faerie Queene also provides countless examples of contrasting
ways of seeing things, Spenser does not at all so consciously
manipulate the perspectives of the characters themselves to
show each of them offering a special interpretation of what
the nature of things is. But throughout *The Tempest* are many
such juxtaposed view points, each with a claim to validity,
and we constantly observe people in the process of seeing things
their own way and then we attempt to make our own judgement[4]
on the adequacy of the images they choose to make significant,
and in which they may be said separately to believe.

Such a process, involving both characters and audience in
constant and uncertain interchange, is obviously much less like
a masque than a drama. Yet an emblematic sense of stable
order does strangely haunt *The Tempest*, and, in combining
elusively with the world of unstable dramatic compromise, tends
to make of Shakespeare's images something close to the traditional 'spiritual vision'—a puzzling inter-penetration of 'intellectual' and 'corporeal' elements. Still, we should be cautious:
although the dramatist manipulates his characters to show them

committed to *their* several visions through images, his *own* commitment is a lot less clear. Shakespeare observes rather than dwells in the image-making process he describes, and *The Tempest* becomes a dramatisation, not simply an expression, of the Augustinian type of theory.

Prospero's famous 'revels' speech is a key example: the 'baseless fabric of this vision', we learn, will all 'dissolve' for it consists mainly of images. We are dreamers in life but our infirmities need the 'cloud-capped towers' and 'solemn temples', the phantasms which mediate values we cannot know directly as pure Form. Shakespeare is careful to place this speech directly after the masque where Ferdinand thinks he is in paradise, for the Edenic vision has traditionally been fundamental to Ferdinand's type of civilisation, for which he must himself soon assume a share of responsibility. Prospero, in passing on the essential 'intellectual' values, resorts to the heightened imagery of the masque, knowing that men need images to embody their highest intuitions but that such images will pass away, 'dissolve', within the dramatic and corporeal contingencies of human existence. All this we could certainly call Augustinian. But whether or not a realm of absolute Truth or Reality does in fact inform the images as Augustine affirmed, neither Shakespeare nor *The Tempest* will say clearly. Nor of course are we told that there is no such Truth at all, or that the images are groundless illusions. Rather, the way in which one partial or inadequate set of images seems to develop throughout the play into a more adequate and coherent one as we move with the characters from their initial pursuit of carnal self-interest towards fellowship and reconciliation, is paralleled by the mystery of 'corporeal' images themselves reaching towards 'intellectual' truths. If we feel the fellowship to which the principals are brought at the end fulfils their essential human natures, then we are likely also to feel that the play's images do mirror an ideal reality, and we will affirm the importance of the masque in Shakespeare's design. If we think the fellowship merely a happy respite in a hard world of political intrigue and that Antonio is the realist, not Miranda, then we are likely to feel that the play's images mainly reflect the attempts of incompatible individual psychologies to cope with the world, and we will stress the importance of Shakespeare's dramatic tensions.

The playwright succeeds in presenting this quandary of image in relation to truth, as I have suggested, by stressing the independence of the characters' several perceptions within a structure which forces their views of things into provocative juxtaposition. One result is that the audience (and certainly the reader) cannot always be sure what is happening in the play, even on the surface. For instance, the storm of Act I seems real enough, with an immediacy of physical and dramatic impact involving the uproarious elements and roused human passions. But the next scene occurs in the almost ethereal atmosphere of Prospero's island, where Miranda strangely falls asleep with the assurance that 'There's no harm done' (I, ii, 13). The world of storm and passion seems distant, even unreal. Later, Gonzalo notices that his clothes have not been affected by the sea: they are even 'rather new-dyed than stained with salt water' (II, i, 64ff.): Sebastian and Antonio mock at him, and we feel at once that Gonzalo, despite his foolishness, has been more perceptive than they in noticing some strangeness in the events. But the play turns this around on us, for Gonzalo assumes there has been a normal physical storm and his partial insight about the strangeness confirms how wide off the mark is his general interpretation. Or again, maybe there *has* been a real storm and indeed the clothes are all ruined, but Gonzalo's slightly senile and forced optimism has tricked him into imagining things: in which case Sebastian and Antonio are closer to being correct after all.

Similarly, the island shimmers to evade our certain interpretation of what it is like: is the ground tawny or green (II, i, 56), does the island have horses or lions (both or neither), and must we reconcile its exotic Mediterranean qualities with its harsher northern ones—its fens, flats, bogs, and inclemency that needs the gathering of firewood, with the situation between Carthage and Milan? And if we suspend judgement here, must we not do so with regard to the particular evaluations the characters make of what is going on in this place which they observe so variously? The play, again, refuses us relief: Gonzalo's commonwealth speech (II, i, 152) with its 'soft' primitivism and sentimental interpretation of what the island can offer to visitors is immediately modified by the plot of Antonio and Sebastian to murder the sleeping king. Caliban soon after gives his view of the same island, and puts the case for an unsentimental, 'hard' primitivism as he curses his master. He leaves us in no doubt that his plans for Miranda remain unchanged should some defect in Prospero's awareness present him an opportunity. Yet Gonzalo's utopian dream and Caliban's flashes of sensitivity to nature cannot be completely rejected either.

So also we compare Ferdinand's attitude as a log-bearer to Caliban's, as we compare Ferdinand's devoted service to Miranda with Caliban's to Prospero, the plot of Antonio and Sebastian to murder the king with that of Stephano and Trinculo to murder Prospero, and the various kinds of illusion to which the characters are subjected by Prospero's magic, to one another. In all this we have a dramatic clash of perspectives in which the poor and compromised expediency of human psychology seems to be the main point: in a world full of individuals there is no general agreement, but a continuing conflict of opinion and ambition. Everybody suffers his own illusion, and this is the world interpreted mainly by the shifting light of 'corporeal vision', where each strives to turn things to his own ends according to what seems to yield best advantage.

Still, the main characters in *The Tempest* do not only suffer such illusions, but also suffer through them, and one important concept underlying the play is that providence acts through time according to the traditional pattern of fall and redemption.[5] From this perspective we recall again that extraordinary contrast in the first two scenes of Act I between violence and calm, danger and assurance, distress and comfort. Miranda asks:

What foul play had we that we came from thence?
Or blessèd was't we did?

and her father replies:

By foul play, as thou says't, were we heaved thence,
But blessedly holp hither.   (I, ii, 60–63)

The patterned lines suggest the fortunate fall, and throughout *The Tempest* Shakespeare examines this theme by having people's partial visions constantly interact to produce opportunities of reconciliation unforeseen by any of them. The play hints that the wisdom of all together can illuminate the deficiencies of each. The snag of course is that no character can force such a reconciliation upon any other, for none can force an acceptance of the forgiveness on which it depends. Basic to Prospero's development is his acknowledgement of this point. So he must leave Antonio to himself, and the masque-like depiction of perfect fellowship with which the play ends is compromised by the particular dramatic option of this individual to stand outside it. The play, again, does not reduce simply to allegory or emblem, yet the powerful attractions of 'intellectual' vision are never underestimated. The originality of *The Tempest*, we conclude, lies in Shakespeare's capacity to dramatise the mystery of spiritual vision itself, and the enduring proclivity of the human mind for 'believing in' its images.

PROSPERO: KING AND MAGUS

Prospero, who controls most of the action within the play is clearly under a good deal of strain, for the control he must exert is not easy and he is often testy and irascible. He draws attention almost immediately to his special consciousness of the pressures of time, telling Miranda ' "Tis time/I should inform thee farther' (I, ii, 22–3), and as he recounts how they came to the island an excitement enters the rhythms of his speech to measure something of the effort he experiences in bringing the varied strands of his plot together, in time:

Hear a little further,
And then I'll bring thee to the present business
Which now's upon's; without the which this story
Were most impertinent.   (I, ii, 135ff.).

Against Prospero's excitement is Miranda's curious somnolence. At the end of the speech she falls, magically, asleep. It is her father's doing, but nonetheless he commands her attention with some unfeigned impatience at her nodding off. Admittedly, the plea for attention is obliquely directed by Shakespeare at an audience which must listen through a long exposition reconstructing the passage of twelve years, but we also see something of the strain imposed on the magus as he works, slightly at cross purposes, to inform Miranda while also needing to have her asleep.[6] Prospero's art puts too much pressure on him, and he is caught doing too many things at once so that he almost doesn't do them right. A similar pressure is felt in his dealings with Ariel and Caliban. He controls them, again, only by an effort of unremitting vigilance and concentration. The language he uses to restrain Ariel's desire for liberty is time-conscious ('Before the time be out? No more!'

[I, ii, 246]) and violent ('Thou liest, malignant thing!' [I, ii, 257]), and reduces Ariel to timorous deference. Caliban is incipiently rebellious and is kept in check by torments which, likewise, do not always command our admiration. Even at the play's end Prospero's Christian forgiveness is oddly tense with peevish resentment:

> I do forgive thee,
> Unnatural though thou art   (V, i, 78–9)
> For you, most wicked sir, whom to call brother
> Would even infect my mouth, I do forgive
> Thy rankest fault—all of them   (V, i, 130–32)

Such charity is decidedly hard won, and the effort expended by Prospero in bringing his enemies within his power is measured only by the effort he must make to let them out of it.

The strain in all this is eminently human, individual, interior and dramatic. It presents us with the portrait of a powerful but difficult old man in the process of learning wisdom and overcoming some personal flaws. He, like all the visitors to the island, is trammelled by consequences of his own way of seeing things, and his perception of the world is clouded by the same kinds of opaqueness which attend the image-making of the others. This is Prospero by way of dramatic portraiture, fighting against others to impose his will upon the material world and shape corporeal things to his own design.

Still, there is another and no less important side to Prospero, for as well as being an enterprising magus under pressure, he is the divine king returning to restore order in the state. As he does this, the tensions of conflicting viewpoints and the pressures of time are released, and the play momentarily assumes the quality of a beautiful emblem, showing forth the lineaments of an ideal order where everybody (almost) finds his place and acknowledges the place of his fellow. In the unfolding of such a design, Prospero's dedication to Miranda assumes a special, exemplary significance. To underline his daughter's innate worth, her *melior natura*,[7] Prospero insists on the good quality of her lineage (I, ii, 56), and in the masque where the high values have found embodiment fit to inspire the troth-plight of Miranda and Ferdinand, Prospero too seems to stand illuminated by the ideals for which he has so long struggled. These are mirrored alike in the elevated imagery of the masque, in the betrothal, and in his own momentary, beneficent selflessness. Here, indeed, we are most apt to feel some praeter-natural design has attended Prospero's actions all along, and that Shakespeare really did intend us to read an allegory. Only, on reflection, we cannot be sure. The images may well have brightened towards some higher meaning, but certainty eludes them, for the play, we recall, also needs the dramatic Prospero, the difficult old man in the uncertain process of learning, and, ironically, Miranda's very *melior natura* as we have seen makes her vulnerable, however much it gives her the advantage over Caliban in the skills and arts of learning and civility.

Yet at the opposite pole to Miranda is not Caliban, who has in him simply more of the anomalous and unregenerate elements of Nature, but those who have enjoyed the advantages of the higher good and corrupted it. Such especially are the usurpers Antonio and Sebastian, and to a lesser degree Stephano and Trinculo. Caliban consequently sees more at the end than they do, and throughout the play he is given the dignity of verse and speaks some beautiful lines. His concluding avowal, 'I'll be wise hereafter/And seek for grace' (V, i, 295), is thus important for two reasons. It shows that some process of regeneration has begun in him, and it may well be the slow process of the civilisation itself, in which Prospero believes. It therefore shows also that Prospero was wrong about Caliban's completely unregenerate nature, for Caliban has moved a tiny step towards the higher values. The final stage of Prospero's education is to acknowledge the Caliban in himself: 'this thing of darkness I/Acknowledge mine' (V, i, 275–6). Much as Prospero fought and spurned and even perhaps thought his 'secret studies' could free him from such a realisation, he finds in the end that Caliban is at home in the human breast.

After the masque, when Prospero says to Ariel, 'Spirit/We must prepare to meet with Caliban' (IV, i, 165–6) he describes, in a way, this discovery by his own spirit of Caliban in himself, and soon he will make the point explicit before the others. The line offers, therefore, an important comment on the masque which Prospero has just presented to Ferdinand and Miranda. Despite the dramatic sense of urgency, there is no actual threat from Caliban, whose plot is defused well in advance and who is grovelling in the mire, drunk, with his bumbling companions. But thematically the breaking of the masque is significant for what it says about images and reality. The masque above all confirms, with its splendid embodiment of reconciliation, fruition, and order, the high dream with which the children co-operate. Ferdinand thinks he is in paradise and in this context confirms his commitment to Miranda. The images have captured the allegiance of the young people who give their assent to maintaining into the future the imageless vision they imply. But the conspiracy of the beast breaks the dream, not because of an imminent and actual intrusion of the monster and his cronies, but because human ideals cannot sensibly be pursued without acknowledging that, in human nature, the spirit must always prepare to meet Caliban. The images will not always appear so transparent to transcendent dimensions as in the masque, but will often be muddied and dramatically confused in the moil of corporeal human experience. The huge sadness of the 'revels' speech follows quite logically. Prospero has shown the young people the 'transparent' images but knows that Ferdinand can no more 'live here ever' than Gonzalo can actualise the golden world he dreams of. That is why Prospero insists so much on the 'sanctimonious ceremonies', the 'holy rite', and the 'contract'. He knows that the children will, sometime, face disillusion, the tempests of their own 'corporeal' natures which for the moment they do not see. When this happens they must fall back on the painfully achieved institutions—the marriage contracts, religious rites, and so on—to help them sustain the values which they once saw imaged so movingly before them.

The richness of Prospero's speech therefore comes from the fact that he can accept the images while knowing they are transient. Prospero as magus must learn to shape his human perceptions and strive to command and subdue their 'corporeal' component. As king, he must attend to the ideal, transcendent 'intellectual' element, and mediate it, but without forgetting the imperfections of the earthly society to which he belongs. Together, the perspectives of magus and king constitute a total experience, dramatised, of 'spiritual vision' itself. It is, throughout, interpreted by Prospero according to intellectual ideas and in the service of Miranda, but its successful use depends, paradoxically, as Shakespeare forces us to see, on the corporeal Caliban also being given his due.

MIRANDA: THE PLAY'S FOCUS

I have said that Prospero's main commitment is to Miranda and that Shakespeare suggests through her some of the play's centrally implied values. I do not mean that Miranda is an allegorical figure, for the two main elements of *The Tempest* which I have described, one masque-like and the other dramatic, continue their subtle interrelationship within her. We have seen how her idealised responsiveness to the 'many goodly creatures' is checked by other perspectives which show it as naïve. Yet her love, the kind that redeems, is patient, and sees things new, continues to move us despite her simplicity and vulnerability, and a person of the early seventeenth century would readily have found a word to describe it. Miranda, more fully than any other character, shows forth, not perfectly but on occasion clearly enough, the root virtue of Christianity itself, namely *caritas*. Prospero's assertion, 'I have done nothing but in care of thee' (I, ii, 16) thus carries overtones suggesting his dedication to the basic ideal of the Christian society wherein he is king by divine right.

On the emblematic level this reading will appear straightforward, but by showing Prospero's interior struggles for humility and mercy as he strives to restore the kingship to his daughter, Shakespeare raises the further, and timely, question of what the magus can legitimately do by way of exerting power over corporeal nature to bring men to the paths of traditional virtue. Miranda thus becomes the focus of the play-as-masque in representing the central virtue to which Prospero's Christian society is dedicated, and of the play-as-drama in raising the problem of the self-sufficient power of the magus, newly aware in Shakespeare's day of his ability to control physical nature as well as engineer political intrigue. On the one hand she marries Ferdinand and in so doing reunites the broken kingdom, symbolically restored to order under the divinely sanctioned dispensation of the rightful monarch. On the other, she inspires her father's magic and provides an impetus for his complex plan to bring the malefactors into his power, so ensuring his daughter's succession to the kingdom. Although both of these functions relate to Prospero, they do so in different ways. In the manner of a court masque, when Ferdinand and Miranda are betrothed and then afterwards disclosed to their parents, a series of significances is revealed to the audience for their collective participation. One imagines that the 'unmasking' discloses also the identity of Miranda and the Princess Elizabeth (whose betrothal the play celebrates), and that James I would be pleased to see himself in Prospero, the wise king whose divine right is gloriously celebrated at the same time. On the other, dramatic, side is something a bit different. Through his struggle to settle the wild island and the wild human natures who are shipwrecked on it, we watch Prospero evolve from the contemplative, aristocratic student of the early days in Milan. He learns a practical magic (distinct from the magic of Sycorax) which he at last puts off, presumably having learned the wisdom to do without it. The pressures of time and circumstance which bring him to this decision, the testiness and anxiety he experiences as the moment of crisis draws near, are centrally relevant to his education as a magus, for they explore something of the limits and boundaries of the natural magician's endeavour.

I have now suggested a series of correspondences between masque and drama, king and magus, and the two ways in which we see images consistently throughout the play in relation to transcendent values and material nature. For Prospero, as king, the images of sense are subsumed and made meaningful by the imageless realm of higher ideals which they mirror truly but imperfectly. For the magus, personal ingenuity and learning give power over a material nature which the images of sense relay, likewise imperfectly, and which we may conquer and use according to our desires. That Shakespeare seems to manipulate the tension between these tendencies suggests that *The Tempest* to some degree reflects pressures under which a mediaeval 'spiritual vision' was being put by the secular and empirical innovations of Shakespeare's own time. Two figures at the court of James I can represent the increasingly divergent tendencies within the culture at large to interpret images predominantly in the 'intellectual' or 'corporeal' directions; that is, towards an otherworldly spirituality, or an empirical materialism. The first is Inigo Jones, who was centrally important in the development of the court masque, of which James I had become increasingly fond since about 1605. The second is Francis Bacon, whose court career also flourished most splendidly in the decade after 1605. Bacon was swiftly promoted, first to Solicitor General and then to the clerkship of the Star

Chamber, so that by 1611 the high opinion in which he was held by King James was a conspicuous fact.[8] Yet the ideas and personalities of Inigo Jones and Francis Bacon, despite their joint favour in the eyes of the king, were profoundly antithetical. In their peculiar complementary opposition we can discover something of the cultural context which helped to engender the character of Prospero.

INIGO JONES: THE IDEA OF THE MASQUE

Inigo Jones, hailed as 'Vitruvius Britannicus', is part of a Renaissance revival of Vitruvius in which that ancient authority on architecture is treated in a deeply magical way.[9] In England, this revival had occurred relatively late and was especially the work of one man, the Elizabethan magus John Dee, whose *Mathematical Preface to Euclid* delivered the entire panoply of the magically interpreted Vitruvius to artisans and designers of Elizabethan theatres, and especially to Inigo Jones,[10] in his heyday when Shakespeare wrote *The Tempest*.

The Hermetic tradition which Jones inherits from Dee is heavily Neo-Platonist and aristocratic. The secret knowledge of the Hermetic magi was the possession of a few adepts or *illuminati*, comparable to the sages of antiquity whose knowledge was hidden from the vulgar.[11] Such secrecy bred suspicion, especially among uninitiated ecclesiastical authorities, and even the strongest distinctions Dee cared to make between natural and demonic magic did not prevent him from being accused of conjuring. The first such allegation came in connection with a theatrical performance, where, in a play by Sophocles, Dee shocked his audience with a flying scarabaeus he had invented as a prop.[12] No doubt his name was much maligned subsequently, and the image of Dee as a conjurer has remained most prominent until quite recently. Still, his own secrecy, stemming from his view of the magus as a special *illuminatus*,[13] and his Agrippan account of conjuring angels, did much to foster this reputation. In elaborate detail, he tells how 'holy Angels . . . have used to inform me',[14] and the arcane dealings between Dee and the spirits by way of Edward Kelly, a medium of doubtful reputation, seem to confirm Dee's serious entertainment of a most befuddled chicanery. But recent research has helped to show that the unfavourable reading is not the only one, and that Dee is also a considerable figure in the history of Renaissance thought. He is the first European type of magus in England, and this helps to put his angel-conjuring, with its connections to the aristocratic Hermetic cult of the *illuminatus*, in a more understandable context.

Certainly, Dee's influence was much alive in the reign of James I, and Inigo Jones was, by this means, the eager inheritor of an aristocratic Neo-Platonist magic which flourished in the milieu of the court masque. Thus, Jones became the architect-magician satirised by Ben Jonson as 'iniquo Vitruvius', who, with a band of 'Mathematicall Boyes',[15] brought the conjuring effects of John Dee's primitive scarabaeus to a height of enchantment and perfection at the court of the king. Indeed, the enthusiasm of James I himself for the masque stemmed largely from the fact that he saw it in a support for his own aristocratic, magical view of kingship.

Holding not any longer to the old mediaeval and Bractonian concept, according to which the monarch is greater than any of his subjects but not greater than all (*rex sub lege et Deo*), James I embraced instead a more modern absolutism, and in this merely followed his predecessors, the Tudors. At the end of the sixteenth century, Hooker still spoke elegantly for the old theory based on custom, Natural Law, and the king's function as executive rather than innovative power. But Tyndale, among others, spoke louder for something different, and in *Obedience of a Christian Man* (1528) we learn how 'The King is in this world without lawe and may at his owne lust do right and wrong and shall give accounts to God only': a statement welcomed with open arms by Tyndale's monarch, Henry VIII.[16] James I, in his turn, was unwilling to yield much on this point, and believed himself truly the vehicle of a special dispensation which sets rightful monarchs apart from their subjects. He advised his son that a king is created not only as 'a man' but also as a 'little God',[17] with unique powers for mediating the Divine Law to his people. This explains how, even though James I notoriously hated necromancers and magicians, Francis Bacon could write a complementary dedication addressing the monarch as Hermes Trismegistus.[18] To James

I, royalty is magical and creative, and its power should not be assumed by those who do not properly inherit it.

The masque, then, fraught with the traditions of Florentine Platonism and Vitruvian magic interpreted through Dee and adapted to the theatrical constructions of Inigo Jones, becomes a celebration of the king's divine right. It is on one level simply a compliment made real by an ideal Platonist participation: Prospero *is* James I, for, as Rosemond Tuve points out, when we view a masque we look 'with the eyes of the mediaeval realist, or the Platonist', and not with the eyes of 'the deep-dyed nominalist (or positivist)'. The pictorial counterpart is Botticelli's Neo-Platonist allegory, for the masque presents a series of fixed significances which do not interact dramatically but which lead to an expected unveiling of some general truth. So, says Tuve:

> The masque as a genre is peculiarly suited to this unveiling or discovery of the true nature of things through images; its high moment is commonly a sudden disclosure of the masquers, when as in a vision the key to full meaning and application opens the image wide.[19]

But as Enid Welsford and Stephen Orgel elsewhere suggest, the court masque was also an important means of preserving a sense of collective life and order increasingly threatened in the world of the Stuarts,[20] and for Frances Yates, who confirms this point, the masque is really a 'vast moving and changing talisman which should call down divine powers to the assistance of the monarch'.[21] The masque for James I is therefore more than just a celebration: it is an exercise also in propaganda, and to some extent an exploitation of the old images, the Neo-Platonic spirits 'tapped' to put them to the practical use of promoting the monarch's divine claims. It is easy to see why Miss Yates goes on to compare Prospero directly to John Dee.[22] The secretly learned magician, conjuring up an airy spirit, raising a storm, and yet involved with matters of navigation and presenting masques with curious magical effects, suggests the career of Dee himself. Just as the magus must manipulate his spirits to have them work, so, increasingly, must the king. To some degree magus and king alike are up to an equivocal modern practice of exploiting the festive spirits for special and private ends.

FRANCIS BACON: THE MATTER OF THE DRAMA

Paradoxically, but with certain energy, the English king also espoused a view seemingly quite opposite to the one just described, for he shared, anxiously, a widespread Protestant apprehension about the popular use of Hermetic magic. To many Protestant reformers the magus had seemed simply to usurp and then to perpetuate the power of the priest. The manipulation of material nature by the spiritual power of the magician seemed akin to transubstantiation, and the priest therefore seemed a kind of secretive adept, or conjurer. Calvin repudiates the practices of Catholicism and of the magi with the same voice. Thus, the consecration is virtually equivalent to 'magic incantation', and the Roman church labours under 'the error of a magical conception of the sacraments'.[23] In the teaching of St Paul, unlike that of Rome, 'we should not imagine some magic incantation, supposing it enough to have mumbled the words, as if they were to be heard by the elements' (4, 17, 39). Calvin fears that somehow divine life could be channelled into the elements by human intervention, as the Renaissance magus espoused. So he repudiates any Neo-Platonist conception (and here we can imagine Ficino and Agrippa and Dee) of the interpenetration of spirit and matter: the clamor of some 'about a secret inspiration that gives life to the whole universe . . . is not only weak but altogether profane' (1, 5, 5). Such teachings set up 'a shadow deity to drive away the true God, whom we should fear and adore' (1, 5, 5). The one time Calvin mentions Hermes Trismegistus in the *Institutes* is to equate him with Servetus, who was burnt at the stake by Calvin as a heretic (4, 16, 31).

Reflecting this tradition in England, Anthony à Wood tells of Puritan raids on the Oxford Library in 1550, wherein books containing mathematics were burned as magical, and their magic was suspected of being 'Popish or diabolical'.[24] Even in the reign of Charles I, when Nicholas Ferrar, that refined Christian spirit from Little Gidding, burned all the 'vain books' in his library, the Puritans thought him to be burning his 'conjuring books'[25] which they associated with his suspected Papist leanings. In the earlier generation, James I maintained this same Calvinist conviction. His condemnation of necro-

mancers in the *Daemonologie* is linked directly and frequently
to his fear of Papist superstition and idolatry, and he talks
of 'much muttring and murmuring of the conjurers; like a
Papist priest, dispatching a hunting *Masse*'.[26] Transformations
wrought on natural bodies are 'like to the little transubstantiat
god in the *Papistes Masse*' (40), and 'in the time of blinde
Papistrie', the devil and his minions, the necromancers and
witches, walked most freely 'in these Countries' (54). Still,
despite these repudiations, James goes on to confirm the widespread and familiar distinction between natural and demonic
magic, and wishes clearly to separate 'vnlawful charmes, without
naturall causes' from a philosophy which can 'abide the true
toutche of naturall reason' (11). He describes mathematics in
astronomy as 'not onelie lawful, but most necessarie and commendable' (13). Astrology also uses mathematics and depends
on the knowledge of influences and 'the course of the seasons
and the weather'. These concerns are 'not vnlawful, being
moderately vsed', but are 'not to necessarie and commendable
as the former' (13). Only the trust in such influences to reveal
the future is 'vtterlie vnlawful' (14), and James singles out
Cardanus and Cornelius Agrippa for censure on this account
(13).

King James I seems to trust, therefore, in mathematics (used
scientifically, not as numerology) and in natural reason as sup-
ports for his Calvinist repudiation of the magi. Indeed, the
practical Puritan world was, for the monarch, a real political
concern, and the *Basilikon Doron* is alive to the new, middle-class
world on which the king has to keep a weather eye.[27] There,
a man's career can be made or broken by his own enterprise
and choice: it is the world not of the masque but of the
drama, with Machiavellian malcontents and individual portraiture. It is Rembrandt as distinct from Botticelli, and it can
be summed up in the figure of Francis Bacon,[28] whose star
rose at court no less brightly than that of Inigo Jones in the
years between 1605 and 1613.

Bacon himself, it now appears, also has something in him
of the Renaissance magus, for he desired to have a controller's
power over nature.[29] But Bacon turns another corner in Renaissance thought, for his direction is away from the Agrippan
Neo-Platonist tradition characteristic of Dee and towards the
nominalism of a future Royal Society.[30] Like James I, he attacks

with 'Calvinist rigour Agrippa, Cardanus, and their brood: 'Agrippa ... is not fit to be named a controversialist, but a trivial buffoon, relying on distortion and ridicule',[31] while 'Jerome Cardan ... like Aristotle, is at variance with facts and with himself.'[32] He singles out others but concludes simply that 'alchemists grow old and die in the embraces of their illusion', and the 'achievements of the magicians are unsure and fruitless".[33] In particular, he heaps scorn on the magicians' cult of aristocratic secrecy. Their sense of being an elect group with arcane powers had led Calvin and James I to compare them to priests and condemn them as idolators. Bacon sees their secrecy also as pride, the root of idolatry. Thus Paracelsus is 'conspicuous for his braggart air. His presumption calls for a particular reproof',[34] and the whole of natural magic is 'beneath condemnation' because such 'Imposture dresses things up to seem more wonderful than they would be without the dress.'[35] Those practices are 'openly convicted of vanity',[36] and the secret and 'remote and lofty tower' of the magician's pride must be abandoned if he is to come 'close to things'.[37] The real obstacle, says Bacon, 'lies ... in human pride .... It is this pride that has brought men to such a pitch of madness that they prefer to commune with their own spirits rather than with the spirit of nature.'[38]

The 'lofty tower' seems also to encourage the magus in a life dangerously remote from the actual world. This tendency, we learn, originates in Plato, who 'turned our minds away from observation' and 'taught us to turn our mind's eye inward and grovel before our own blind and confused idols under the name of contemplative philosophy'.[39] Such philosophy, 'originating in Greece', issues mainly in 'pride and show',[40] and by adopting it, the magus repeats Adam's sin. True philosophy, on the other hand, 'tends to equalize men's wits and capacities',[41] and depends on patience, humility, and discipline, for 'men's wits require not the addition of feathers and wings, but of leaden weights. Men are very far from realising how strict and disciplined a thing is research into truth and nature.'[42] Time, patience, and a sense of one's common humanity are necessary if man is to be 'delivered' from the 'enchanted glass'[43] of his own mind.

All this sounds like a blueprint for one side of Prospero, in particular the dramatic portrait as distinct from the masque-

like representation of the king desiring to celebrate a universe
of stable values. First, the aristocrat devoted to 'the liberal
arts' (I, ii, 73) is rudely awakened. As Bacon understands
and Machiavelli explains, a sign of the times is the brothers'
rebellion against their monarch. Yet Prospero struggles to come
to terms with such a situation, and in doing so learns his
true powers as king, magus, and person. He learns, first of
all, patience and humility, which enable him to put off pride.
As Augustine points out,[44] a manifestation of pride is anger,
and Prospero, testy from Act I, must resist the impulse of
anger toward revenge: 'The rarer action', he concludes, 'is/In
virtue than in vengeance' (V, i, 27–8). That Prospero's anger
breeds impatience is equally plain, for the play insists on the
maturation of things in good time and pays consistent attention
to the passing of time by enacting its processes in Prospero's
chafing and impatient mind. Bacon also understands that
patience is of prime importance in bringing to maturation the
unripe,[45] a process which cannot be rushed, for once the die
has been cast, success 'depends only on human patience'.[46]
This Prospero finally learns, as he comes to terms with pride
and impatience in his symbolic acknowledgement of Caliban:
'this thing of darkness I/Acknowledge mine' (V, i, 275–6).
The sadness of the 'revels' speech is therefore deepened by
Prospero's understanding that it involves not only the transience
of images, but that such an understanding itself implies the
surrender of his status as an adept or *illuminatus*:

> I'll break my staff,
> Bury it certain fathoms in the earth,
> And deeper than did ever plummet sound
> I'll drown my book.   (V, i, 54–7)

However, to Sebastian Prospero can now conclude, 'I do for-
give/Thy rankest fault—all of them' (V, i, 131–2). Here he extends
human and royal forgiveness rather than magical or priestly
absolution, and his Neo-Platonist magic is good finally because
it enables him to understand enough to forgive his enemies.
But the forgiveness again is less than festive, and an audience
is relieved to see the book buried. Prospero indeed has been
involved with traditional images in the service of the traditional
values of love and forgiveness, but he has also been dabbling
with these in disquieting ways. In a world that cannot do
without the old values yet sees them darkening, *The Tempest*

renders them important once more by making them exciting, the subjects of magical art and contrivance. Spirit is saved by making it matter, but it is open, in consequence, to manipulation no less by the magus than by the scientist or absolute ruler.

Shakespeare may, therefore, capitalise on the appeal of Hermetic magic by way of the masque to celebrate a world of collective value, but we can feel the reservations everywhere. We are wary of the magus as secretive power-hungry adept (Dee according to Bacon); of the propaganda and despotism that lie not far beneath the surface for a monarch too convinced of divine right (the Stuart use of the masque); and of secular impulses no less bent on the control of nature for its own sake (Bacon in modern dress; *The Tempest* without Miranda). Yet Prospero as we see does forgive, and although the play has acknowledged the human hazards and characteristic illusions of the titanic magus, it manages also to show with great subtlety the process of Prospero's education as he spans the poles from Dee to Bacon. As I have suggested, the touchstone in this education is Miranda.

MIRANDA: THE MAGIC OF CARITAS

Miranda belongs with Cordelia, and with those other several women in Shakespeare whose innocence and purity hold a power over the play far in excess of the number of words they speak.[47] Cordelia's love, which is 'Nothing' or no-thing, and which knows 'no cause', is the gracious gift of charity which she herself represents. So with Miranda, who represents the wonder of this same virtue as distinct from the *cupiditas* and *luxuria* which are as obviously present in *The Tempest* as in *King Lear*. Again, I do not claim a simple allegory any more than I do for Cordelia, but rather attempt here to account for an experience of heightened significance which attends Miranda, and which seems to depend on Shakespeare's ability to draw provocatively but consistently upon traditional images to suggest that through her the redeeming and essential virtue of *caritas* is expressed with special clarity. Miranda's delicacy at any rate should not be lost, despite the analysis, and just as Prospero stands elusively poised between king and magus,

Botticellian masque and Rembrandt-like drama, so does Miranda between redemptive ideal and vulnerable girl.

Shakespeare first of all gives an important and fairly conspicuous hint about how we can read Miranda-as-emblem by stressing so strongly the theme of her chastity, and Prospero's insistence on his daughter's virginity brings to mind the commonplace Renaissance equation of *castitas* and *caritas*, an association partly invited by the similarity in spelling and partly by the Platonist conviction that to move towards God was to renounce the flesh.[48] The equation is at the centre, for example, of Milton's *Comus*, a work influenced by *The Tempest*, and which cannot be adequately understood apart from the tradition that would read the Lady's chastity as Christian charity.[49] The significance of this familiar combination would certainly not be lost on Shakespeare's audience, for his play underlines is plainly. Also, the one point in *The Tempest* where Shakespeare seems to allude to the *Confessions* of St Augustine, a seminal work for determining the content of the Christian experience of *caritas* in the Middle Ages, is in Ferdinand's courtship of Miranda. Ferdinand complains 'There be some sports are painful, and their labour/Delight in them sets off' (III, i, 1–2), recalling Augustine's passage:

> Yea, the very pleasures of human life men acquire by difficulties . . . . It is also ordered, that the affianced bride should not at once be given, lest as a husband he should hold cheap whom, as betrothed, he sighed not after.[50]

This passage, which describes Ferdinand's situation in *The Tempest* so exactly, occurs in context of a discussion on 'what . . . takes place in the soul . . . on recovering the things it loves', where Augustine alludes to a 'storm which tosses the sailor, threatens shipwreck', but which issues eventually in peace and joy. The passage is preceded by a discussion of penitence which leads to the supreme experience of 'holy charity'. The allusion in Ferdinand's speech and the context in the *Confessions* are both significant: the storm threatening shipwreck and the journey through penitence and hardship (holding back the affianced bride) to charity are strikingly similar in both works. An understanding of this single allusion together with the *caritas–castitas* association may help us to see a further pattern of traditional significances which can be developed under three headings: the association between *caritas* and 'wonder'; the association

between *caritas, castitas*, and 'castigate'; and the relation between
caritas and Venus.

That Shakespeare puns throughout *The Tempest* on the name
'Miranda', which means 'wonder', scarcely needs discussion
('O you wonder!' [I, ii, 427]; 'Admired Miranda!' [III, i,
37]; 'I will . . . bring forth a wonder' [V, i, 169–70]; and
so on). But there is a less generally acknowledged, though
commonplace, association between faith, love, and the marvel-
lous, for the redeeming, miraculous love of *caritas* is often conceived of as especially 'wonderful', and consequently (via the
Latin pun) 'admired'. St Paul, for instance, writing to the
Thessalonians, commends the faith and 'charity of every one
of you all towards each other' (2 Thess., 1 :3), promising
that Christ will 'be admired in all them that believe' (2 Thess.,
1 :10). The Douai version renders this 'made wonderful', and
the Vulgate has 'admirabilis'. This grouping of words is conventional: in his universally read *Of the Imitation of Christ*, Thomas
à Kempis has, for example, a chapter specifically 'On the
wonderful effect of divine love' (III, 5), and he engages in
several deliberate plays on the relationship between *caritas* and
mirabilis. 'Behold love's revelation! . . . O how admirable (*admirabilis*) is Thy work . . . For the charity (*caritas*) of Christ is
never diminished' (IV, 2). He commends the 'admirable' grace
of the sacrament which 'enkindles . . . love (*affectum*)' earlier
described as 'charity (*caritas*)' (IV, 1).[51] In a similar vein we
may recall John Donne's discussion of charity in *Holy Sonnet*
XI: 'O let mee then, his strange love still admire', or again
Holy Sonnet XII, where he exhorts himself (and his readers)
to 'wonder at a greater wonder', namely God's redemptive
love.[52] Although the association I am suggesting extends to
The Tempest by inference, it does nonetheless offer grounds
for a coherency in the 'Miranda-Wonder' wordplay by permit-
ting us to see Shakespeare's pun in context of a fuller meaning
consistent with the play's total action.

Returning now to the Augustinian passage on penitence pre-
ceding *caritas*, we can suggest another widespread Renaissance
tradition which, assuming the association of *caritas* and *castitas*,
in turn associates *castitas* with 'castigate'. The theme of the
castigation (rendering chaste) of passion leading to a concord
of higher love (*caritas*) has been documented in detail by Edgar
Wind.[53] He adduces many examples from the visual arts, though

they are also plentiful in literature, perhaps the most obvious literary example being the career of Britomart in *The Faerie Queene*. As an overt representative of chastity, she castigates and chastises with vigour for her entire maidenly career. However, Titian's celebrated painting of 'Sacred and Profane Love' provides a more tractable example for the present context. (See plate 8.) The figures of higher and lower Venus sit on a sarcophagus which is full of water and on which are depicted scenes of violent physical chastisement. Although Wind does not mention it, the sarcophagus may represent the body of death in which we are buried with Christ 'by baptism into death' (Rom. 6:4), and from which we emerge, chastened, as 'new men' dedicated to the admiration of Sacred Love or *caritas* and not to Profane Love or *cupiditas*. In *The Tempest*, certainly, the theme of restoration from death and the ordeal (chastisement) by water is of obvious importance. So also is the ruling of Ferdinand's passions—he is a 'patient log-man' (III, i, 66) in service of Miranda, 'lest too light winning/Make the prize light' (I, ii, 452–53), as Prospero says. Prospero himself is dedicated to chastising the other aberrant characters so that they may repent, and in his 'nurture' of the higher spiritual love which Miranda represents, the activity of castigation and of repentance and forgiveness is of central importance. As St Augustine concisely puts it (referring to I Tim. 1:5), 'the end of every commandment is charity', and the 'Greatest of all alms is to forgive our debtors and love our enemies'.[54] Specifically, he says that charity is manifest in forgiving those who have done us wrong, and thus, in pronouncing 'I do forgive/Thy rankest fault—all of them' (V, i, 131–2), Prospero is again acting 'in care of thee', as his anger turns to forgiveness and charity.

Finally, the relation of passion (the Profane Love of Titian) to Venus and to the sea storm is a familiar theme, and Shakespeare draws on it. The association of Venus with the sea is of course basic, because the myth attributes her origins to that element. Botticelli's 'Birth of Venus' is perhaps the best known explicit example of this story in the visual arts, though during the Renaissance the moist element is continuously associated with venery. So Desdemona's 'moist Palm' (*Othello*, III, iv, 32), is a sign to Othello (a moor, after all, of 'Venus') of her libidinous nature, and in *The Tempest*, which assumes this association, the cupidity and lust which come in various forms from the sea to the enchanted island must be 'castigated' and 'made new'. Here Prospero's masque is again significant, for Venus is banished; 'now' (IV, i, 88) there is no passion and Cupid 'Swears he will shoot no more' (IV, i, 100). Instead there is a 'contract of true love' (IV, i, 133), and the clear opposition at this point of *caritas* and Venus seems deliberate. As the language implies, Ferdinand may *formerly* have been prone to what Prospero calls, before the masque begins, 'fire i' th' blood' (IV, i, 53), but now he appreciates the higher love of *caritas*, the wonder of Miranda. The clarification of Ferdinand's attitude to love during the masque in turn helps to reveal a further pattern of allusions to *caritas* in many of his addresses to Miranda. 'The mistress which I serve quickens what's dead' (III, i, 6), he claims. Miranda is 'worth what's/-Dearest to the world' (39), and he has never loved anyone 'with so full soul' (44). 'Hear my soul speak' (63), he says, and promises Prospero, 'I ... shall never melt/Mine honour into lust' (IV, i, 27–8), thus opposing his love to *cupiditas*, the passion of Caliban.

To summarise: first is the Augustinian nexus of sea-storm, labour, penitence, and *caritas*, which the play seems directly to invoke. Second is the traditional Renaissance emphasis on 'chastity' and the link between *castitas* and 'castigate'. Third is the pun on 'wonder' and the association of wonder with *caritas*. Fourth is the opposition of sacred and profane love in relation to castigation, along with the opposition of Venus to Miranda in Prospero's masque, which in turn recalls the association of Venus to the sea. Finally is the dedication by Prospero of his every act to the nurture of Miranda and his final emphasis on forgiveness, the consummate art of charity. All this suggests that the intuitions of value imaged forth in Miranda are, not unreasonably, summarised by the traditional *caritas*, and that in some masque-like sense they echo through the entire fabric of the play. By this account, Miranda is also Shakespeare's central unifying principle, for by using the conventional Renaissance idea of charity dramatically, he boldly solves some of the academic problems of presenting his magus on stage. Charity is precisely the virtue to which the magi, and in particular Dee and Bacon, with their antithetical yet subtly interrelated views of how the material world can serve the spiritual progress of man, appeal in common.

For Dee, an irenical thinker who envisages a universal Christian religion based on love,[55] *caritas* is fundamental to every Christian endeavour. He sees his entire philosophy as following the path of 'all true, devout, zealous, faithfull, and constant Christian students',[56] and laments the lack of 'true faith and charity'[57] in judgements about his work. Dee particularly regrets slanders which, as one direct consequence of the loss of charity, have branded him a conjurer: he believes that only the wise, the 'godly and charitable',[58] will see the true meaning of his thought. Elsewhere, he hopes that the 'chief authorised' will use 'charitable discretion'[59] in judging his work. The influential *Mathematical Preface* makes a fundamental appeal to Christian charity for a basic understanding of Dee's scientific and religious thought: 'For no man (I am sure)' he tells us, 'will open his mouth against this Enterprise . . . who . . . hath Charitie'.[60] Indeed, Dee's life ambition, prayerfully expressed, is to be found not only a true student 'in the schoole of *Verity*' but an 'Ancient Graduate in the Schoole of *Charity*',[61] which truth must serve.

For Francis Bacon charity is also the highest Christian virtue: it is 'excellently called the bond of perfection, because it comprehendeth and fasteneth all virtues together'.[62] The Scripture, says Bacon, 'saith excellently, *knowledge bloweth up, but charity buildeth up*. And again the same author doth notably disavow both power and knowledge such as is not dedicated to goodness or love.'[63] All types of knowledge, even 'though they advance nature', are 'subject to excess; only charity admitteth no excess'.[64]

For Bacon the naturalistic magus, as for Dee the aristocratic Hermetic magus, *caritas* is the true end of science, and consequently by appealing to it Shakespeare can reconcile the dramatic education of the magus in naturalistic Baconian terms with the aristocratic magic of the masque which descends from Dee. The nominalism of those whose interpretation of the world stresses the basic importance of our separate corporeal visions, merges with the Platonism of those for whom the stability of the divine Ideas is more important. Shakespeare thus presents us with a 'spiritual vision' poised between intuitions of the timeless transcendent, and the experience of a dramatically contingent world. Charity reconciles the opposites because it is something which everyman must learn to nurture and at the same time a central support for the rights of kings. And though it promises the gift of transformation, charity entails for king and ordinary citizen alike a dedication in which the aspirations to higher things do not obviate an equally significant acknowledgement of Caliban.

Yet perhaps I am too facile in my readiness to have a solution: of course charity is important, and who does not exalt it? Still, we have noticed too that the traditional icons are not so much explicit as tacit and elusive, and that Miranda is vulnerable, and herself no simple emblem. Just as the spiritual powers throughout *The Tempest* are subject to manipulation, so too might be the power of selfless love if we insist that Miranda embodies it. Consequently we are anxious for her, because we cannot be sure that she will not be abused, or the value for which we suspect she stands speak loudly enough for itself. There is a kind of moral anguish throughout this play from which it does not come finally free, as Shakespeare's last hero states how he believes that the old images have value, while nevertheless standing curiously outside them, not wholly their servant. This tension between deploying images as the vehicles of meanings which they truly represent, and using them to promote beliefs from which they are felt to be separable is central to my general theme, and is taken up by all authors with whom this study deals.

On this question, Shakespeare's attitude, it seems clear, is closer to Spenser's than to that, say, of John Locke. In both *The Faerie Queene* and *The Tempest* the imagery carries overtones provocatively metaphysical and seems to mediate, however imperfectly, the mysteries upon which time and space and the shadow world of human dreams and exiled wanderings are founded. If in Red Cross Knight we have stressed the way of the cross towards a promise of saving knowledge, in *The Tempest* we have stressed the way of redemption through the value represented in Miranda, and the two are complementary. Ephesians 6, the account of spiritual armour on which Spenser bases his description of St George, concludes by reminding us also of charity, the end to which these arms are wielded, and in the poetry of *The Faerie Queene* and that of Shakespeare's last play, we find a similar, complementary relationship between

faith and charity. Still, this similarity does not amount to identity, and the burden of the opening section of this chapter
has been to show how Shakespeare dramatises the process itself
of the mind's interpreting subjective impressions as objective
facts, and even in the act of configuration to distort, not truly
represent, nature observed. Even though the play is redolent
of traditional values and ideals, the question is not shrugged
off whether or not these too may be expedient ways simply
of our shaping the world, and that they may not tell us much
about its real constitution. Prospero is thus disquieting as we
watch him at work in some infinitely poignant fashion with
the great traditional affirmations of love, truth, and Christian
charity, while at the same time he is also a manipulator at
whose hands we feel the traditional values lose something of
their stability as part of a divinely ordained and inclusive universe. Yet Shakespeare allows the old sense to sound continually
in musical counterpoint with the new, and to echo, for instance
through the masque and the icons of *caritas*, as a kind of moral
and spiritual memory that shows us how acutely he sees the
difference between Prospero's power and the claim of the images
themselves to embody real spiritual truths. Through this delicate
counterpoint runs a cognisance of past experience and future
cultural developments which Spenser's poetry does not reach.
The effect is unsettling—this is part of the play's achievement—
and we can feel that for Shakespeare a critical rift has opened
to check the traffic of free correspondence between the forms
of nature and visions of the mind, but he calls nonetheless
for our acknowledgement of the highest and best that the great
images express, for we cannot do without the wisdom they
contain, and we cannot be sure either that they do not indeed
tell us the Truth. Shakespeare we might say believes his images,
but does not, like Spenser, believe *in* them—his characters,
with Prospero a doubtful case, do that.

4 Richard Crashaw and the Capucins: Images and the Force of Belief

Richard Crashaw is a most peculiar poet who tends to stimulate among his critics either extremes of revulsion or of deliberately argued admiration. This sharp division in taste tends to correspond also to a methodological distinction between 'modern' and 'historical' approaches to his work. To those who read his poems without concern for devotional conventions the images of wounds and mouths and blood and nests are soon revolting and the sense grows strong of something awry in the poet's sensibility, something smacking of perverse eroticism. Those who wish to defend Crashaw nearly always begin by acknowledging the lurid and sensuous qualities and then, producing a range of examples from contemporary Baroque devotional practice, go on to say that the sensuality must be understood not literally, but as emblematic of certain spiritual states.[1] One critic claims that the images should be read with no corporeal significance attached to them at all,[2] and in this light Crashaw becomes less an enraptured mystagogue and more a careful and intellectual manipulator of conventional materials: a cool and aloof arranger of brightly coloured beads,[3] not a febrile and over-excited case of arrested development.

I do not wish to spend time discussing the history of Crashaw criticism and assessing the degree to which, inevitably, the various scholarly opinions refuse to belong exactly to one of these camps or the other. An appendix to the most recent book on Crashaw very helpfully does make such an assessment, and, even while aware of the fine points, is prepared to state in summary that 'without too much straining, one can arrange almost all the critics in two camps: those who are cognizant of the purely symbolic and emblematic nature of Crashaw's imagery and who are familiar with the history of Christian thought and devotion; and those who are unable or unwilling to assume the necessary historical orientation'.[4] Though Mr Bertonasco's own position is clearly enough implied in his concluding phrase, it does not particularly help his argument to make the division: he simply notices something which to a striking degree is characteristic of Crashaw's readers. But the peculiarity itself suggests how, in terms of our present study, Crashaw's poetry is of special interest, for the key problem which divides the critics and indeed seems to determine their taste, is how *actual* they think Crashaw's images are. If the referent is the actual physical world, the images reveal a disgusting sensibility, but if the referent is spiritual they assume a quite different significance and reveal a quite different caste of mind. The kind of relationship, in short, which we posit between Crashaw and the physical world is of signal importance for what we make of his poetry.

It is attractive, if bland, when faced with this kind of polarity to attempt to take the middle road, but with Crashaw the problem is that he pulls us so strongly in one direction or the other. John Donne's *A Litanie*, on the other hand, gives us lines like these:

My heart is by dejection, clay,
And by selfe-murder, red.[5]

The image is striking, but we do not experience a great deal of perplexity about how, basically, to read it. We are never tempted to imagine the speaker's heart as literal *terra cotta*, or to think of a literal suicide. Rather we see a reference to the Fall of Man: the word 'dejection' contains the latinate implication of throwing down, the clay heart suggests the melancholy humour, cold and dry, which follows upon the human realisation of fallenness, and the self-murder confirms the general theological interpretation by referring to the original transgression by which man, by his own hand, brought death into the world. The further combination of 'clay' and 'red' suggests

a pun on the Hebrew *adom* or 'red earth' from which, by
tradition, the first man was moulded and which the poem
develops in the following line, 'From this red earth, O Father,
purge away/All vicious tinctures'. Thus the clay heart and
the red colour are effective because they are such enlivening
ways to deepen our understanding of original sin.

But when Crashaw writes of, say, the wounds of his crucified
Lord, the relationship of image to concept is much less readily
ascertained:

Lo! a mouth, whose full-bloom'd lips
    At too deare a rate are roses.
Lo! a blood-shot eye! that weepes
    And many a cruell teare discloses.[6]

The transpositions are obtrusively anatomical. The body's integrity is violated, both by crucifixion and by the distortion of
normal physical functions which follow on it as wounds become
lips ('full-bloom'd') and eyes ('blood-shot'). Our first reaction
is to recoil from the physical horror as the poem shows us,
presumably, Magdalene ('O thou that on this foot hast laid/Many
a kisse') who is kissing a mouth and commiserating with a
weeping eye, actions which the poem depends on us seeing
as normal—except that these consolations have for their objects
the physical distortions caused by the maiming of Christ's body.
Magdalene, we come to see, is licking Christ's wounds, and
with an ardour of erotic concern.

On reflection, however, it may seem that the poem operates
by playing deliberately with our attitudes to harsh physical
facts. We have to note and accept that kisses and tears are
normal manifestations of pity in order to appreciate the abnor-
mality of Magdalene's actions, in physical terms. In our recoil,
and partly dependent on it, we begin to reconsider what we
have been reading, for the suffering of Christ, in theological
terms, is the act which uniquely causes us to take stock again
of the meaning of all human suffering. The eloquence of grief
in those wounds, theologically understood, will direct us to
the significance of the event which is the poem's true subject.
There is a clue in the last stanza:

The difference onely this appeares,
    (Nor can the change offend)
The debt is paid in *Ruby*-Teares,
    Which thou in Pearles did'st lend.

The word 'difference' is ambiguous. On one level (the actual–physical) it indicates that Christ's weeping is in blood while Magdalene's is in water. But on another (the imaginative–symbolic), it has to do with the value of rubies and pearls in relation to the implied theme of payment for the 'debt' of the third line. The transformation from blood and water to rubies and pearls, things familiarly physical, fluid and impermanent to things rare and more enduring, suggests a scale of values rising towards the eternally transforming and redeeming act of the crucifixion itself, whereby human and physical suffering is endowed with meaning in relation to the most enduring, because spiritual, values.

Crashaw's poem is thus about the spiritually transforming effects of the crucifixion, but the sense of what the crucifixion means in spiritual terms depends on our reaction away from the grotesquerie of the sheer anatomical actualities which the poem evokes. On this point, the critics who argue that we should not visualise Crashaw's images are on weak ground, and their very insistence tells against them. There is clearly little need to argue in this way about the degree to which we should or should not visualise Donne's clay heart in the lines I have quoted earlier, and the same would go for much that we have read, for example, in Spenser. When the two trees, Fradubio and Fraelissa, talk, do they have mouths? How does Amoret recover so swiftly from the incisions into her heart by Busyrane? How does Florimel breathe under the sea? Spenser critics do not waste time on questions like these because they are the wrong sorts of questions. The 'dark conceit' does not work that way, and neither do the lines from Donne's *A Litanie*. But Crashaw's critics argue about this kind of question all the time, and the insistence of some of them that we should not actualise the images underlines the fact that the images cry out for us to do so.

At this point the historians will often adduce examples from Baroque tradition, to assure us that Crashaw wrote in a milieu where aesthetic tastes and expectations were less ready to be revolted by such physical actuality than is the case today. By this argument they attempt to reduce the full impact of the physical component, and I am unconvinced. In a great deal of Crashaw, as in the poem 'On the wounds of our crucified Lord' revulsion from physical grotesquerie remains essential and should not be explained away. Nor will it do to say that Crashaw is aware in a particularly acute manner of the physical in relation to the spiritual life, and that the poems show how peculiar as a result are his perceptions of things. His poetry shows more than that too. Crashaw rather attempts to convince us that the physical seen by itself really *is* horrid, and a very important dimension of his spiritual meaning involves our recognising, simply, the distortion of a physical world seen without God.

HYPOTHESIS: CRASHAW AND THE CAPUCINS

The technique of spiritualising the physical by 'referring' the creatures to their divine source is an age-old convention of Christian devotion which Crashaw would have known very well. We 'refer the things that we use', as St Augustine says 'to the enjoyment of the goodness of God',[7] and proper enjoyment is the key to charity, against which the love of creatures without referral—the 'worshiping of any creature or any part of any creature as though it were God'—is idolatry or cupidity.[8] Thus the famous canticle to the sun, in which St Francis addresses the creatures, attempts to draw us to a heightened awareness of the divine glory and confirms the Augustinian principle of using things to praise the creator. The same insight underlies a poem like George Herbert's 'The Starre',[9] where the star-beam is praised as an analogue of the source of all light, physical as well as spiritual. The star referred to its maker 'wilt joy, by gaining me/To flie home like a laden bee', as its 'use' in creation is appreciated by man praising its beauty in God. As I have argued elsewhere,[10] George Herbert writes within a Franciscan tradition, the roots of which extend mainly through the English religious lyrics of the Middle Ages, and he is partly nourished also by continental sources through the Franciscan-based writings of Juan de Valdés who was highly valued by the Little Gidding community. Crashaw, clearly enough, has a place here; he was a dedicated admirer of George Herbert, and the title of his first volume, *Steps to the Temple*, is a compliment and avowal of deference to the author of *The Temple*, whose poems were formative for the younger writer.[11] Crashaw, moreover, joined practice to precept, for he became intimate with the Gidding community and his spiritual life at Peterhouse was moulded on what he learned from the Ferrars.[12] But however much Crashaw seems influenced by *The Temple*, there are striking differences. Certainly there is nothing in Herbert of that technique which I am claiming for Crashaw of using the traditional doctrine of creatures to stimulate our revulsion from the physical object seen as an end in itself.

At this point I can suggest a means of reconciling my critical conclusion (that Crashaw's poems attempt to give us a sense of the distortion of the physical world seen without God), and what seems to make sense historically (that Crashaw uses physical things emblematically, as signs to be referred in the conventional Augustinian manner to a higher spiritual reality). Crashaw, I suggest, does stay faithful to the main traditions of Augustinian devotion, but develops them in a form consistent with his leanings to Roman Catholicism as well as his debt to Herbert. A type of spirituality which enabled him to do this had evolved in France among the counter-Reform branch of the Franciscans, *Ordinis Sancti Francisci Cappuccinorum*, better known as the Capucins, and was readily available to Crashaw in England during his most active period as a poet.

A number of advantages attend this suggestion. First, it helps to relate Crashaw to the traditions of English devotional poetry in his period: both George Herbert and the community of Little Gidding shared an inheritance of native English Franciscan devotion[13] which they attempted to adapt to the needs of a reformed church. Crashaw follows in their path, developing their insights in a direction separate from, and yet continuous with, theirs. Second, it demonstrates the extent and energy of Capucin influence in England: the concern of French spirituality in *le grand siècle* in relation to English devotion is almost entirely unwritten, but, as I shall suggest in this and in a subsequent chapter, is of signal importance for clarifying the concern expressed in English devotional literature for the new philosophy of Locke and the eighteenth century. Third, it helps to explain Crashaw's path Romewards: Capucin thought has certain close links with England so that the path by that route from Anglicanism to Romanism could be taken without suggesting that Crashaw's sensibility is basically European and not

English.[14] Fourth, an allied but minor point, has to do with Crashaw's biography. His eventual end at Loreto assumes a particular significance because the Holy House at Loreto was given to the Capucins in 1608 as a special favour acknowledging their missionary zeal.[15] Loreto is also sacred to St Mary Magdalene who is said to have died there after the pilgrimage of her long penitential life, and in giving Loreto to the Capucins, the Holy See was acknowledging not only the success of the new movement, but also the special Capucin devotion to Mary Magdalene.[16] It is fitting, and to a degree poignant, to think that Crashaw, himself so warmly espousing such devotion, should in his last days be directed towards one of its most hallowed shrines. Perhaps Cardinal Palotto, who is said to have been a good man though his corrupt servants endangered the life of the saintly English exile,[17] saw the appropriateness of finding Crashaw a place there among the Capucin fathers.

Lastly, and most important, my suggestion clarifies Crashaw's special use of the doctrine of referring the creatures. In Capucin devotion the central act of the will, the Augustinian *conversio* or turning towards the good, is developed through a unique emphasis on the horrors of physical nature seen literally, and without God. The Capucin referral of the creatures thus assumes peculiar mystical overtones by exploiting the actualising powers of imagination, and the results are strikingly similar to Crashaw's poems. In light of this point my argument provides a way for reconciling the divergent tendencies of the two camps of Crashaw criticism. We *should* visualise the images, and even recoil from them, but we should not too simply think Crashaw uncontrolled on that account: his aim is to edify by exposing us to a certain kind of horror, and his technique is wholly characteristic of a devotional tradition to which, I have suggested, he might well be expected to show sympathy.[18]

I cannot hope that this perspective will make Crashaw an acceptable poet to all his readers. But for those who remain unsympathetic, it may at least demonstrate something of the shock which in Crashaw's time a great number of spiritual people experienced on seeing the physical world bright and threatening simply as object, something 'other', and not immersed with the warmth of a sign in the glory of God's creative light. As Bacon and Descartes moved their cool intellects against the relevance of final causes for scientific knowledge, the spiritual vision of many gifted men, Crashaw among them, glimpsed at what would be left, and they saw with horror something simply and intensely inane.

THE CAPUCIN SPIRIT

The Capucins had their origins in Italy, in the district of the Marches, in the early part of the sixteenth century.[19] They are the last of a series of reform movements asserting the desire to live according to the primitive simplicity of St Francis's rule against the more worldly-wise and established ways of the parent body. This ideological split had its origins at the very beginnings of the Franciscan movement when St Francis, an advocate of the simple life, was followed by Brother Elias, an advocate of 'establishment', and the two groups who followed these leaders became separate as Conventuals and Observants. The Observant reform was in turn redefined by a number of further splinter groups: Recollects, Zocolanti, Alcantrines, and finally the Capucins.

To confirm their observance of the rule to the letter, the new friars wore a habit which was supposed to be the original form of Franciscan dress. From it, describing the pointed hood, the popular name 'Capucin' derived. The new group proved itself able and disciplined, and in 1528 Clement VIII released it from the official parent body and it became a distinct family with constitutions drawn up to ensure the primitive observance. The Capucins attracted many adherents, though they suffered a setback when their third Vicar General, Bernardino Ochino, joined the Protestant Reformation in 1543 and departed for England, where his sermons were popular.[20] Ochino was an intimate of Vittoria Colonna from whose patronage the Capucin order found support, as did the spiritual family of Juan de Valdés,[21] whence a further line of diffusion may be traced in England to Little Gidding and George Herbert. Following the defection of Fra Bernardino, however, the direct intervention of Vittoria Colonna helped to prevent the Capucin order from being dissolved in uproar. It managed to survive, and it grew. In 1536 there were 500 Friars, and in 1587 there were nearly 6,000.[22] By the end of the sixteenth century the Capucins had become famous throughout Europe for their extraordinary zeal as preachers, for the austerity and simplicity of their life, and for the courage with which they ministered to the afflicted during pestilence, famines, and war. In deference to their reputation and to meet the alarming spread of Calvinism in her own country, Marie de Médicis called them to France in 1574.[23]

As one historian points out, the influence of the Capucins on a particular culture was never greater than that exerted on France in the seventeenth century.[24] Under the leadership of Père Honoré de Champigny the Capucins at Paris made the city a renowned centre of religious reform, and around Père Honoré grew 'as remarkable a company as could be found anywhere in Christendom at that time'.[25] Ange de Joyeuse, Benet of Canfield, Joseph le Clerc, Yves de Paris, and Zacharie de Lisieux were men whom the whole nation apparently came to regard 'with awe or respect'.[26] Certainly they were men whose careers embraced extremes of dedication, men often from the top drawer of the French nobility, like Ange de Joyeuse, who left the order under dispensation to rule as governor of Languedoc, and then to serve under Henri IV as Maréchal of France. Or like Joseph le Clerc, whose amazing austerities of spiritual self-abnegation combined with a flair for international politics: he became Richelieu's right-hand man, and a diplomat of powerful influence.[27]

Although the extraordinary religious revival spearheaded in France by such figures was not solely the work of Capucins, the formative energy largely did emanate from them. The spiritual lives of Mme Acarie, of François de Sales, Pierre de Bérulle, of Fénelon, Mm. Guyon, Jansenius, and Pascal, were all formed in some significant way by the Capucin fathers.[28] And if we were to isolate one figure among the Capucins of whom we could say that his example was basic, it would be Benet of Canfield, whom many years ago Brémond named 'master of the masters themselves.'[29]

BENET OF CANFIELD

Benet of Canfield was an Englishman, born in 1562, whose legal name was William Fitch.[30] His father was a landed gentleman, and at some time between 1578 and 1585 the young William was sent to London to study law. But a growing interest in religious affairs led to a crisis of conscience and eventual conversion to Roman Catholicism, and William departed for France in 1586. Soon afterwards he entered the Capucin novitiate, was given the name Benedict (though it has become customary to use the shortened form Benet) and, as usual among Franciscans, the name of his birth place was added. William Fitch had become Benet of Canfield.

The young friar's novitiate was difficult, partly because he was tempted to leave the order and partly because he was visited by ecstasies and raptures which aroused suspicions among his superiors and caused severe mortifications to be imposed on him. But Benet's spiritual gifts eventually were acknowledged as genuine. He was ordained in 1591–2, and by 1594 had become Guardian of the convent at Orléans. By 1597 he had been sent to Paris where he was appointed Definitor of the Province. During these years Benet also managed to gain for himself a reputation as a spiritual director, and his fame extended not only throughout France but Europe.[31] The vehicle through which this unimposing and obscure English exile's influence managed to reach out so powerfully and so widely was the circle surrounding the no less remarkable figure of Mme Acarie.

Barbe Acarie,[32] a woman of noble birth and marriage, at the age of 22 had discovered a capacity in herself for religious ecstasy. Her experiences caused distress, for she did not know their provenance—God or the devil—and only after she had been treated, with the usual brutalities, for various physical illnesses was Benet of Canfield called in. Her lifelong friend and biographer, André Duval, says that Benet 'lifted a stone from her heart',[33] and Mme Acarie emerged as a woman of radiant saintliness, attracting to her household in Paris a group of people of high intellectual gifts and religious ardour. The spirituality thus formed and directed by Benet of Canfield reached directly to Pierre de Bérulle,[34] François de Sales,[35] and the baron of Maffliers himself, Joseph le Clerc,[36] all of them influential men and the chief instruments of a far-reaching spiritual reform. The phenomenon which Brémond describes as 'l'Invasion Mystique' in seventeenth-century France had thus as its leading light a Capucin, and an Englishman.

The teachings of Benet of Canfield reflect his psychology, his vocation, and his circumstances: they are, in other words, mystical, Franciscan, and counter-Reform. The result is a blend of traditional elements in an original synthesis of distinctive quality. As missionaries and preachers particularly concerned to deal with the revolutionary emphasis given to the inner spiritual life by Protestant reformers, the Capucins revived and assiduously taught the practice of mental prayer, especially in forms deriving from the Bonaventuran and Victorine traditions which were important in the early history of the Franciscan order.[37] Benet of Canfield in particular welcomed this emphasis for it gratified certain needs of his own, and he added to it a deep reading of Dionysius the Areopagite, together with the English author of *The Cloud of Unknowing* and the Flemish mystics, especially John Tauler and Harphius. The result, in Father Benet's writings, is an extreme theocentric emphasis, accommodating a traditional Franciscan devotion to the passion of Christ and a characteristic Augustinian stress on referring the creatures.[38]

Although theocentricism is a hallmark of mysticism in general, Benet's manner of presenting it was revolutionary. His disciple and founder of the French Oratorians, Pierre de Bérulle, in adapting the master's teachings, said that they effected a 'Copernician revolution'[39] in the life of the spirit. Benet's main work, *The Rule of Perfection*,[40] published in the first French edition in 1609 best shows the main points of his novel teaching. The book is in three parts, each dealing with a phase of the spiritual life which Benet names as active, contemplative, and supereminent. Although he has the spontaneous, confident spirit of the Franciscans and advises 'abandonment' of one's self to God, Benet produces a masterpiece of compact structure and scholastic lucidity.[41] He is constantly aware of the scheme of his argument and follows his divisions faithfully. Yet he continually reminds us that the experience towards which all this is reaching defies and absorbs all schemes, being like 'the maine Ocean', which is 'without any variation, change of object, or multiplicitie' (6). Throughout his work, images of fluidity continue to suggest how intellectual calculation is subsumed, with individual selfhood, in the encompassing divine mystery which remains Benet's central preoccupation. Also important, but subordinate, is a concern for the dynamic movement itself into God, and for the ambivalence of particular human beings faced with this challenge of transformation.

Benet leaves little doubt about the centrality of his God-centred viewpoint: all he has to say reduces 'to one only point', namely 'the *will of God*' (2). This emphasis is specifically opposed to the anthropomorphic tendencies of the Jesuits.[42] Granted, Loyola dedicates his work to the greater glory of God, but his *Spiritual Exercises* stress the training, discipline, and achievement of the individual will through intense self-analysis. There is self-mastery even in the self-renunciation which Loyola advises, and the soul nourished on the *Spiritual Exercises* strives energetically towards God, acknowledging its own weakness and hoping to imitate Christ. Benet seems to have such techniques in mind when he writes:

> A man may doe his worke for divers intentions, as to exterminate vice, to attaine unto vertue, to avoid hell, to come to heaven, to imitate our Saviour's example all which are good though some more perfect then others: but to doe his worke only for the *will of God*, and only to please him, is an intention farr excelling them all.   (23)

Benet never ceases to affirm, in this vein, that 'Our worke taketh her goodnes of the end for which it is done' (22), and he discourages intense self-scrutiny of the 'Ptolemaic' sort, emphasising instead a 'Copernican' release and abandonment of one's self in doing God's will. Here he deploys the Dionysian language of annihilation and the negative way:

> but I say wee must behold the worke or intention as the verie *will of God*, which is God himself, whoe by his presence doth annihillate in this respect both the worke, and intention or will of man; ... because though in it self the worke be some thing, yet considered in the *will of God*, it is nothing, but even the same *will of God* into which it is transformed, and so of death and darknes is made life and brightnes, and that which in it self was corporall, in the *will of God* is made spirituall.   (88)

Benet alludes to Dionysius on a number of occasions (30, 111, 113) to develop the kinds of emphases we find in this passage, and in the *Rule* anthropocentric devotion remains suspect. The soul finds God its true light, joy, and life 'not whear shee thought, nor whear ordinarily men seeke him (namely) in our selfes ... but whear shee thought him not to be ... (to weet) in renouncing our selfes' (120–21).

As is clear from the above passages, Benet's stress on the

will as the seat of desire for God is traditional, and also paradoxical. We become most ourselves when we cease loving ourselves,
and this emphasis can be seen as an extension of the Augustinian
dilige, et quod vis fac, except that Benet pushes the conventional
paradox much further and argues that our truest love is accompanied by the complete absorption of our independent faculties,
and indeed of our very capacity itself for loving. If we do
something for the will of God, Benet claims, it is God's will,
not ours, which effects the action: a man must realise that
'it is not his will that doth the worke, but the *will of God*;
nor his spirit, but the spirit of God; and by consequence that
it is not himself but God which doth the same' (86). Benet
insists that we must not see the work as somehow 'containing'
(87) the will of God: the object is not a human work at
all, and we 'should not behold it as the worke, but as the
will of God' (76). Only by seeing it in such a way do we
annihilate the work and make the corporeal act spiritual.

From this view of the will, Benet moves towards a highly-
charged version of the conventional Franciscan teaching on
referral of the creatures. By refusing to allow the will to see
corporeal 'works' as autonomous he leads us to appreciate
how the physical world itself most truly exists as a capacity
for spiritual meaning. It is not that we must reject the corporeal,
and Benet warns us against such an attitude, 'that none may
think the corporall to be lesse then the spirituall; and to touche
the deceipt and common error heerin of many spirituall men'
(67). We should indeed attend to 'Accidents' (68)—colours,
sweetness, bitterness and so on—but in order to consider how
they 'ought to be in my soule' (68). The exercise of the three
mental faculties of Intelligence, Memory, and Will should thus
'digest, worke, and metamorphose' the corporeal into another
form whereby the veil of the image is put off, and the object
is brought to a 'pure abstraction' (68). So, 'the worke that
seemed corporall' is 'turned wholie into spirituall' (69) and
in being transformed the essence of the work is appreciated
as adhering to the will of God. This activity Benet describes
as a kind of prayer and offering of 'pure love and charities'
(117), and although it entails a simplifying and centering of
the soul's powers on an imageless experience of God's will
(117), it does not deny the creatures. God 'in whom is no
Accident' (129) nonetheless uses the accidents of corporeal cre-

ation to lead men to Himself, and the process whereby this transformation is effected, Benet claims, is the very key to the contemplative life: 'wherefore I wish it may be well heeded' (135).

Yet Benet does not leave it at that. Although simplification of the spirit may entail the loss of all 'impression . . . and image of the worke' (135), a sense of delight in such 'annihilation' is provided by two characteristic means. The first is by an appeal to images which suggest the absorption of physical into spiritual by describing things which are fluid, as we have seen, and in which the familiar and hard contours of corporeal forms are transfused and interpenetrate. The second is by evoking the spiritual senses: far from being negated, physical pleasure is intensified and becomes, on the spiritual level, quintessentially penetrating and exquisite.

Benet's images of fluidity often relate to the sea. Our soul should seek to navigate an ocean where there is no 'variation, change of object, or multiplicitie' (6). The will of God is 'a spirituall Sea' (8), or a 'celestiall Ocean' which we, in the midst of a land-locked and fixed world of hard objects, cannot apprehend. But when the will of God 'overfloweth the darknes of our proper will', we lose all sight of the land and sink 'in the depth of this will', where all things are then transformed and, instead of darkness, is a 'heavenly shining light' (9). Benet has a good deal else to say about this 'spacious Oceane of the *will of God*' (134), and the image recurs in various forms: it can be an 'abysse of the inaccessible eternall light' in which we drown (130), a process of assimilation wherein we are 'swallowed up' (130), or a 'heat' which 'melteth and dissolveth mee like wax before the fier' (146). In the language of the canticles, which Benet also uses consistently, it can be the passionate marriage to the Bridegroom in the 'ardour and lively flames of love' (93).

From here Benet moves readily to descriptions of a sublime spiritual sensuality where the 'sweete pleasure of God' is tasted and savoured (146). There are 'apples of odoriferant prayers' which are as pillars to bear us up, 'hard as Adamant, high as heaven, of depth bottomlesse' (146). The soul enjoys an 'extreame sweetnes' which 'so inebriateth her' (158) that she forgets the world and the creatures and 'remaineth wholly fixed in this fountaine of joye' (159). Once we have 'tasted' the spirit of God, 'all flesh fayleth', and we exult and rejoice, 'having experimented that thy teates are better than wyne' (155). The soul is subjected to 'a torrent of delights' (140) which make her drunk so that she is 'melted and dissolved into a sea of sweetnesse' (140), hearing the 'delicious and mellifluous speaches' (136) of the spouse, receiving his 'sweet kisses' (136) and his 'secret touche' (135). In the end she is 'as one wholly dissolved into sweetnes, and inflamed with love' (151). Clearly, one of Benet's favourite words is 'sweet', and images of touch and taste and smell add further excitement to the fluid transformations of corporeal to spiritual signified by the impersonal images of ocean and abyss.

Benet's sense of the suffering involved in this kind of transformation into God causes him to look, in a typically Franciscan manner, also towards the cross. In expecting God we must be content to remain 'at the foote of the Crucifix' (118), and especially in the third section of the *Rule* Benet insists on the importance of meditating on Christ's suffering: 'God wishes us to place the red and bloody passion of Christ in the window of our inward house . . . to the end that we may always meditate upon it and contemplate it.'[43]

Part of Benet's stress on the cross results simply from his awareness that it expresses the problems of faith and doubt. He is particularly aware (his biography confirms it) that in the spiritual life the way to selflessness is plagued with uncertainties. Part of his procedure in composing the *Rule* is therefore to raise questions which he calls simply 'doubts', and then to suggest solutions. Most of these questions have to do with the single fact that it seems impossible to perform many physical acts 'only and purely for the *will of God*, without somme mixture of affection or sensualitie' (41). We must therefore be reminded that 'This desert is the penitent life' (40), that mortification may not be avoided, and that 'The afflicted spirit is to God a sacrifice' (40). In meditating the cross of Christ, these painful conditions and unavoidable liabilities of human nature are brought home to us.

But here a special kind of problem arises. On the one hand is a strongly urged theocentricism, expressed in the language of Dionysius and requiring abandonment of the self so that the will may be transformed into the imageless will of God. On the other is an insistence on lively meditation of the passion and the cross. These two themes are not necessarily incompatible, for Dionysian mysticism and Christocentric meditation had been reconciled in Christian devotion long before Benet of Canfield. But, as Aldous Huxley argues, in the main line of Dionysian mysticism (as for example in the *Cloud of Unknowing*, a copy of which Benet owned) meditation on the cross or involvement with corporeal images and 'distractions' is merely a prologue to the 'simple regard' and one-pointedness of the vision of God (47 ff.). Discursive meditations are a stage on the path of spiritual progress, and of most use to beginners. Benet departs from the main line of this tradition by insisting that 'the practice of the passion' be continued even in the most advanced stages of contemplation: 'One should not leave the passion to contemplate the divinity, but one should continue both simultaneously' (75). Father Augustine Baker, a contemporary of Benet, in a commentary on the *Cloud of Unknowing* points out specifically that Benet departs from tried practice on this point. 'I ask you to observe', he writes, 'that he [the author of the *Cloud*] leaves no room for the exercise of the passion, so long as one is enabled in this exercise of love. This love is directed to the pure divinity, without the use of any · image, either of our Saviour's humanity, or of any other creature . . . wherein we differ from the opinion of Father Benet Fitch in the third book of his *Will of God* and from some others also, who would have some exercise of the passion in all states' (73–4). Huxley argues from this that Benet, by turning back 'from ultimate reality towards a particular manifestation of reality' (75), did irreparable damage to the traditions of genuine Christian mysticism. Because of his great influence, Benet managed in consequence to distort the spiritual impulses of those who followed him and to produce a mere 'personalistic theology' (81) often accompanied by a gross and carnal pseudo-mystical fervour.

Against this it might be argued that if we turn to the earlier mediaeval Franciscan tradition within which Benet was writing we find something not unlike the emphases of the *Rule*. For instance, the final chapter of St Bonaventure's *The Mind's Road to God* reminds us that even in the last stage of mystical elevation 'He who with full face looks to this propitiatory [Christ] by looking upon him suspended on the cross . . . makes a passover . . . that is, the phase or passage (Exod., 12:11) with Him.'

For Bonaventure the cross remains of special importance even at this height of mystical elevation. However, Bonaventure also assures us that in the vision of God and in the crossing-over that leads to it, 'all intellectual operations should be abandoned, and the whole height of our affection should be transferred and transformed into God.' The process 'is mystical and most secret, which no man knoweth but he that hath received it.' He then cites Dionysius to confirm that the senses have no part at all in this final operation.[44]

Father Benet, in likewise carrying his exercise of the passion to the final stage of contemplation may simply be continuing the Bonaventuran tradition. But it must be granted in favour of Huxley's argument that Bonaventure draws a firmer line between meditation on the cross and the necessary abandonment of such 'distractions' than does Benet, who insists that both cross and Godhead be contemplated simultaneously. Though the Franciscan tradition helps to explain something of Benet's concern for the passion, it does not fully account for the peculiar lengths to which he sought to extend it. Yet Benet in the end does accede that the experience of God is imageless, and Huxley may be drawing far-reaching conclusions from a difference which is less one of kind than degree. Still, his feeling that the history of European spirituality does take a unique turn with the *Rule of Perfection* is not unjustified, though I would explain the main causes in different terms.

Abbé Brémond provides a clue when he suggests that Benet's refusal to relinquish the principle that the word was made flesh and crucified was really a special attempt to avoid pantheism or quietism.[45] As it turned out, these were very real consequences of the spiritual revival in seventeenth-century France, and it is an attractive suggestion that Benet was especially aware of the dangers of otherworldliness. A recent book on French moralists of the seventeenth century[46] makes clear how the loosening of scholastic categories, together with an increasingly confident secular materialism, caused considerable problems for the spiritual writers of the entire period, and indeed precipitated the quietist heresy. First there had been a widespread revival during the Renaissance of Neo-Stoicism which exerted a profound influence on the theories of the passions, and which soon passed into handbooks of spiritual direction. According to the Neo-Stoic teaching (heavily overlaid with Florentine Neo-Platonism), rational appetite is set over and against the physical passions which cannot have immaterial objects. The rational appetite alone can have for its object 'something which the senses cannot perceive' (118). This division undermines the old scholastic insistence on the psycho-physical unity of man, according to which the will can be drawn to an object desirable either to the passions or imagination. Thus in St François de Sales, who is influenced by the Neo-Stoic theory, a division occurs between physical passion and spiritual affection: the latter belongs to rational appetite and is directed to the love of God, while the former is confined to sense pleasure (118). Likewise in Bérulle, Yves de Paris, Charles de Condren, and so to the Jansenists and Quietists, there is a growing tendency to insist that the will, in loving God, functions independently of sensible stimulus. The result is an upsurge of Neo-Platonist mysticism purged of all traces of naturalism: 'The supernatural is no longer added to the natural as another tier, nor does it merely merge with it; it replaces the natural altogether. This is the significance of Condren's central doctrine of annihilation, his 'néantisme'. Not only has he made Plato anti-naturalist, but he has associated him with fideism and with a love of God which, divorced from all sensible satisfaction, has become akin to "pure" love' (204).

The central problem, in all this, had to do with the function in the spiritual life of the material world itself. Nor was this 'material' the *prima materia* of the scholastics, but the new, objective 'extension' of Cartesianism. The clash between old and new on this question became especially clear in theories of medicine and physiology which focussed on the relation of human passion to the mechanics and chemistry of the body (234 ff.). Certainly by 1637 Descartes had, in the *Discourse on Method*, proclaimed a clear connection between morals and medicine and argued that the mechanistic approach to morality could promote man's spiritual perfection (248). Yet this kind of theory had been long in gestation, and seeds can be found in Montaigne's demonstration of how physical environment affects social customs and, consequently, morality (238). Again, the encroachment of mechanist theory upon a realm traditionally the province of religion further encouraged the distinction made by spiritual writers between passionate desires which may be determined by physiology, and mental desires which may not. Significantly, the most coherent statement of physiological determinism is accompanied, in Descartes, by the clearest distinction between extension and thought.

All this relates to Father Benet in a direct, even dramatic, way, through an event which was a turning point in his career. In 1599 Benet became involved in the official investigation of a young woman who was said to be diabolically possessed.[47] He was a member of an ecclesiastical tribunal which, although appointed to examine the girl, soon became involved in matters much more wide-ranging, dangerous, and complex. Marthe Brossier had been placed under civil arrest because her ecstatic behaviour and inflammatory statements about Huguenots were creating political disturbances. Ecclesiastical authorities contested the legality of the arrest, protesting that it constituted an infringement of immunities. Tension was heightened by the fact that medical authorities, who were also appointed to examine her, delivered a decision contrary to that of the ecclesiastical tribunal. The doctors said that Marthe was physically ill, and the priests, Benet among them, said she was possessed. The upshot of the confrontation was a victory for the civil authorities, and as a result Benet left Paris. Probably desiring martyrdom, he set off for England, but by an irony of fate his spiritual ardour had outdone itself. His fame was already sufficiently widespread even in England that the authorities who arrested him would not believe that his arrival among them was not part of some high-level intrigue. His life was spared, though he was imprisoned, and in confinement wrote the *Rule of Perfection*.[48]

It is not difficult, from all this, to make a suggestion about Benet's peculiar, atypical insistence on the physical passion of the cross. He was a mystic who knew himself to be writing in the Counter-Reformation tradition to redeem souls not only from the German heresy, but also from the spread of libertinism and scepticism. Yet Benet must also have recognised the dangers of ardent theocentricism and teachings on 'pure love' in a society already disposed to polarise secular and spiritual, material and mental, and where the scholastic synthesis was already yielding to a new eclecticism programmed to confirm the distinctions rather than mend them. Had he not seen an example at close range, in the case of Marthe Brossier, of physiological determinists arguing about medicine and the passions and usurping the judgement of men gifted in discernment of spirits? His situation was highly paradoxical: his revivalism depended on the effective promulgation of the theocentric, mystical emphasis on the will of God, but too incautious an emphasis here would defeat his purpose by leading to quietism and indirectly promoting the concerns of the physiological determinists. Benet's strenuous demand that we never relax our attention from the cross of Christ can therefore appear as an attempt to redeem, for the purposes of spiritual ascent, the material world itself.

The real difference between St Bonaventure and Fr Benet is thus not so much in their teachings on the cross as in their attitude to things corporeal. In Bonaventure there is no strain. It is extremely difficult to decide when he is describing physical objects as distinct from the perception of God in them: 'since with respect to the mirror of sensible things it happens that God is contemplated not only *through* them, as by His traces, but also *in* them'. The interpenetration of 'through' and 'in' is never examined in detail, and does not present itself as a special problem. Although we are advised to refer to God our apprehensions 'through the doors of the five senses'[49] by a process similar to that described by Benet, there is an altogether more comfortable optimism in Bonaventure as he describes how 'the whole world can enter into the human soul through the doors of the senses'.[50] Throughout Benet's writing, as we have seen, are repeated warnings against looking upon the corporeal object 'as the work' (26) separate from the will of God. Bonaventure does not seem threatened in the same way by the object 'in itself'. But for the author of the *Rule*, the physical object can be a peculiarly ominous threat to spiritual well-being. The realm of extension, of corporeal 'works', of physical objects, has assumed in the mind of Benet of Canfield a new and disturbing brightness and threatening autonomy. That he saw this clearly and addressed himself to it boldly is perhaps the key to his great influence and significance for his times. But it caused him to put the traditional Franciscan and Dionysian conventions under particular strain, which shows in two tendencies which give to the whole of his writing a distinctive quality.

The first is a way of seeing the cross as a highly ambivalent symbol of the perpetual war in the human being between senses and spirit wherein pleasure and pain are strangely mixed. Benet insists that this conflict is 'the verie knott of the spirituall life' (44), and so must be understood thoroughly. When 'sensuality' seems to usurp reason, we must proceed by 'making of necessitie a vertue in accepting the same sensualitie or affection ... not as a pleasure but as a paine, not as sensualitie but as the crosse of *Christ*' (44). The result is a deliberate confounding of pleasure and pain, by which Benet attempts to stimulate the higher or spiritual sense to absorb and transform experience of the corporeal. Benet instructs us carefully in the procedures of thus taking 'such pleasure for paine and as the crosse of *Christ*', for this technique, he says, leads directly to the 'true *will of God*' (123). In consequence the lavish and fluid images of taste and touch and burning and erotic delight which are deployed throughout the *Rule* are often complicated by images of wounding and pain to remind us of the sacrifices and discipline which are necessary prologues to the mystical state. So the 'extreme sweetness' (158) and 'fountain of joye' (159) strikes and painfully wounds the heart. Amidst the 'apples of odoriferent prayers' and wax-like melting, the soul is pierced with an arrow and languishes of 'wounds which love hath made in my heart' (148), yet in such sweet exultation (155) that the 'dolour of Abnegation' is assuaged as the heart's bitterness turns sweet (156). The ambivalence of this painful delight measures, for Benet, the condition of humanity itself, trammelled by passionate sensuality which it cannot well distinguish from the soul's capacity for God.

The second of the two tendencies is that Benet reacts to the soul's propensity to see the object 'in itself' by attempting to let us glimpse the emptiness and revolting inanity of a world thus perceived without God. To perform works only according to such things as 'the motion, tract, and impulsion of pleasure and sensualitie' is to be 'insatiable and brutish' and not better than a hog in a trough (73). On the other hand, even things which seem revolting, such as kissing and licking the sores and ulcers of poor men can become a 'pleasant and sweet thing' (104) if not seen merely by exterior sense. In his descriptions of mortification Benet's main emphasis is therefore not on expiation of guilt and his main awareness not penitential: rather he is concerned with expunging the meaningless distractions constituted by things-in-themselves seen by exterior sense

(103, 60). But Benet also sees that for most people there is
a shock involved in realising the kind of point he is making
on the beggar's wounds, and he describes the 'extreame astonishment' (145) of a soul so transformed from material to spiritual
regard. Again, the solution is quite clear—we must 'behold
the worke, not as the worke' (75); none can see God 'which
will only see the worke' (76); the soul should not look upon
her act and 'behold it as the worke' (76); she must do what
she can 'not to see the worke as the worke' (77). Throughout
the *Rule* this point almost tiresomely underlines the acute, and
I believe novel, awareness Benet has of the threat of things
'in themselves'. Counteraction is taken first by fervent evocation
of the delights of spiritual sense and then by insisting on the
ambiguously pleasurable pain of crucifying oneself to this world
in order to refer it to the will of God.

The *Rule of Perfection* is, as Benet's contemporaries immediately
realised, a unique and timely blend of traditional materials
and gifted insight. It synthesises the high mysticism of Dionysius
with the ardent devotions of Bonaventure and the Franciscans
on the cross and on referring the creatures, in support of a
highly abstract, theocentric ideal. There is little of the usual
'application of the senses', and Benet's emphasis is on transcendence, on the selfless abandonment and absorption of individual
will into the will of God, rather than on straining to train
the ego by exercises in self-scrutiny. Physical passion is turned
to spiritual affect as literal works become emblems of divine
love,[51] and Benet dwells on images which suggest the fluid
transformations of hard and objective realities into sweet and
delightful experiences of God.

To avoid the danger of quietism or of spiritual otherworldliness which may attend this opposition of material to spiritual
and of passion to affect, Benet tries hard to demonstrate the
importance of the creatures. He does so by placing unusual
emphasis on the cross, thereby stressing the importance of incarnation and of the deeply mysterious relations of physical to
spiritual. He thereby underlines the ambivalence of human
nature itself, and by confounding the emotions of (literal) pain
and (spiritual) pleasure through the cross, he helps further
interfuse the complex experiences of our physical and spiritual
natures. For Benet, as for most Christians, the final end of
mankind is the ineffable vision of God. But Benet appreciates,

with original insight, that over and against God stands the world 'in itself'; not simply the creatures but the realm of hard objects, the realm of extended material reality which human beings readily idolise and in which they can become disastrously all-engrossed. The high abstractions, the strain, the dramatic exploitations of pleasure and pain, the insistence on not seeing works 'in themselves', the appeals to astonishment and horror, are all essentially the passionate assertions of a traditional Augustinian spirituality in face of a modern epistemology already well set to undo it. Benet's programme for interpreting St Augustine to a modern world, as I will show more fully in the chapter on John Norris, was not a success, but it is founded on genuine spiritual perceptions and on powerful intellectual abilities. The result is remarkable in a high degree.

ZACHARIE OF LISIEUX AND REMI OF BEAUVAIS

Though the influence exerted by Benet of Canfield was extensive, his most gifted followers made personal adaptations of what they learned from the master and it is hazardous as well as difficult to reduce to uniformity the eclectic spirit of French devotion in the seventeenth century. Yet among the Capucins the main emphases of the *Rule of Perfection* do remain distinctive. The works of Zacharie of Lisieux and of Remi of Beauvais provide two examples which can lead us conveniently to Richard Crashaw.

Zacharie of Lisieux (1596–1661) was a gifted and- learned Capucin preacher and author of sophisticated prose satires attacking social vices of his times. He was also attached for twenty years to the Capucin mission to England, and his main work, *La philosophie Chrestienne, ou persuasions puissantes au méspris de la vie* (1639)[52] is dedicated the Henrietta Maria, the French Queen of Charles I. Zacharie encourages her to continue, by good example, to convert her English subjects (6), and offers her the advantages of his Capucin method of spiritual exercise (11).

The *Philosophie Chrestienne* shows all the hallmarks of Benet's influence, even to exaggeration on certain points. As the title implies, Zacharie is concerned to engender in his readers a thorough despisal of worldly living, and this to the end that the soul may aspire to the imageless (681) infinite sea (682) of God's transcendent and simple purity (679). It is essential to understand, as we pursue the path of mortification and abnegation, that 'la creature ne doit pas presumer de se regler soy-mesme; ... & qu'elle se rend criminelle, si elle ne prend Dieu pour son prototype' (493–4). Zacharie's assault is remorseless and consistent: the senses bring us to unhappiness (1) for they tyrannise our souls by imprisoning them and starving them and reducing them to indigence (47). But Zacharie does not desire to encourage hatred for the good things of God's creation. There are two ways, he says, of loving the body: one is to give it all it wants of sensual gratification (280), and the other is to sanctify it '& pour luy conferer la.pureté' (281). Zacharie claims, as does Fr Benet, that by the second means sensual passion can be transformed to delicious spiritual affect. To evoke the process, he deploys a series of heightened images of sensual pleasures combined with suggestions of fluidity and interfusion to give an impression of the intense delight of spiritual self-annihilation. We are like waves in the sea (691), like sailors learning to love the sea while abandoning the restricting pleasures of land (566) as we enter the vast ocean of the Godhead (682). Zacharie's sensual descriptions are more lavish even than those in the *Rule of Perfection*, as he appeals to spiritual taste and smell and sound and touch (699), repeatedly engaging images from the canticles (557) and endlessly reiterating the favourite suggestions of 'douce' and 'delices' (577, 673).

To help keep this paradoxical blend of matter, spirit, and sense before us, Zacharie also lays heavy emphasis on the cross. He devotes a chapter to explaining how 'Jesus-Christ mourant pour les hommes les a tous obligez de mourir pour luy' (548), and how all Christians must strive to imitate the passion (585). Our ambivalence among the obscure paths of sensuality while we seek the all-absorbing simplicity of heavenly glory is very much Zacharie's preoccupation. To the heightened description of spiritual sense he adds a whole range of images which confound pleasure and pain and confirm the peculiar interrelationship between our necessary suffering and spiritual joy. There is no way, Zacharie insists, to avoid pain in this life, and he has a chapter entitled 'Necesité de souffrir en ce monde, & pour quoy la vie et la douleur sont inseparables' (276). To his images of fluidity he adds the especially ambivalent image of tears, developed emblematically to show us our sorrows and joys together. Tears burn like fire (703), and are pure as snow (706). Shed in penitence they witness our wounding by the fiery arrow of God's love (576), a love which, bleeding on the cross, has told us from each wound as from a mouth (550) that we must also seek to die like this. Yet the death of the body even in these conditions can be a religious ecstasy (311), for though charity is in one sense Neronically cruel (573), it is also the quintessence of sweetness and leads to heavenly delight.

The ambivalent conflation of pleasure and pain is drawn to great lengths by Zacharie, and his work shows a quality of exaggeration which is absent from the more abstract Benet. Particularly, Zacharie exaggerates Benet's idea that the physical world seen in itself constitutes a special kind of horrifying threat to the spirit. Zacharie uses the same image as occurs in the *Rule (Avant Propos*; 675), warning us of the dangers of fixing attention on material accidents rather than spiritual essence. A soul fixated on physical objects soon regards earth as its proper centre (46), and God is forgotten. Moreover, the object seen in this way is also repellent. Think what medical doctors do to the body: hideous and vain acts for which one 'doit auoir de l'horreur, & conceuoir de la crainte' (13). So in physical nature a landscape of dead things can be redeemed and animated only by our seeing it in God. The gaze of the senses upon a world of objects in themselves is like the basilisk's eye: 'elle tue tout' (493). In such a situation, mortification may involve a shock to the senses as they perceive the horror of a dead universe before experiencing revivification by divine grace. Zacharie's description is precise, and of some interest:

Il est vray que la mortification a quelque chose d'abord qui estonne ceux qui la contemplent, comme ces tableaux dont les racourcissemens ou les ombres choquent les yeux qui ne les ont pas encor bien considerez, & qui demandent du loisir, & de l'attention, pour se faire estimer ce qu'ils meritent; elle n'expose pas du commencement tout ce quelle a de consolations, par ce qu'il n'est pas raisonnable, que ceux qui sont encores foüillez, & à demy prophanes, entrent tout d'un coup dans ce Sanctuaire ... Mais aussi apres qu'on a passé les premieres difficultez, qui estonnent les sens, & qui arrestent les deliberations de la volonté, l'ame ne

trouve plus que du plaisir; on vient aux roses; apres les
espines; & on cognoist par experience; que toutes ces peines
n'estoient que les preparations d'une felicité qu'on n'esperoit
pas, comme les tourmens de la faim qui picquent l'estomach,
sont les dispositions de la volupté qui charme le goust, quand
nous prenons nostre nourriture.   (564–65)

This passage prescribes that our senses *should* be shocked so
that in our recoil we can discover how our initial experience
of the brute physical prepares us to appreciate the real significance of what we have seen, in God. Here Zacharie seems
also to confirm his allegiance to Benet, for this technique, as
we have seen, is of basic importance to the *Rule*.

My final example is not a devotional treatise but a poem,
La Magdaleine, written by the Capucin Remi of Beauvais
(1568–1622). Mary Magdalene had become a favourite subject
for Capucin writers in the seventeenth century, and, catching
the spirit of his times, Remi of Beauvais wrote a 746-page
poem on her life. Originally the work was intended for a pious
lady, Marie de Langueval, but it was published in 1617, enjoyed
considerable popularity, and was much imitated.[53] Brémond
suggests some reasons why Mary Magdalene should have held
such a special appeal for the Capucin fathers.[54] First, her physical
beauty seemed a striking complement (highly suggestive to
writers interested in emblems) to her sublime sainthood. Second,
her penitence demonstrated how effectively she triumphed by
humble self-abasement over sensual pleasure to which, by
natural endowment, she had good cause to be attracted. Third,
she was by tradition especially the saint of pure love and mystic
passivity, and popular accounts of her raptures and ecstasies,
of her suffering, proverbial tears, and her presence at the cross
of Christ, rendered her attractive to writers influenced by the
kind of devotion described in Benet's *Rule*.

Epically long, Fr Remi's poem recounts how, after the death
of Jesus, Mary Magdalene is set adrift in an open boat. She
arrives at Marseilles, and preaches there before retiring to a
desert grotto (presumably the later Loreto) to lead a life of
penitence and contemplation. In her longings and laments for
Jesus she is sometimes visited by angels, and for spaces of
time is 'absorbée en Dieu' in ecstatic rapture. The poem then
doubles back to reconstruct Mary's early life, describing her
historical encounters with Jesus, her penitence, her devotion

Plate 1.   Woodcut (1558). Artist unknown

Plate 2.   Giovanni da Modena, Fresco (1421)

Plate 3. Wood Panel, 'The Crucifixion' (fifteenth century), artist unknown. Courtesy of the Art Institute of Chicago

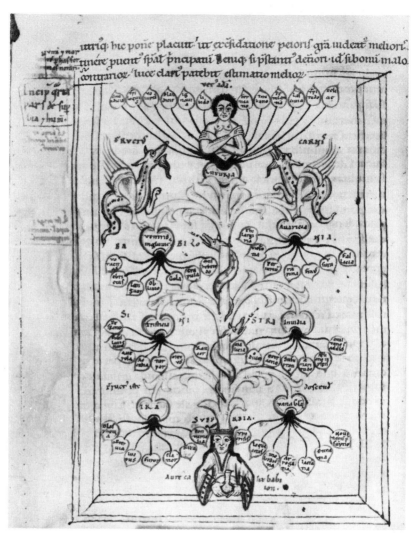

Plate 4.   BM Arundel 44, f. 28v, 'The Tree of Jesse'

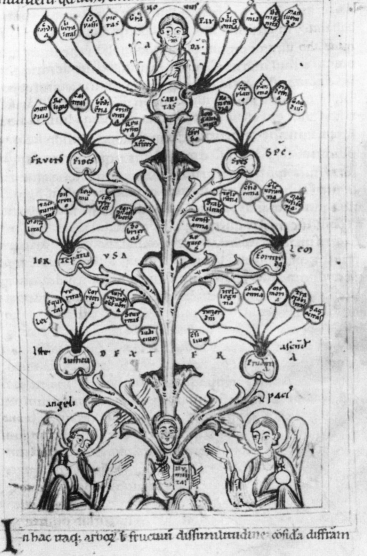

Plate 5.   BM Arundel 44, f. 29r, 'The Tree of Jesse'

Plate 6.   BM Royal 2A XVIII, f. 5v, 'St George and the Dragon'

Plate 7. Vittore Carpaccio, 'St George Slaying the Dragon'

Plate 8. Titian, 'Sacred and Profane Love' (c. 1515)

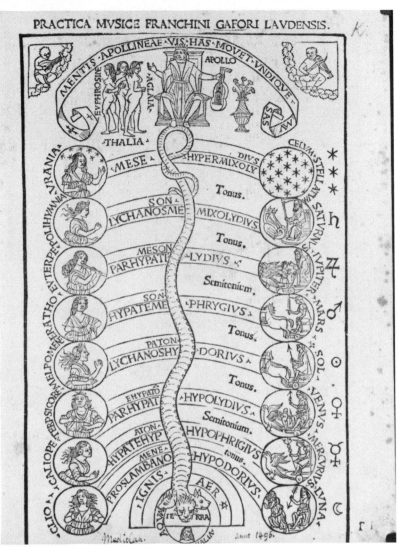

Plate 9.   F. Gafurius, *Practica Musice* (1496)

Plate 10. Giovanni Rost after Angelo Bronzino, Tapestry, 'The Vindication of Innocence'

to him, and her presence at the crucifixion.

Throughout, Remi is concerned to highlight the mixture of suffering and ecstatic joy in Mary's experience, and to dramatise the ambivalent status of her humanity devoted to pure love of God while forced to live in the world of creatures. The high points of Mary's experience are her Dionysian mystical flights, and several times Remi describes how she is rapt into God's inscrutable immensity:

L'immense Immensité, l'abstruse profondeur,
L'abysme, l'infiny, l'inscrutable grandeur
De son essence.   (151)

A margin note summarising the passage as a 'union sureminente de l'Ame a Dieu' (177), indicates that Remi is drawing perhaps on Benet, or certainly from some source in the Dionysian tradition. In the main body of the poem, this kind of transformation also draws lavishly on imagery from the canticles, and on suggestions of sweetness and erotic sensuality:

Dieu mesme, qui (navré de ton oeuil qui luy touche
Au fond du coeur) accouple à ta bouche sa bouche,
Te caresse en ces bras, te paiste de ce miel doux
Qui coule de sa léure &, comme un chaste espous,
Te flatte en te nommant, ores, sa toute-belle,
Ores sa mieux aymée, ores sa colombelle,
Son espouse, sa soeur, sa douce & tout cela
Que recherche, en amours, une Ame qui est là.
O! faveur, ô! douceur, ô! Grace inesperée,
O! Baiser, que n'és tu d'eternelle durée?   (177)

Transformation of the corporeal into such ethereal delight occurs frequently, and is often accompanied by images suggesting a fluid change of literal into symbolic realities. The hard and alien physical world melts into seascape, first the sea upon which Mary is set adrift, and then the sea of God's immensity: 'Dans ce grand Ocean, dans ce fleuve sans rive/Que l'homme ne pourra profonder tant qu'il vive' (151). The motif of tears, of which Zacharie and Benet were both fond, is again subjected to extraordinary treatment. From literal water drops tears become pearls, spring showers, cosmic principles of regeneration distilled in the planets of Mary's eyes. They are crystals, they scald, and they are streams of gold, ocean water, precious balm, and delicious wine. They burn like choirs of seraphim, and fall on Jesus' feet which are marble, ivory, lilies, 'la

doux-flairante gloire/D'un parterre esmaillé de cent mille cou-
leurs' (142). Along with her tears falls Mary's hair, and she
is tied by it to Jesus—'voy! Seigneur, je me lie, m'attache
a tes pieds'—as the box of perfumed ointment which she applies
to his feet blends its savour with the unction of her tears,
the balm of her thoughts, and aspirations of her heart to which
the box is directly compared: 'ce vaze est plein d'odeurs/Et
mon coeur est confit en faëves ardeurs', and so on (154).
The hypnotic and slightly breathless rhythm of all this is best
shown by a few lines together. These on the pearls are characteristic:

> Larmes? non! je dis mal, Marie ce n'estoient
> Des larmes, ains plustost des perles, qui sortoient,
> Rondes, grosses, de chois, claires, blanches & nettes,
> Nourriës à l'humeur des humides Planettes
> De tes yeux, pour orner, pour broder tout autour,
> Les pieds chers de celuy qui te brulle d'Amour.   (140)

After such a blending and flowing of substances comes the
final 'saint aveuglement' (145) of love which bears the soul
above the senses, 'pardessus les sens', and into the paradise
of heavenly Ideas (150).

Despite such sublimations, Mary's grief and suffering remain
real, even necessary, and are bound up paradoxically with
her joy. In Book 12, for instance, she conducts a long debate
with Christ in which he attempts to convince her that the
cross is necessary for human salvation. Mary tries, but cannot
dissuade Christ from his suffering, and her traumatic, vicarious
endurance of his passion becomes the means of her own initiation
to the heavenly mysteries. Eventually, in 'ravissement' (153),
her own body appears dead, even frightening, in the clutch
of a 'mort affreuse' (153). But physical appearance is a
dangerous deception. So, as Mary sees Jesus die, the physical
horror causes in her a revulsion which consumes her with a
hatred of life. But when the body it taken from the cross,
the initial shock is transformed, and she kisses the wounds,
attempting even to kiss Christ's heart through his side:

>   elle baise
> Ou croyt baiser son coeur: & (jaçoit qu'a mal-aise
> Et par ou le dur fer de la lance est entré)
> Insere dans son flanc à dessein fenestré
> Sa bouche.   (593)

The literal is transformed by surrender to its redeeming spiritual significance, but surrender and significance alike in this poem, as in the other Capucin materials we have examined, depend on a prior dramatic recoil from the physical-in-itself.

Remi develops this theme elsewhere. The physical extravagance of Mary's anointing Christ's feet, for instance, repels Simon the Pharisee, but Jesus indicates the emblematic significance of what she does, distinguishing it from the literal 'work in itself'. The streams of gold which fall from Mary's eyes, the poet also tells us, would be shocking if we saw only literal gold according to the profane imagery of poets (143); so we should not see it finally that way. The sea, where bitter waves seem a mortal threat to Mary's well-being (380), in fact symbolises absorption into the Godhead; so our first, and literal-minded, reaction to her peril must yield to a more comprehensive understanding. Remi, in short, is aware, in giving us such directives, of deploying the kind of technique we have seen in Zacharie and Benet. All of them exploit physical 'workes' to promote our self-abandonment to God's will.

CRASHAW'S POETRY

As I have already suggested, Crashaw inherits a native English and Augustinian spiritual tradition which he is at pains to adapt and interpret for a new age. Yet the chaste and chiselled style of other writers who took up the same challenge, for instance Valdès, Ochino, or Herbert, is not that of Crashaw, or the Capucins we have been examining. I suggest, therefore, a more direct line of influence between Crashaw and seventeenth-century Gallican spirituality.

Even before Henrietta Maria arrived in England in 1625 with her retinue of Oratorians, who were soon replaced entirely by Capucins, the counter-Reformation mission of Franciscans in England had been growing vigorously. Fr John Gennings, the Franciscan provincial, had taken advantage of the leniency of Charles I towards the English Catholics, and between 1630 and 1640 six new districts were added to the Capucin mission already in existence at London and Reading.[55] The Franciscans, thus encouraged, were involved not only in a ministry to Catholics, but in the production and dissemination of literature. Before

1649, more than 50 Franciscan books and manuals were printed at the Friary in Douai[56] for use in England. Puritan concern about the toleration of priests and this new flood of Catholic literature was soon reflected in complaints from Commons to the Lords. When we consider that Joseph du Tremblay, the dedicated Capucin proselyte of Father Benet and right-hand man to Richelieu, as well as Pierre de Bérulle, had been allowed to visit England,[57] it does seem probable that, with the king's approval, some serious gestures were being made towards reconciliation and that Puritan alarm, so certainly felt, was not without cause.

In such a context, Crashaw could well have fallen under French Capucin influence. As his several poems and dedications to the Queen suggest, Crashaw was an especially devoted subject, a fact which Henrietta Maria was later to acknowledge in recommending him to the Pope.[58] It is improbable in such circumstances that Crashaw was unaware of the activities of the Queen's Capucins and of their far-reaching political influence and devotional zeal. Further, Crashaw was a fellow of Peterhouse while John Cosin was master, and in this most Royalist and Laudian of the colleges, tendencies towards Catholic devotion were pronounced.[59]

Still, such speculation, even if correct, does not explain Crashaw's reasons for writing a Capucin-inspired poetry, and I return to my point that he, like George Herbert and the Ferrars, was dedicated to maintaining, in face of an emergent modern world, the religious practices of what can broadly be called a mediaeval and Augustinian devotional tradition. In embracing the unique synthesis of the Gallican Capucins, Crashaw responded to a particular programme for doing just this, and at least part of the reason why Crashaw's poems fail wholly to engage the modern reader lies in an equivalent failure of Benet of Canfield and his followers to solve the spiritual problems of their times, especially in relation to the new scientific materialism which they attempt to engage.

The synthesis I am attempting to suggest here between the Capucins and Crashaw is in the end vindicated not by things we cannot know (why his sensibility was attracted) or by probabilities we can suggest (the historical and social context), but by the degree of cross-diffusion that seems to exist between the writings of the Capucins and the poems themselves.

In the opening pages of this chapter I suggested two conclusions from my examination of Crashaw's poem on Christ's wounds. First that we are meant to see the wounds symbolically, and to appreciate the poem as a description of Christ's love, so that the physical actuality of the images is spiritualised. Second, that the poem exploits our reactions to normal and abnormal physical stimuli, and plays upon our revulsion from the literal grotesquerie in order to give us a sense of how distorted a traditional symbol becomes if seen without spiritual significance. These effects should now appear peculiarly close to the achievements of Benet of Canfield, Zacharie of Lisieux, and Remi of Beauvais. The kissing of wounds, the tears, the mixture of pain and erotic pleasure, the centrality of the cross, the absence of self-scrutiny or autocentricism, the fervid abandonment of the Magdalene, the technique of recoil, and the fluid transformations as literal is transmuted to symbolic sense, have all the hallmarks of Capucin influence. As we look further in Crashaw's poems, we find they conform consistently to these general tendencies, which now we can consider briefly according to the headings I have used to describe the *Rule of Perfection*: first, the theocentric emphasis; second, the dynamics of transformation; third, the ambivalence of the human being faced with the challenge of personal change.

Crashaw's poems try, centrally, to arouse in the will a desire for God and for annihilation by His infinitude. The way is through 'Delicious deaths, soft exhalations/Of soule; deare, and divine annihilations/ . . . /An hundred thousand loves and graces, /And many a mysticke thing' ('On a Prayer Booke', 129). In his evocations of mystic theocentricism, the language of transcendence, fraught with highly abstract metaphors and paradoxes, recurs frequently, and Crashaw's debt to Dionysius the Areopagite is plain. One poem even directly addresses 'The right-ey'd Areopagite' who teaches the path to 'mystick day' through obscure explorations of 'negatiue light' ('Epiphanie', 259), and elsewhere we catch the characteristic Dionysian language of superlatives and negative intuitions, abstractions and conceptual paradoxes cryptically challenging us with the limits of what language can say. So, for instance, God is the 'vnbounded NAME' ('To The Name Above Every Name . . .', 239) at the soul's centre where 'Aeternall worlds' have their seat ('To the Countesse of Denbigh', 238), and here the poet finds 'bottomlesse treasures' both 'Boundlesse and infinite' ('On a Prayer Booke . . .', 130), but beyond the limits of language: 'O what! aske not the tongues of men,/Angells cannot tell' ('In memory of . . . Lady Madre de Teresa', 134). Yet a way can be found towards this 'faire Center' ('Psalme 23', 104); it lies both in love and in self-annihilation, and especially in realising that the 'whole SELF' (240) of God makes the personal ego both nothing and empty (240). Man is a 'Hyperbolized nothing!' ('Upon Mr. Staninough's Death', 175) given definition by God ('On Hope', 143) whose 'incomparable Light' ('On the Assumption', 141) he must seek with dedication and self-consuming love. The aspiration to die for love is itself the essence of love's 'hard command' ('Sancta Maria Dolorum', 285) and, as mystics from Dionysius to Benet confirm, it involves the annihilation of personal will before the all-consuming refulgence of God's 'full fac't Glories' ('It is better to go into Heaven with one eye, etc.', 93):

> That lost again my LIFE may proue
> As then in DEATH, so now in loue. ('Charitas Nimia', 282)

The nature of true desire, both uncompromisingly theocentric and demanding an abandonment of self-will, is expressed in Crashaw's punning and epigrammatic commentary on Matt. 6:22:

> Yet if thou'lt fill one poore Eye, with thy Heaven and Thee,
> O grant (sweet Goodnesse) that one Eye may be
> All, and every whit of me. (93)

The biblical image of entering heaven with a single eye suggests the one-pointedness of mystical vision and the absorption of partial sight in the 'All' of God's light. Also, by the two senses of 'Eye' (indicating the organ of sight and the ego, 'I'), the surrender of self-regard to God's will also becomes central to the poem's meaning.

Such preoccupation with theocentric self-abandonment draws Crashaw especially to St Teresa and Mary Magdalene, in whom the combination of devotion and self-abnegation produces unusually striking examples of 'death more misticall and high' ('In memory of Lady Madre de Teresa', 133). Even the Preface to *Steps to the Temple* makes clear how fundamental to Crashaw is his 'Copernican' focus, not only for dictating his choice of subject matter, but for the language of poetry itself. All his poems, he says, direct us to 'that other state' (75), and poetic language attempts merely to approximate the higher and intuitive language of angels—'the Quintessence of Phantasie and discourse center'd in Heaven'. (75)

In describing the dynamics of the soul's transformation into this higher state, Crashaw, like his Capucin forebears, draws heavily on images of fluidity in which literally-apprehended meanings change into symbolic evocations of eternity and in which the mortification of carnal passion is accompanied by an enlivening of spiritual affect. As in Benet, Zacharie, and Remi, the sea for Crashaw is a favourite image for representing the absorption of ego into Godhead. Thus the streams of Christ's blood blend into 'a generall flood' and a single mystical red sea: 'I counted wrong; there is but one/But ô that one is one all o're'. In the midst of an overwhelming tide the blood itself is transfused to blessed and 'living Waters' ('On the bleeding wounds . . .', 102). Elsewhere, Crashaw tells us that by reading St Teresa his exposure to a 'Faire sea of holy fires' has totally 'transfused' his spirit ('An Apologie . . .', 136). Again he becomes 'a melting sacrifice' ('To the Morning', 185) as partial intimations of God's high mysteries are absorbed in an ocean of mystical awareness:

Tast this, and as thou lik'st this lesser flood
Expect a Sea.   ('Our Lord in his Circumcision', 98)

In the famous meditations on Mary Magdalene's tears Crashaw, like Remi, is fascinated by the multifold transmutations of 'milky rivers' ('The Weeper', 79), alternately dew and wine and amber and gold, flowing towards the 'Christall Ocean' (79) of sweet Heaven. Such images, in which tears and blood mingle and blend 'in one flood' ('Upon the Infant Martyrs', 95) and where bitterness is transformed to an inebriating joy remain favourites, and with all of them at the centre we observe, as in an emblem, the literal sense become symbolic. Thus the water of Christ's baptism, in washing 'Is washt it selfe' ('On the water . . .', 85); by the miracle of the loaves 'food it selfe is fed' ('On the miracle of multiplied loaves', 86); when we think of Christ's sepulchre, we see that 'the Grave lies buried' ('Vpon the Sepulchre . . .', 86). In these literal objects spiritually observed the subtle miracle of divine grace enacts an enlivening metamorphosis: things, as Crashaw puts it,

> Are in another sence
> Still legible;
> Sweet is the difference.   ('On the still surviving
>   markes of our Saviours wounds', 86)

In attempting to express something of this 'difference', Crashaw's poetry fully exploits the implications also of 'sweet'.
His indulgence of spiritual eroticism is well known, and he
draws often on the canticles to convey a sense of 'Amorous
Languishments' ('On a Prayer Booke', 128) which accompany
the mystical state. The 'divine embraces' of the 'deare spowse'
(129) are an inebriating blend of 'sweet Light' ('An Hyme
of the Nativity', 107), perfume (106), and seas of virgin's milk
(107). Here belongs the music that sings tears to sleep (108),
chastened 'With many a rarely-temper'd kisse', and all in the
snug warmth of a 'perfumed' or 'Balmy Nest' (107), incompar-
ably delicious and full of 'An hundred thousand loves and
graces,/And many a misticke thing' ('On a Prayer Booke',
129). In such lavish exploitations of the full range of sensual
experience for spiritual ends, Crashaw achieves effects as peculiar
and remarkable as those of the French Capucin fathers.

   In all this, Crashaw remains acutely aware of the ambivalence
of the human being challenged by God's love in a world given
over to distractions and falsity. The condition of man, 'Whose
DEFINITION is a doubt/Twixt life and death, twixt in and
out' ('To the Countesse of Denbigh', 236) is never far from
his mind as he writes of the 'strange warres' (237) of spiritual
life. Christ's wounds in particular are symbols of the relationship
Crashaw constantly sees between self-mortification and spiritual
joy. Thus the extended meditations on the cross do not involve
a strenuous composition of place prior to self-scrutiny as in
the typical 'Ptolemaic' devotion. Rather, as with the Capucins,
they are directed at a 'Copernican' realisation of how the
'purple Rivers' ('On the bleeding wounds', 101) can wash
away and dissolve the puny assertions of self-will in a sea
of cosmic consciousness. Crashaw devotes a series of poems
to the Office of the Holy Cross and he writes also on the
Stabat Mater Dolorosa, a traditional Franciscan theme which
especially heightens the ambivalent human suffering of the Virgin at the crucifixion. Love's trials for her are especially 'sweet
bitter things' ('Sancta Maria Dolorvm', 287), and Crashaw
is fascinated by the mixture of pleasure and pain which accom-

panies the *via mystica* in light of the paradox of the 'sad, sweet TREE!' ('Evensong', 273). His poems feature plentiful sweet woundings and there is a special stress on arrows. St Teresa's heart will 'Kisse the sweetly-killing dart' and deeply embrace its 'delicious wounds' (134). The dart is itself dipped in a rich flame (133) which melts the sweet mansion of her soul 'Like a soft lumpe of Incense' (134). She experiences 'sweet deaths of Love' (137), full of 'subtile paine' (134) and 'intollerable joyes' (134). The Countess of Denbigh also is wounded by love's dart, an 'arrow of light' and 'healing shaft' (237) that penetrates her soul's centre (238). Love's martyrdoms are an entire 'sweet inciendary' of 'mystick DEATHS' ('The Flaming Heart', 326) where blood becomes purifying water, fire becomes ardour, and pain pleasure. Substances mix in extraordinary ways, and like the snow that blends with fire to express the mystery of the Incarnation, they give us a sense of the puzzle of human nature itself: 'Aeternity shutt in a span' ('In the Holy Nativity', 250).

This leads to my final point, namely Crashaw's exploitation of our recoil from many of these images literally conceived, so that our initial shock may be read in 'another sence' ('On the still surviving markes . . .', 86) and thereby even seemingly repugnant things find meaning in God. The technique of the poem already discussed on the wounds of his crucified Lord represents Crashaw's standard procedure on this kind of subject matter. Take as another example the divine epigram on Luke 11, 'Blessed be the paps which Thou has sucked':

Svppose he had been Tabled at thy Teates,
Thy hunger feeles not what he eates:
Hee'l have his Teat e're long (a bloody one)
The Mother then must suck the Son.   (94)

The poem assumes a conventionally acceptable analogy between Mary's nourishment of Christ's vulnerable human flesh at the nativity, and his sustaining of our weak spiritual natures at the crucifixion. But we are asked to take this symbolism literally. The first line makes a hypothesis which we should imagine in actual terms: the concrete and domestic 'Tabled' enforces this sense, and the reader takes the place, momentarily, of a nursing mother. But when Christ himself grows a teat which gives blood (presumably the wound in his side) we are repelled, partly because wounding mars the body's integrity, and partly because our literal imagination forces us to see the unnaturalness of a man with a teat. When the mother now undertakes to suck the son, the literal imagination is pushed beyond endurance, and our mixed revulsion from the imáge of Christ's side turns to shocked rejection. We can actually imagine and perhaps accept ourselves as mothers, or that Christ's side-wound is like a teat. But we balk, and I think Crashaw intends us to, at Mary consoling herself at Christ's side literally in the manner suggested. As we thus refuse to see the traditional image as a literal 'worke in itself', we acknowledge again, with relief, the spiritual meaning of what, in literal terms, involved only an escalation of horrors. The poem, after all, turns out to be an affirmation of spiritual nourishment, redemption, and the paradox of the Incarnation which uses Mary's dependent and weak flesh as a vehicle for the triumphant cross to extend divine love to men. So, for instance, tasting the blood of circumcision and desiring then to drink seas of it ('Our Lord in his Circumcision', 98), ceases to be upsetting as we reject the actual implications in favour of the spiritual sense. And the blood of the 'self-wounding Pelican' ('Adoro Te', 293) which transfuses its 'benign flood' to the gasping heart also becomes increasingly difficult to accept 'in itself' if we move away from the spiritual reference to the cleansing action of grace on the sinful soul. In all these examples the traditional symbol, if simply reified, becomes as Crashaw says, a 'Brooding Horror' ('Psalme 23', 103) which must be transformed again by referral to the 'faire Center' (104),

> Fresh from the pure glance of thine eye,
> Lighting to Eternity.   (104)

Yet the perspective on eternity must not blind us either to actual sufferings attendant on the human condition, and, paradoxically, the engendering of a spiritual awareness in Crashaw's poetry confirms also the obtrusive facticity of physical realities. The impact of things remains 'still legible' even in the spiritual sense ('On the still surviving markes . . .', 86), and Crashaw's insistence on avoiding complete otherworldliness remains, as in other aspects of his poetic technique, close to the Capucin example.

Crashaw's 'The Weeper' combines most of the characteristics which I have now exemplified from the poems in general. He is indebted to a variety of sources in this famous work,

but his treatment, like Remi's, shows Mary Magdalene yielding to passionate longings for her lover, as her penitence and self-abasement triumph over the world by absorbing its coarse sensuality and referring it 'Vpwards' (309) to Heaven. The image of transcendant 'Waters aboue th'Heauns', represents the ineffable source in God to which other images of fluidity in the poem strive to blend. Crashaw indeed uses almost the same repertoire of metamorphoses as the Capucin poet, as tears become pearls, spring showers, cosmic principles of regeneration, crystals, streams of gold, rivers, wine, and the food of angels. The literal significance of these comparisons of course is transformed as they become symbols of penitence redeeming the world, and the abandonment of herself to God in sorrow and longing thus allows Magdalene unselfconsciously to draw the physical world towards God. They are a great many references to 'sweetness' in the images which describe this referral, from the 'sweetest Lippes' (309) of the cherub to 'clouds of incense' (313), dew 'Nuzzel'd in the lilly's neck' (310) and the coy droppings of balsam-sweating boughs (310). Such spiritual joys also reduce temporal reality to a simple, delightful eternity enjoyed in contemplation. The anguished round of sunrise and sunset (309), changing minutes into hours and months into seasons, is measured by tears but then transformed in turn by penitence into the ineffable mystery of the timeless ocean: 'Waters aboue th'Heauns' (309). Yet Mary remains human throughout her bittersweet joy: the word 'sorrow' recurs almost as often as 'sweet', and the poem suggests the fair penitent is exemplary in her ambivalent 'Sweetnesse so sad, sadnesse so sweet' (309). In such a context we are *meant* to discriminate between the inappropriateness of comparisons literally conceived when they show the anomaly of things-in-themselves, and then move to the relief which spiritual significance provides. Thus the famous 'walking baths; two weeping motions;/Portable, and compendious oceans' (312) are intended to suggest cleansing tears in relation to the absorbing cosmic sea, but I am not sure that we are not meant to notice (as throughout Remi's poem) how outlandish the comparison would be in itself. Crashaw gives a hint when, after the opening two stanzas of similarly outlandish conceits ('Euer bubling things!/Thawing crystall snowy hills!' (308) and among other things, stars), he writes:
    But we are deceiued all,

Starres indeed they are too true,
  For they but seem to fall,
  As Heauen's other spangles doe:
It is not for our Earth and vs,
To shine in Things so pretious.   (309)

The conceits have not been actual comparisons at all, and
our earthbound imaginations are too literal-minded. Yet the
poetic imagery is not without actual foundation, for in a sense
the eyes are even more star-like than stars, and this we can
see if we look spiritually. The argument here may not seem
anything more than the old mediaeval convention that analogies
are real, but there is one important difference: Crashaw deliberately manipulates our reaction to move us away from a nominalist
interpretation to a realistic one. He depends on the powers
of our reason to diagnose the unacceptability of the actualising
imagination, and thus to move us to the spiritual sense. Such
a view of the physical world is the characteristic contribution
of Capucin spirituality to the Augustinian tradition: it is a
striking innovation, with far-reaching implications.

In attempting to explicate Crashaw's poetry in light of French
Capucin spirituality I do not hope to reduce his work to dependency on a particular source, or to denounce critical views
which relate Crashaw to other aspects of his culture. Mainly,
I hope to clarify Crashaw's place in the history of English
devotional poetry, and to suggest that his work shows, in one
way, how the new materialism affected the use of traditional
images in devotional literature. I have stressed the continuities
extending to Donne and Herbert because their tradition precipi-
tates the very departures which Crashaw makes from it. In
attempting to maintain the techniques of Franciscan devotion
through the pressures of seventeenth-century secularism, Crashaw resembles these earlier writers, seeking a timely solution
to traditional problems. Yet he is more willing also to risk
new departures, and in this he resembles Henry Vaughan,
who, to the same end, looked to the novel insights of Hermetic
philosophy, or Thomas Traherne, whose highly personalised
and radiant thought is a unique departure from a tradition
which nonetheless continued to nourish his work. But the important point for the present study is that Crashaw found in the
Gallican spirituality of the Capucins a unique prescription for
interpreting St Augustine in the age of Descartes. From Little

Gidding, where the influence of Franciscan reformed devotion was already felt, to the atmosphere of Peterhouse and the influence of the court and the Capucin mission, a series of relationships can be established to suggest how readily Crashaw could have found a path from George Herbert's *Temple* to the concerns of Père Zacharie, until at the end of his life he made his way to the Capucin house of Loreto itself. At the centre, however, is simply the question of whether or not the main Capucin emphases—the theocentricism, the self-abandonment, the debt to Dionysius, the evocation of the spiritual senses, the fluid images of transformation, the devotion to the cross, the concentration on the ambivalence of ecstatic experience, and the technique of stimulating a reaction away from the thing-in-itself to centre the will on God—seem sufficiently peculiar and clearly enough shared by Crashaw and his Capucin antecedents to compose a tradition, as I believe they do.

My argument, if thus accepted, helps also to establish the place of Crashaw in the scheme of this study. The world of materiality is experienced by him in a manner new to English poetry. As Ruth Wallerstein[60] some time ago pointed out, Crashaw learned a great deal from Spenser, but Crashaw is a much more deliberate and calculating writer. There is a sense in his poetry of a cool manipulator of effects, and there is a sense too of a man aware of himself in the spiritual life in a new way standing over and against a world of thwarting materiality. The thing-in-itself never appears in Spenser, but in Crashaw it is recognised and exploited for particular effects as we have seen. His poetry exists partly because in the world of ideas a critical dislocation had occurred, and was increasingly affirmed in complex ways by society at large, between our images and material substance. I have tried to show how such an innovation was pertinent for Crashaw's poetry: certainly his effectiveness depends greatly on how we interpret his treatment of images in relation to material things. As we have seen, his works exploit traditional types and images so that we first see them literally, and then we move, driven by the reified image itself, as it were, to seek relief in reaffirming the spiritual significance which absorbs us with a sense of affective participation in the mysteries. This act of 'vertical transcendence' to which Crashaw so unremittingly forces us, requires a special technique whereby the spiritual meaning of images is rescued in the end by giving them first a desperate injection of concreteness. Augustine's 'spiritual vision' here has become self-conscious to the point where the corporeal element must be *forced* to reveal the intellectual truth. So we are recalled to our awareness of the spirit by the very fact that the split between object-in-itself and the image as acceptable spiritual sign is made the ground of the poem. Crashaw's indebtedness to the Capucins for this technique therefore carries over into his poems something of their concern to meet the challenge presented by scientific materialism to the older, traditional ways of knowing the world. Crashaw, like them, uses his images in a novel manner to command our belief, and the next stage of this story, in which the demise of the Augustinian tradition in English devotional writing itself can be told, lies with John Norris of Bemerton, with whom I will deal in the closing sections of this book. He too inherited the poetry, as well as the parish, of George Herbert and he embraced, like Crashaw, the teachings of Gallican spirituality, bringing the heritage of Benet Canfield, as interpreted through the Oratorians Pierre de Bérulle and Nicolas Malebranche, to bear directly on the new and empirical philosophy of John Locke.

5 Time and Temptation in *Paradise Regained*: Belief and the Single Image

TIME AND MATTER

There is not much sense of history in Richard Crashaw. As a Neo-Platonist he simply does not engage as a problem the historical facts of the saints' lives with which he deals.[1] The enduring and transcendent significance of a life as exemplar is, for Crashaw, what really matters. Yet Christianity has always insisted on joining Crashaw's kind of Platonic speculation with the Hebrew sense of uniqueness in temporal events, even though the measures in which the ingredients are mixed have varied a great deal in the history of Christian thought.[2] In the early church, which lived with a strong sense of impending apocalypse, history was especially important, whereas the church of the high Middle Ages, dominated by Platonism, stressed more firmly the a-temporal quality of saving truth. The central rite of the mass in particular symbolised a continuing transection of time by eternity, and the resultant sacramental emphasis highlighted a conception of the world structured hierarchically towards the changeless Ideas in whose image the realm of shifting material things was created.

Clearly, these different emphases imply different interpretations of the value and meaning of the physical world itself. For the Greeks, the physical and temporal are both impediments to clear apprehension of Ideas, whereas for the Hebrews things and events are valued as a medium of God's ministrations to man. The dominant hopes and aspirations of an early and a mediaeval church, respectively, for the second coming (Hebrew) and the bliss of contemplative vision (Greek) reflect their divergent estimates of the ways in which material creation can promote the fulfilment to which faith directs us. Not surprisingly, in the Reformation, a period which saw a profound shift in received ideas about physical nature, there was again an oscillation from Greek to Hebrew time among theologians who sought to accommodate, among other things, the new, positive attitudes of science towards the bounty of God's physical creation. The Hebrew linear emphasis was once more widely asserted, with accompanying attacks on Catholic sacramentalism and on the Neo-Platonic hierarchies of Being. The mediaeval ontological emphasis was replaced by a historical and psychological one, and theories of a millennium at the end of history became a special preoccupation of Protestant preaching.[3]

Some of this we have seen reflected in Spenser and Crashaw, whose poetry shows little historical sense and a strongly exemplarist interpretation of the physical world. By contrast, John Milton, the main subject of this chapter, considers historical process with as much care as Crashaw contrives to ignore it, and, in particular, *Paradise Regained* shows how time in Milton's theory influences profoundly the relationship in his work between images, bodies, and the content of faith.

MILTON AS HISTORIAN

Milton's *History of Britain*, like most of his work, sets out to adapt traditional wisdom to modern innovation. On the innovative side it shows the influence especially of an attitude to history which had grown up through the Renaissance and which had Petrarch as one of its earliest main exponents.[4] In *De Viris Illustribus* Petrarch first of all shows a revolutionary awareness of how, in the historical past, perspectives were conditioned by social and cultural circumstances different from his own. Careful study of original documents and concern to establish reliable texts he sees as a means of making available accurately the different viewpoints of past ages. He is first among historians to suggest the development of European civilisation in terms of the now familiar scheme of an ancient world, a middle age, and a modern period, and in approaching history through textual study and in breaking from the mediaeval scheme of creation—redemption—judgement, he shows himself the harbinger both of a modern historical sense and of modern methods in historical criticism.[5] Still, in a manner congenial to the old ways, he continues to see history as exemplary, insisting that the past should be studied for whatever moral lessons can be derived from it, just as mediaeval writers had always taught. Petrarch remains Augustinian in his conviction that the true end of history is the City of God, and that the story of human society provides examples of how time is moving towards that sublime conclusion. He does not feel that the theological is opposed to the objective and scholarly, and there is little strain between these two elements in his writing.

Milton carries on the main traditions of Petrarch's humanist historiography, and his *History of Britain*, first published in 1670,[6] is scholarly and edifying. It draws on the exemplary history of the universal chronicles[7] still popular in the England of his day, and from the new secular method promulgated by the labours of translators and by those new independent men concerned to scrutinise the traditional claims of monarchy by the light of hard facts. The result is that Milton's work, though unfinished, is a careful and judicious interpretation of original documents which are examined for reliability, and to provide an objective outline of national history; a 'view of what with reason can be rely'd on for truth.'[8] But Milton does not hesitate to draw edifying conclusions and to suggest providential parallels between the errors of past times and those of the present. For instance he claims that after the Roman Conquest Britain suffered a demoralisation equivalent to that caused by 'the late civil broils' (103), and from 'two such remarkable turns of State' he ventures that we may deduce something of the national character, approach some 'high point of wisdom' in self-knowledge and also demonstrate how 'accidents' can yield 'exemplary' lessons.

Although there is a typically Renaissance blend here of an objective search for reliable facts with a readiness to conclude that such facts will reveal God's design, the note of restraint and scepticism also runs deep in Milton's scholarship. For instance, there is little faith that the 'good of the *British* Nation' (3) is served by the outlandish figments (4) so often grafted on to its legends and allowed to pass for truth. Milton states flatly that what happened in Britain before Julius Caesar must remain uncertain for it is hopelessly entangled with fables. Throughout his own investigations, by contrast, he remains concerned to establish the 'surest Authors' (123), noticing their consistency, their anachronisms and discrepancies. Thus he concludes that who King Arthur was 'and whether ever any such reign'd in *Britain*, hath bin doubted heertofore, and may again with good reason' (127–8). Arthur's chief historian, Geoffrey of Monmouth, is condemned out of hand as a fraud (113) and Milton observes that this historian's conclusions are severely undermined by taking seriously achievements 'more renown'd in songs and romances then in true stories' (123). Modern critical method here clearly opposes the songs and romances to actual facts, and one reason for Milton rejecting his own proposed plans for an Arthuriad (he also had a plan to start with Brut)[9] was his discovery that Arthur's place in history was so uncertain.[10] The Protestant scholar who stressed the importance of history must have found the mediaeval confusion of Arthur with mere fable uncomfortably akin to the similar fabulous theories of divine and episcopal rights, equally based on non-verifiable claims to authority and equally rooted in legendary constructions upon a counterfeit past.

Milton, as we might expect, moves with confidence to apply the lessons of his *History* to theological imbroglios in contemporary politics. For example, his scorn of the 'inconstant, irrational, and Image-doting rabble'[11] who protect the false authority of their king is supported by a battery of citations from history to demonstrate that kings never were, in God's declared purposes or primitive practice, exempt from secular jurisdiction. The history of the early British Church affords many further examples of ecclesiastical authority usurping secular justice, and one especially important ill consequence is the superstition, advanced as historically valid in Charles I's *Eikon Básilike*, that the king rules by divine right alone. Milton's reply in *Eikonoklastes* clearly announces the intention to break such superstitious images to pieces, and it is easy to see how the scholarly historian combines here with the advocate of Protestant individualism against the Catholic institutions of Royalty and Episcopacy. For Milton, the mysterious transection of time by eternity, the mystery celebrated and renewed in the bloodless sacrifice of the mass and explained by social theory in terms of divinely sanctioned and priestly functions, results only in a travesty of human justice. It must be replaced at all costs by a system in which each man experiences God as God intended he should, unmediated by the pomp and circumstance of human pretension and idolatry: 'all corporeal resemblances of inward holinesse and beauty are now past.'[12] The static hierarchies of Neo-Platonism are therefore replaced in Milton's view by the dynamic-progressive movement of history. His poetry shows the consequences of this shift in perspective, for the change affects not only Milton's interpretation of material creation itself, but how he may disclose its meaning in images.

MATTER, TIME, AND THE SINGLE IMAGE

As I have indicated, Milton does not wish to surrender the main traditional insights of Christianity, and so does not allow his emphasis on history to usurp the belief that God eternally has ordained all things. The completeness of divine fore-knowledge is made baldly explicit in *Paradise Lost* and *Paradise Regained* where, before the action of either poem begins, God describes the outcome which he knows fully and outside of contingencies by which the humans come to discover it. Yet Milton insists equally on human freedom, and the paradox of fore-ordination and freewill is maintained by him in line with the mainstream of Christian teaching, as a mystery.[13]

Though Milton thus retains the notion of an eternal design at work in time, he was never able to write successfully on the main symbol of this paradox, namely the cross. His early poem on the crucifixion, 'The Passion', is incomplete, and a failure.[14] It gropes awkwardly towards the subject, with the poet describing himself about to write a poem, but never actually engaging its central event. Christ remains the 'Most perfect Hero' (13) rather than sacrificed God at once divine and human, with the mystery made present to the senses through meditation. Milton's later emphasis on Christ as an exemplary man among men, who has deliberately put off his Godlike knowledge, is already in germ here. By having Christ more nearly like other men, albeit heroic, Milton was able to highlight what was for him the important thing, namely Christ's moral nature in a historical context, rather than evoke the less important mystery of an eternal God incarnate and suffering in time.[15] So, just as Crashaw we might say upsets the balance of traditional meditation on the crucifixion by concentrating on the vertical axis, Milton tends to over-stress the horizontal. The imbalance becomes clear when, on closer examination, we find that Milton does not really embrace the conventional Christian definitions of time and eternity, even though he does continue to use the terms and subscribe to the basic ideas.

In the traditional Christian explanation, time begins with Creation and will come to an end in the *nunc stans* of eternity.[16] Milton consistently avoids this definition: eternity is not an 'enduring present' but 'signifies *always existent*.'[17] An eternal thing has neither beginning nor end, but this does not mean it exists in a realm divorced from time. Milton thus suggests that motion and time could have existed before the creation of the world, as they may exist after it. In *Paradise Lost* Raphael assures Adam that 'Time, though in Eternity, appli'd/To motion, measures all things durable/By present, past, and future' (V, 580–82), and both epics describe time and motion in heaven. Milton also argues that matter could not be created from nothing, as the traditional Augustinian account again suggests.[18] For Milton, it must 'either have always existed independently of God, or have originated from God at some particular point of time' and he concludes that 'like the form and nature of the angels itself' matter proceeded from God and so can never be finally annihilated.[19]

Not surprisingly, these attempts to de-emphasise the 'vertical' Neo-Platonist mystery are accompanied in Milton by progressivist tendencies which stress human fulfilment horizontally in history, and in material terms. In his earlier career Milton, with many another hopeful Puritan, saw Cromwell's revolution as harbinger of the millennium itself. The 1000 year rule of saints predicted in the book of Revelation as a preface to the second coming of Christ seemed close at hand: on these grounds Cromwell's chaplain had even argued for the execution of the king,[20] and *Areopagitica* is vibrant with optimism about England as the chosen nation to prepare the 'lovelines' of her 'Masters second Comming.'[21] Although Milton experienced the disillusionment of such hopes by the restoration of Charles II, *The Christian Doctrine* still looks forward to the coming reign of Christ, which is to be on earth for a thousand years. True, in *Paradise Lost* the war in heaven is a lesson against trying too closely to determine God's purposes in the thick of temporal events,[22] but Milton never doubts such purposes, which, he stresses repeatedly, will be unfolded in history and fulfilled in time. Milton insists also on the material conditions of this fulfilment, and on the material composition of the resurrection body, thereby again taking a direction contrary to the main mediaeval tradition.[23] St Augustine had played down the apocalypse and had spiritualised the Heavenly City, which endures in eternity. He had, in general, discouraged curiosity about millennial expectations and interpreted the book of Revelation as an allegory for individual spiritual experience rather than a literal prophecy of historical events.[24] But Milton, with a whole rank of seventeenth-century divines (and peculiarly in their company on this question, Thomas Hobbes)[25] had insisted not only on a much more temporal but also more material interpretation of the teachings of faith on the question of Last Things. His reasons come clearest if we consider the question from a political perspective, for the argument that we are not mysteriously in touch with the crucified saviour at every holy mass but will be actually so at the time of the second coming is really an effective way of attacking the old authoritarian political system based on hierarchical and Platonist principles. Here Milton's theories of material creation and his sceptical, scholarly study of history blend once more with his Protestant faith in the new Jerusalem to produce a unique synthesis of traditional Christianity and modern secular egalitarianism. As E. L. Tuveson has demonstrated, the combination of new philosophy and Protestant millennialism was essential to the modern secular ideal of progress,[26] and in the history of this development Milton occupies a significant place.

Milton's theories of time and the material world have profound consequences also for his poetic practice, and particularly his attitude to images. As with Crashaw, it is easy to feel in Milton's poems a curious, obtrusive physicality in descriptions of things which we do not usually associate with the physical. In Crashaw, as I have shown, we recoil from carnal literalism in order to discover the transcendent bliss of spiritual affection. In Milton, an analogue is the war in heaven where we are asked to consider some oddly palpable angelic wounds and the process of their healing, or Raphael's discourse on food, where we are told of angelic digestive tracts. The presentation of God the Father has of course been widely criticised for its literalness, and Dante's suggestive indirection admired by contrast.[27] I have suggested that a similar response to the world newly constituted of quantifiable material reality causes Crashaw and Milton alike to strain in representing the spiritual in physical terms. Yet their responses to this challenge are diametrically opposite. Crashaw rushes to a Catholic sacramentalism and the Platonist traditions of the Capucins to transubstantiate the physical 'vertically' into the higher mystery which spiritualises it. Milton rejects such a Neo-Platonist ontology with its accompanying sacramentalism, and his 'horizontal' spirituality is oddly mixed with the physical, not because the soul is unlike matter, but because it is similar.

The exegetical theory behind Milton's attitude to poetic imagery, which consistently reflects these other concerns with matter and time, history and progress, is well described by William Madsen.[28] He contends that Milton's 'shadowy types' should not be read as Neo-Platonist intimations of higher ineffable mysteries, but according to Protestant methods of Biblical exegesis, as foreshadowings, just as the types of Old Testament history indicate things to come. Milton uses imagery in a Platonist sense only to describe Adam's condition before the fall and the 'grateful vicissitude' of heaven, where time, unbroken by sin, moves in cycles. But in fallen time such perfection is seriously damaged, and is restored by Christ. Before the Incarnation, human history provided only *shadows* of truth, a series of images and types of what will happen in the fullness of time. Then, with Christ, such images and types are abolished and he alone is 'the image, as it were, by which we see God' and the 'word by which we hear him'.[29] The useful function of images is not, in consequence, denied by Milton, for they still can be used like types of the Old Testament to enliven and illuminate truths already known in Jesus. Read in this way, Milton's imagery, like his theories of time, matter, politics, and history, again turns out not to be 'mysterious' in the Neo-Platonist sense, for in his poems the thing pictured, the event alluded to, the tableau exquisitely presented, do not mediate any transcendent Idea, and the emphasis is historical and psychological. Imagery, in short, becomes primarily a test of faith in Christ the redeemer, not a real mediation of mysterious divine realities. The mystery is broached directly by the single image of Christ, in which alone, says Milton, we may believe, but even in Christ the image is accompanied by the word through which he operates in the Spirit, without images, directly upon our souls.

In *Paradise Regained* this range of attitudes combines in a complex but lucid unity. The poem is centrally about time, and about faith. In it the theories of Milton the secular historian, anti-sacramental polemecist and millennial materialist combine with traditional teachings on providential history and Christocentric belief. In keeping with the first 'modern' group of tendencies, the peculiarly imageless rendition of Christ and the oddly non-mysterious quality of the encounter with Satan have obscured the degree to which Milton also enriches his poem through the second 'traditional' element by drawing on a conventional iconography of time as the medium of Providence. Yet, although Milton does use conventional icons for time, he also wrests them away from their conventional function of representing the vertical mystery of eternity, to apply them to his own ethical and horizontal explication of Christ's discovery in time of his own Godlike purposes. The icons are developed with a consistency that shows time the vehicle of providence, but they are stripped of accretions suggesting that images of material things are real representations of transcendent Ideas. So, in explicating the iconography of time in the following pages I intend to demonstrate not only that it is an important implicit principle of organisation for *Paradise Regained*, but also that this very implicitness in relation to the poem's major images can show how Milton's more modern perspectives on time, material nature and faith have affected his poetic practice.

PARADISE REGAINED AND THE ICONS OF TIME

A main problem for critics of *Paradise Regained* has grown simply from the general unpopularity of the poem's subject matter in Christian art and letters. The cross has inspired countless artists; the temptation hardly any.[30] But Milton's success is not just a token of his originality in dealing with a new subject: rather, it is in large measure dependent on his ability to bring this subject into fruitful relation with literary and iconographical traditions already well established in the Renaissance. The assessment of Milton's achievement has produced many theories about the number and kinds of temptations in *Paradise Regained*, the main ones being by Elizabeth Pope and Barbara Lewalski.[31]

Miss Pope explicates the Patristic background, arguing that the traditional association of Adam's temptations with Christ's provides the 'triple equation' on which *Paradise Regained* is structured. Milton, however, following Protestant exegesis, interprets the stones-to-bread temptation as a test of faith, not of abstinence as was traditional, and innovates by providing the banquet to tempt Christ to gluttony and by developing the tower temptation into an identity test. Both Pope and Lewalski agree that Milton's Christ is not omniscient and must discover his true nature: during the poem he is in process of finding out his mission and his identity as Son of God. Lewalski argues further that Christ's self-discovery involves specifically the roles of prophet, king, and priest, about which the Son finds illumination as he resists Satan. *Paradise Regained* deals with these three roles in turn, and this scheme is the inner structure of a poem which, in broad terms, is modelled on the sub-genre of the brief epic.

Both critics do much to illuminate the rich traditions which have moulded Milton's sensibility on various levels. Both, however, render it difficult for the reader to assess which elements of the complex and learned background Milton may have isolated for the deliberate structuring of his particular work. All that Lewalski suggests in her synthesis of the criteria for the brief epic, the process of Christ's self-discovery, and the prophet-king-priest sequence, is no doubt there, for Milton was exceptionally learned, but the clarity and elegance of *Paradise Regained* suggest some more direct and uncomplicated controlling principle than her complex analysis indicates. In a later article she has also gone on to examine the importance of time and history for the poem, but comes short of suggesting, as I now wish to do, that a traditional iconography of time provides a sound principle for poetically motivating the temptations. Milton, moreover, may be expected to exploit such conventions in a work so fundamentally concerned with history and typology as *Paradise Regained*: as another critic has argued, 'the cornerstone of Christ's rejection of the temptations' is his attitude to time, to 'the proper moment',[32] in contrast to Satan's importunity.

First, in general terms, there is a clear opposition throughout *Paradise Regained* between the Son's and Satan's views on the meaning of time and history. Christ's trust in the 'fullness of time' is contrasted repeatedly to Satan's trust in fortune and chance. The Son interprets time as the context in which God's purposes are declared, and through which man will be redeemed in the 'due time' which Christ equates with 'providence'.[33] In such knowledge Christ finds strength to 'endure the time' until 'my season comes', for he believes 'All things are best fulfill'd in their due time' (III, 182). Without this sense of participation in the divine plan time becomes chaos, as it is for Satan. He does not know the meaning of Christ's coming, and consequently is at the mercy of the seemingly random moment that brings his downfall. Satan's knowledge of the prophecy (as Milton confirms in *The Christian Doctrine*)[34] serves only to pain him, and his first question to the Son reflects his total point of view: 'Sir, what ill chance hath brought thee to this place?' (I, 321). For Satan, time is the realm of 'ill chance', of fortune, of accident: a category which he attempts to use, exploit, and turn to his own ends. 'But on Occasion's forelock watchful wait' (III, 173), is, in this respect, the burden of the tempter's advice to Christ. Yet in the course of *Paradise Regained* time runs out for Satan because it has no purpose. His extemporising, like Iago's, confines him increasingly to cares of the moment and this draws him ever deeper into delusions of a self-sufficiency as meaningless as time itself viewed without the perspectives of providence.

In terms of commonplace iconography, Satan seems to rely, foolishly, on time the destroyer, while Christ trusts in time the revealer. As Panofsky points out, time the revealer is well known in the Renaissance 'from countless representations of subjects such as Truth revealed or rescued by Time, Virtue vindicated by Time, Innocence justified by Time, and the like.'[35] On the other hand, time the destroyer, often associated with Saturn who devoured his children, is typically monstrous and self-destructive.[36] This is the sharp 'tooth of time' of Shakespeare's *Measure for Measure* (V, 1, 12),[37] the 'Misshapen Time . . ./Eater of youth' (925-7) of *The Rape of Lucrece* (whose servant in that poem is, significantly, 'Opportunity' [932]).

Milton's early poetry shows his familiarity with these conventions,[38] and they are deployed also in *Paradise Lost*,[39] where prelapsarian time, for example, is presented in the conventional aspect of revealer. Raphael explains to Adam that 'one Almighty is, from whom/All things proceed, and up to him return' (V, 469–70), and suggests that, for Adam and Eve, 'Your bodies may at last all turn to spirit,/Improv'd by tract of time' (V, 497–8). This view of time accords well with the Platonic imagery describing the 'great round' and 'grateful vicissitude' of God's prelapsarian creation. On the other hand, time the destroyer is introduced with the Fall, through Sin and Death. The Saturnian iconography is clear as Sin addresses Death in Book X, instructing him to 'devour unspar'd', 'whatever thing/The Scythe of Time mows down' (X, 605–6). Time with the scythe is allied to the devouring monster, and cannibalism in turn is one of the attributes of Sin in Book II: 'about her middle round,' we learn, 'A cry of Hell Hounds, never ceasing bark'd/With wide *Cerberean* mouths full loud' (II, 654–5). The hounds are begot on Sin by Death, her own son, and return to her womb 'and howl and gnaw/My Bowels, thir repast' (II, 799–800). Here Milton envisages the legacy of Sin and Death in terms of time the destroyer, but seems also to know the widespread iconography representing destructive time as a Cerberus figure. A well known example of this convention is in the 'Practica Musice' (1496) of Gafurius, who presents time as both revealer and destroyer, and also as Cerberus.[40]

In a central emblematic woodcut depicting his traditional interpretation of the music of the spheres, Gafurius shows Apollo enthroned in heaven with his feet resting on the tail of a serpent which is looped to represent eternity (see plate 9).[41] The serpent's body extends from the loop downwards through the spheres, and comes to rest on earth, where the head divides into three. The serpent then becomes a monster, time the destroyer, with the face of a wolf (looking left), of a lion (full face), and of a dog (looking right). The three heads represent time in the three aspects of past, present, and future, and Gafurius equates his three-headed beast with Cerberus,[42] though it derives primarily from the Renaissance icon of a three-headed god from the temple of Serapis in Alexandria. The most influential ancient commentary on this famous Egypto-Hellenic god is that of Macrobius, who explains the Serapis 'Cerberus' in terms of time: the wolf represents time past, the lion time present, and the dog time future.[43] The point is taken up in Petrarch's *Africa*, which describes the three heads in some detail, concluding that they 'represent fleeting time',[44] both monstrous and destructive.

Yet the three parts of time in Gafurius' woodcut also in a sense 'imitate eternity', for the monster remains part of the serpent descending from Apollo's feet. Accordingly, the Serapis 'Cerberus' was (however improbably) subjected to widespread interpretation in the Renaissance as an allegory for the intellectual quality of good judgement, or *consilium*.[45] This in turn was connected with the three faces of prudence, each of which, traditionally, represents one of the divisions of time (past, present, and future), while corresponding to the major faculties of the mind (memory, intellect, and will).[46] Through prudence and good judgement, therefore, the blandishments of fortune may be resisted, and fleeting time become a revealer of eternity.

From the early period to *Paradise Lost*, Milton's poetry draws on these traditions, mainly the themes of destruction and revelation, the self-devouring Cerberus monster, the Saturnian figure, and the unveiler of truth. Milton also was familiar with Serapis,[47] and even if he was not thinking specifically of Gafurius, the 'Practica Musice' provides a convenient example of the type of synthesis wrought from familiar sources in Boethius, Macrobius, Aquinas, Petrarch, and the Renaissance Neo-Platonists, which is uniquely represented, among Milton's writings, in *Paradise Regained*, a poem centrally concerned with the meaning of Christ's coming into history in the fullness of time. But fallen time as we have seen, does not, in Milton, imitate eternity in the Neo-Platonist sense, and nowhere in Milton is much use made of the emblematic beasts or the popular lore that suggests correspondences between the hierarchies of created nature and the transcendent divine being in which they are sustained. Although Milton adopts the traditional three-fold icon of time the destroyer, he dispenses with the popular animal imagery suggesting a Neo-Platonist interpretation. Yet we can also see how readily a structural scheme for Satan's strategy based on time emerges from the opposition in *Paradise Regained* between the tempter's claims for fortune, and the Son's trust in providence. The emphasis is not, however, on *images* of time the imitator of eternity, but on time as the context of the act of faith. So Christ's cool appraisal and clear rejection of Satan's assaults are enliveners of faith, the imageless and personal act which gives the images meaning while robbing them of independent sacramental significance. Likewise, throughout *Paradise Regained* the images do not function to move the reader to a wondering sense of how analogies discoverable to 'spiritual vision' intimate the hidden Wisdom which he may hope to contemplate. They serve to give instead a perspective on ourselves in history, and exhort us to follow Christ's example not to be fooled by Satan into thinking we can determine God's purposes in time, but to have faith that, whatever the confusions and distractions, time will at the end bring the faithful once more to the old heaven on a renewed earth. We can now consider in more detail the main directions of Satan's approach.

TEMPTATION AND THE DIVISIONS OF TIME

The challenge to turn stones to bread, with which Satan begins, is separate from the three main groups of temptation which follow. The first temptation, as Miss Pope and others[48] have pointed out, is of particular significance to Protestant exegetes, and represents a temptation to doubt, not gluttony as in the main Catholic tradition. Here Satan directly assaults Christ's faith, and this attempt underlies the other temptations from which it remains symbolically apart. In relation to the iconography of time, it is significant that Satan should begin by assaulting Christ's faith, for the true objects of faith, as we shall see, are eternal (that is, to do with Providence) not temporal. Satan's assault is therefore logically prior to a series of temptations wrought from within the realms of time itself.

In the three main groups of temptation, Satan, like the three-headed Cerberus,[49] tempts Christ according to the three divisions of time the destroyer, to whose self-devouring ways Satan, ironically, is himself bound. The banquet temptation is a temptation to lust, suggesting the voracious wolf (a common emblem for lust, and often associated with prostitutes),[50] and is related to time past. The second temptation, the wealth-glory-fame sequence, refers to the future, and in it Satan appeals especially to Christ's future need of the power of Parthia, Rome, and Athens. This suggests the sagacious dog, which, Macrobius explains, curiously sniffs the future.[51] The third temptation moves into the poem's immediate present, and Satan, by physical threat, tempts the Son through fear to anger, and then, on the pinnacle, to the related sin of pride. Anger and pride suggest the lion,[52] which symbolises time present.

There is, moreover, precedent for relating the three temptations themselves to the Boethian model of fortune and providence which provides, as we have seen, the language for one basic confrontation between Satan and Christ. In the fourth poem of the first book of *The Consolation of Philosophy*, Boethius argues that a man can resist the storms of fortune, and the fourteenth-century commentator, Nicholas Trivet, explains the passage in these terms:

First of all it is to be observed that the persecution of the wicked is designated in three ways, that is, by the rage of the sea, by the eruption of a certain mountain, and by the stroke of lightning. The reason for this is that the proud are found in three species according to the three kinds of sin which occupy the world as in 1 John 2:16: 'For all that is in the world is concupiscence of the flesh, and the concupiscence of the eyes, and the pride of life.' Certain of the wicked are therefore lecherous, whose persecution is designated by the raging of the sea. ... Others, indeed, are the avaricious whose persecution is designated by the fire from Mount Vesuvius. ... Others are the proud whose persecution is designated by the flash of lightning.[53]

The three sins of concupiscence, curiosity, and pride, are clearly associated with the temptations of fortune. Traditionally, these sins also typify the original temptations of Adam which are, in the fullness of time, endured again by the second Adam, Christ.[54] Milton himself calls our attention on numerous occasions throughout *Paradise Regained* to the typological identity between Christ and Adam.[55] So, just as the sin of Adam introduced time the destroyer in *Paradise Lost*, the prudence and good judgement of Christ, similarly tempted in *Paradise Regained*, revalidates for man the perspectives of time the revealer.

In a scheme apparently so exhaustive as the one I am suggesting for the subsequent temptations, the introductory stones-to-bread episode may at first appear extraneous. But Milton, clearly, must not depart by omission from the Biblical account. Also, he would no doubt prefer to follow the Protestant exegesis and interpret the temptation as doubt, not gluttony, and thereby emphasise the typically Reformation stress on faith. Yet these choices were no mere capitulations to convention: the stones-to-bread temptation, as we shall see, would be unsuitable for presenting gluttony in terms of the temporal scheme which underlies the poem. Nor is the stones-to-bread episode unfunctional: Satan begins by attacking Christ's faith for very good reason.

As Milton indicates in *Paradise Lost*, a test of faith underlies every temptation: Adam tells Eve that she is 'not proof/Against temptation', because 'Not incorruptible of Faith' (IX, 298-9). The tree, for Adam and Eve, was the pledge of obedience and faith (VIII, 325), and with the breaking of faith, time as we know it came into the world. The test of faith is the key also to the fall of the angels, who 'first broke peace in Heav'n, and Faith' (II, 690). Consequently Christ, the second Adam, 'came to preach eternall life by faith only.'[56] All temptations, whether of angels or men, therefore, presuppose the corruptibility of faith, and Milton makes an important but commonplace distinction between 'Historical' or 'Temporary' faith, which is limited in efficacy, and true 'saving faith' which relates temporal concerns to 'eternal life'.[57] Milton is here drawing a distinction which occurs in the broadest spectrum of Christian thought from Augustine to Aquinas and Calvin. Augustine asserts that faith has for its object eternal truth and 'things not seen', but points out also that faith 'is concerned with the past, the present, and the future, all three.'[58] Faith transcends the concerns of fallen time and also subsumes them. Granted, then, that Satan does assault Christ's faith in the first temptation (and here the evidence of Pope and Lewalski seems convincing), it would appear that the tempter is simply working to spare himself the effort of plying further temptations from within the specific divisions of time. He offers first a logically prior temptation which subsumes these divisions, and which, for the purposes of the poem, also serves to introduce them. An 'over-tost faith', Milton tells us, leads to 'mutin against divine providence'.[59] Having failed against providence in general, Satan now turns to time in particular.

There may be some difficulty for modern readers in appreciating how the temptation of lust involves time past. But the special association of sensuality with memory is a commonplace theme in mediaeval and Renaissance literature, and the peculiar presentation of the banquet temptation in *Paradise Regained* strongly suggests that Milton was thinking of this connection. The most influential, and universally read, source treatment of the faculties of mind, and particularly memory, in relation to the divisions of time is the *Confessions* of St Augustine. For Augustine the soul itself is the measure of time. Strictly speaking, time past and time future do not exist, for 'they are not there as future, or past, but present.'[60] Consequently, memory brings past events to present attention, and expectation leads to 'forethinking', but 'that forethinking is present.'[61] Therefore, Augustine concludes, there is 'a present of things past, a present of things present, and a present of things future.'[62] Milton affirms the Augustinian theory in his *Logic*, where he defines time as '[present] duration of things past, present, and future'.[63]

Throughout the *Confessions* these three aspects of time are further related to the three key sins indicated by 1 John: the lust of the flesh, lust of the eyes, and pride.[64] They are, in Augustine's language, the sins of concupiscence, curiosity, and pride, the sins by which both Adam and Christ were tempted. Concupiscence, then, is in one special sense related to the 'present of things past', and is a sin associated with memory. The psychology of this is explained by Augustine's treatment of sensuality, and of the function of reason in carnal temptation. First of all, the things of the flesh are in themselves good, 'For the flesh lusts after nothing save through the soul.'[65] Augustine quotes Paul that 'sin reigneth not in our mortal body' but the consent 'unto suggestions that meet him of each several thing that is seen' is what 'defile(s) the man'.[66] The entire stress is on 'consent of the mind' to the suggestions of sensuality. Ideally, 'our very thought itself, although in a certain way it be touched by their suggestion ... turns away ... that it receive not delight ... that men abide not in them.'[67] In this sense, temptation to lust will succeed if it can cause the mind to dwell on a phantasm which is made present through memory. The man 'who *hath seen a woman to lust after her*', says Augustine, 'has let his thoughts dwell on her with more pleasure than was right.'[68]

A further complication is introduced by the fact that thought itself, in Augustine's theory, is actually formed through memory, as we are led 'by means of outward sensible things which are seen by the eyes of the flesh'[69] to reasoning. The act of knowing involves the past: images are impressed on memory, and 'when the look has been turned upon these by recollection',[70] will joins the two. 'These and other things of the kind', Augustine assures us, 'have their proper order in time, and in that order we discerned more easily a trinity of memory, sight, and love.'[71] Memory, then, is the faculty of mind which, in the act of knowing, refers the phantasm, drawn from the senses, to reason, and allows the mind to remember, and not lose itself in the act of knowing. Also, as we have seen, it permits us to recollect experiences from our past to present attention, thus becoming a 'present of things past'.

Temptation to lust, therefore, operates in two ways in relation to memory. First, in the act of knowing, the phantasm can so overwhelm the mind that it forgets itself, and this is surely the case with those endless parodies of Petrarchan lovers,[72] wandering forgetful, as they do throughout Renaissance letters, distraught, and with their garters loose. It is the source, too, of the tragic dementia of an Othello, who, tempted to lustful jealousy almost wholly in terms of things past, falls into an epileptic fit, symbol of his mind's self-forgetfulness.

No less important as a literary motif is the second process, that of delighting in sense experience, just glimpsed, and then recollected. This process is minutely observed, for example, by Chaucer in Troilus, who languishes over a memory of the glimpsed Criseyde, as does Petrarch, initially, over Laura. Andreas Capellanus talks for all the lovers in this tradition: 'love is a certain inborn suffering (*passio*) derived from the sight of and excessive meditation upon the beauty of the opposite sex, which causes one to wish above all things the embraces of the other.'[73] The whole procedure, as D. W. Robertson says, 'involves three steps: suggestion, delightful thought, and consent or passion',[74] and this describes also the process of recollecting the phantasm we have described from Augustine. Certainly Erasmus, writing against the 'filthy sensuality'[75] of lustful temptation, makes clear that memory is the key to the Christian soldier's defence. 'Remind yourself',[76] he exhorts, of the cares lust brings with it, 'recall'[77] those friends who died suddenly, 'remember'[78] hellfire, 'recollect'[79] the love of Christ, 'recall'[80] the blessings of Christ. Remember yourself, he advises, and do not dwell on recollections of illicit sensual suggestions.

In *Paradise Regained*, Satan's banquet temptation fits perfectly into this general scheme. In fact, only by appealing to such conventions can we make sull sense of Milton's peculiar presentation of the feast in the desert. Even before it begins, Belial, talking of women, draws our attention to traditional ways in which the lures of the flesh act upon men. The mind remembering the phantasm, as Belial well knows, is the source of sin, and in this circumstance men 'with voluptuous hope dissolve' (II, 165) and fall 'with credulous desire' (II, 166). Satan makes the sequence clear:

> Beauty stands
> In th' admiration only of weak minds
> Led captive; cease to admire, and all her Plumes
> Fall flat and shrink into a trivial toy.   (II, 220–3)

Again, the delightful thought, the 'admiring', makes men's minds captive rather than the senses themselves.

Satan, however, is not at all sure that Christ will fall for such a specific temptation as Belial suggests. The approach is too simple, for it is limited to one sensual lure. Satan, more guileful, and not knowing his opponent's particular weakness, prefers to present a banquet with an entire gamut of sensual temptation—food, wine, music, perfume, women, and 'stripling youths' (II, 352). Yet Milton's presentation of these sensual lures is curious, and oddly indefinite. We read of 'Beasts of chase *or* Fowl of game' (II, 342: my emphases) built in pastry '*or* from the spit, *or* boil'd' (II, 343). There are fish 'from Sea *or* Shore' (II, 344), 'of shell *or* fin' (II, 345). The 'Ladies of th' *Hesperides* . . . seem'd/Fairer than feign'd of old *or* fabl'd since' (II, 357–8), while '*Arabian* odors' mix oddly with '*Flora's* earliest smells' (II, 364–5). Allusions abound, and with the same imprecision. We learn of 'Ganymede *or* Hylas' (II, 353), of Diana and Naiades, of 'Knights of Logres, *or* of Lyones,/Lancelot *or* Peleas, *or* Pellenore' (II, 360–1), of 'Pontus *and* Lucrine Bay' (II, 347).

How we are to envisage all these alternatives as part of a sensual temptation, actually presented, is not clear unless we assume that this sensuality is deliberately phantasmagoric. As we read these lines, we are really invited to recall, with Christ, the various centres of sensual attraction present, as Augustine would say, in the recesses of our memories. Since Satan is unsure of Christ's vulnerability to sensual temptation, he evokes the range of what Christ (and the reader) might *remember* as sensually exciting. Satan's task then is, according to the paradigm, to make Christ take 'delightful thought' upon the phantasm. Milton indicates this further process by calling attention to the time sequence—'Such *was* the Splendor, and the Tempter *now*/His invitation earnestly renew'd' (II, 366–7). Satan 'now' attempts to have Christ think about the pleasures which might appeal to him through memory, and Christ rejects them as simply phantasms or 'guiles' (II, 391), which could become significant for Satan's purposes only by Christ recalling them to mind and yielding, as Satan says 'all thy heart' (II, 410).

This entire first temptation to concupiscence, then, is associated, through a traditional psychology of recollection, with time past, or more correctly, with that 'present of things past' in the mind. The allied theme of self-forgetfulness is also represented, as Satan, under the guise of challenging Christ to remember and define his identity as Son of God, in fact urges him to forget his Sonship and relinquish the responsibilities consequent upon that identity.[81] Finally, the logic of placing the banquet temptation (which is, after all, Milton's innovation) at this point in the poem is clearer as we come to understand Satan's approach in the following assaults on Christ, to which we now turn. The relatively elusive psychology of the 'present of things past' achieves plainer significance in the coherency of the total argument of which it forms a part.

The second group of temptations, the wealth-glory-fame sequence, fits more obviously the divisions of time which we are examining. Here Satan refers consistently to time future, and his appeal is to Christ's coming need, for his Kingdom, of the power of Rome, Parthia, and Athens. This entire temptation corresponds to the 'present of things future', the dog of the Serapis figure which curiously sniffs at what lies ahead. Satan, characteristically, promises Christ that 'Fortune is in my hand' (II, 429) as he turns his attention to this next main division of time: 'if at great things thou *wouldst* arrive', he urges, 'Get Riches first, get Wealth, and Treasure heap' (II, 426–7). Admittedly, Satan invites Christ to recall the past glories of David and Maccabaeus, of Scipio, Pompey, and Julius Caesar, but all to the express end, 'So *shalt* thou best fullfil, best verify/The Prophets old' (III, 177–8).

The ensuing panoramas conjured by Satan are also plainly

directed at stimulating Christ's curiosity about future events, and of rousing him to seize occasion's forelock and glorify himself by earthly fame which the future promises. Since Christ's Kingdom is 'foretold' (III, 351) the Son must strive to bring about the prediction, or else, 'Thou never *shalt* obtain' (III, 354). Satan also assures Christ that he is 'worthiest' and '*shouldst* be' (III, 226) a king. 'I *will* bring thee' (III, 244) he claims, to 'Empires, and Monarchs, and thir radiant Courts' (III, 237). Of Parthia, Satan says, 'By him thou *shalt* regain' (III, 371), and if 'thou *shalt* restore' (III, 381) the ten tribes through Parthian arms, then 'Thou/ . . . /*Shalt* reign' (III, 385) on the prophesied 'Throne of *David*, in full glory' (III, 383). Christ, moreover, could easily win the power of Rome, 'and with my help thou *mayst*' (IV, 103).

When the temptations of Parthia and Rome fail, Satan turns to Athens and the temptation of learning. He again appeals to time future: '*Be* famous then/By wisdom' (IV, 221–2). How will Christ rule in the new Kingdom, he enquires, without learning: 'How *wilt* thou reason with them, how refute/Thir Idolisms, Traditions, Paradoxes?' (IV, 233–4). In the schools of the ancient world, 'thou *shalt* hear and learn the secret power' (IV, 254), and 'These rules *will* render thee a King complete' (IV, 283). Christ's rebuttal to the series, though issuing from his opposite position of prudent trust in the Father's providence, centres also on the future: 'And of my Kingdom there *shall be* no end' (IV, 151), for, as he says, 'I endure the time' (IV, 174).

Having assaulted Christ from the points of view of time past and time future, Satan moves, in the final group of temptations, dramatically into the poem's present. He buffets Christ with a storm and places him on the pinnacle. The temptation has been variously interpreted,[82] but it seems less likely that the main aim of the storm is simply to cause Christ to trust fearfully in Satan, than to move Christ, through fear, to anger, symbolised by the storm itself. In the storm, however, Satan certainly does attempt to terrify Christ, and the tempest is raised 'to tempt the Son of God with terrors dire' (IV, 431). But the operative word is 'with', which implies instrumentality. The storm is a means to an end, and through fear Satan hopes to move Christ to the sin which ironically rebounds (as usual) upon the tempter's own head: Satan, foiled, can only 'vent his rage' (IV, 445). The second time 'terror' is mentioned in relation to the storm, the pattern is repeated, as 'the Fiend now swoln with rage' (IV, 499) attempts to reply to Christ. Fear, in short, is a means of tempting Christ to unjust anger, or rage.

In *The Christian Doctrine* Milton describes the human affections and lists fear and anger together.[83] They were, therefore, readily associated in his mind, and in a further analysis Milton differentiates between devout fear of God and mere carnal fear which leads to anger and tyranny. In *Eikonoklastes*, Milton accuses Charles I of fearing men more than God.[84] He distinguishes the king's 'terrible ague' of fear from the 'wise fear' of the parliamentarians, and claims that the king's fear led directly to 'vehemence', 'hatred' and 'revenge'.[85] By attempting to terrify Christ, Satan hopes to effect a similar reaction, and thus to drive the Son through fear to 'vehemence', 'revenge', and 'rage'. Interestingly, when Satan describes the storm, he compares it to 'turbulencies in the affairs of men' (IV, 462), perhaps suggesting that Milton was thinking of the argument from *Eikonoklastes*, of political fear breeding vengeful anger.

The antidote to anger, as Milton also makes clear in *The Christian Doctrine* is 'patience and long-suffering',[86] and Christ's reaction to the storm stresses exactly these qualities. Christ is the 'patient' (IV, 420) Son of God, who maintains in face of terror a 'calm and sinless peace' (IV, 425). This would again suggest that the storm is an instrument to tempt Christ not simply to fear, but to anger.

The ways in which anger relates to pride, the final temptation on the pinnacle, are conventional. Both anger and pride are traditionally sins of the irascible faculty,[87] and anger is a manifestation of pride. St Augustine's sermon on the Lord's Prayer provides a useful illustration. Augustine has dealt with the devil's three temptations, the first to lust (where a person 'has let his thoughts dwell' on a phantasm 'with more pleasure than was right'),[88] the next to 'hope of gain',[89] and the third to a temptation of which Augustine asks: 'What then is that frightful temptation ... that grievous, that tremendous temptation, which must be avoided with all our strength?[90] His answer is anger, because it pridefully usurps God's justice, and because it precludes a man from saying, 'Forgive us our debts, as we also forgive our debtors.'[91] 'When that power is lost',

Augustine claims, 'all sins will be retained; nothing at all is remitted.'[92] Here, again, are the three temptations, and Augustine centres on anger as the most important. It is the sin associated with pride, the present, and, by analogy, with Satan's final temptations of Christ in the storm and on the pinnacle where, as interpreters of the poem have amply illustrated, the Son is tempted to 'vainglory'.[93]

CONCLUSION

To summarise: in *Paradise Regained* Milton seems especially interested to present the meaning of Sonship in terms of Christ's interpretation of the achievements of men in time. Such achievements are presented by Satan in the series of historical panoramas depicting Parthian might, Roman justice, Greek learning, Hebrew prophecy and kingship. Christ, by interpreting history 'redeems the time' (Eph. 5: 15–17), and endows it with meaning. Christ is the person (as Satan learns) before whom you most fully discover, in time, who you are. In a poem so deeply concerned with such meanings, and also so coolly articulated and severely disciplined I suggest that a principle of organisation which is itself simple and yet closely integrated with the poem's central concern with time deserves consideration as an underlying plan deliberately adapted by the poet. Such a plan is implicit in the arrangement of the temptations to correspond first to faith which 'is concerned with the past, the present, and the future, all three', and then with each of these temporal divisions in turn.

The confrontation between Satan and Christ in terms of fortune and providence can be associated, through Milton's early writing, with the conventional imagery of time the destroyer and time the revealer. Milton also shows interest in destructive time as a Cerberus figure, the three heads of which, in terms of a further Renaissance tradition involving the Serapis 'Cerberus' iconography, represent time as the wolf (past), lion (present), and dog (future). The Boethian fortune, on which Satan clearly relies in *Paradise Regained*, is readily associated also with the three temptations of Adam and Christ, and it seems plain, in a poem so concerned with typology and history, that Milton has, on one level, arranged the temptation of the

Son in terms of these Renaissance conventions for representing time. He uses the themes of fortune and providence, of revelation and destruction, and the main divisions of time itself; the past, future, and present, which correspond to memory, intellect, and will, and the three sins of lust, curiosity, and anger (pride). But lest this analysis appear arbitrary, one striking analogue from the visual arts to the structure of Milton's poem will provide a conclusion.

The tapestry known as 'The Vindication of Innocence', by Giovanni Rost, based on Angelo Bronzino, and at present in the Galleria degli Arrazzi in Florence, shows Justice, bearing a sword and scales, rescuing Innocence from a serpent, a wolf, a lion, and a dog.[94] (See plate 10). In the background, the figure of an old man, winged, and with an hourglass, unveils a girl. He represents Time (without his scythe or other destructive aspects), unveiling Truth, as Innocence is rescued by Justice from the sins of the world. Panofsky points out that the attitude of Justice is that of Christ rescuing souls from Hell, and, using Ripa, he interprets the animals as anger (lion), perfidy (serpent), greed (wolf), and envy (dog).[95] But, it might now be suggested, since Justice, in the attitude of Christ, is about to slay specifically the serpent, that the serpent is Satan, and the three emblematic animals represent time without truth—the past, present, and future with their three sins of lust, anger, and curiosity. Just as the stones-to-bread temptation underlies the others in *Paradise Regained* and remains symbolically apart, so in the tapestry the serpent (Satan) alone rears up against Justice (Christ), and remains apart from the wolf, lion, and dog. So also, in the tapestry, as Christ confronts Satan, the figure of Innocence is caught between time the unveiler of truth and time the destroyer, just as the reader is caught in the final two books of *Paradise Lost*, and just as are the disciples in *Paradise Regained*. And, significantly, the disciples, our human reference-point in Milton's brief epic, express their human doubt in terms of the major attitudes to time which this chapter began by noticing. As they 'Began to doubt, and doubted many days' (II, 11), they are caught between alternatives: one of wondering, in the language of fortune, 'what accident/Hath rapt him from us' (II, 39–40) and the other of trusting God, and of committing 'all our fears' to 'his Providence' (II, 53–4). The position of the apostles thus corresponds to that of the reader challenged to make his own act of faith in the confused context of fallen time. But a main difference between Rost and Milton lies in Milton's rejection of the Neo-Platonist and emblematic imagery even while he adapts the conceptual scheme. This is at one with Milton's entire secularised and scholarly attitude to history, his unwillingness to admit a realm of eternity as *nunc stans* mysteriously mirrored by human time, and his millennial and mortalist opinions which suggest a material and timely fulfilment of God's providence. The realist view of images which characterises mediaeval thought has altered to one where images are the test of an inner faith that, in a world newly secular and materialist, such a providence will one day come to pass.

So in *Paradise Regained*, when Milton deals with the relationship of time to eternity, he avoids suggesting in the manner of Gafurius and Rost that the material component of his imagery embodies, as in the old 'spiritual vision', a higher, Ideal reality. As a thinker, historian, and politician, Milton had encountered the new philosophy in forms which made it impossible for him to affirm uncritically a linguistic theory of the Augustinian type, and, like Crashaw, he rang important changes on the view of images which characterised mediaeval practice. As religious poets, both men tried to make their images express the spiritual by confirming the material in new ways, but Milton's technique is the opposite of Crashaw's, for Milton dislikes mystery and holds out against it, except in the 'single image', Christ. Otherwise, his emphasis is 'horizontal', as Crashaw's had been 'vertical': not to escape from the thing-in-itself through an ecstasy, but to claim that an ecstasy is an escape from the thing-in-itself. Although these two poets remain different, they nonetheless are challenged alike to show how imagination serves belief, and each, we might say, gives his own answer to problems presented by *The Tempest* on how images interpret the real structure of things. Both believe the image is a means to a spiritual end, but each questions critically the corporeal element, thereby shaping it to serve higher truth. Insofar as their poetry expresses the process, or the results, of such questioning, it shows how speculation in the realm of ideas, while not determining the content of literature, can nevertheless profoundly influence literary practice.

6 John Norris and the Oratorians: belief and the Images in God

The externals of John Norris's (1657–1711) biography are unspectacular. His tombstone bears the words 'Bene latuit'[1] and the assessment is apt: Norris shunned fame and glory, sought retirement and solitude, and seems to have resented even the intrusions of the small number of his parishioners at the tiny living of Bemerton—'It's too busy here', was the burden of his complaint.[2] His writings, and there are plenty of them, have managed in turn to conform to the retiring habits of their author, and have followed him fairly successfully into obscurity. Yet for a while Norris had been read by an interested public, and his works have been always available in many editions for scholars or others who may have wanted to take him up.[3] Few have cared to do so, and it may be that the world has been hard on John Norris.[4] Or perhaps he merely joins the great company of those who have published books which after a topical reputation have passed from view. Certainly the Age of Enlightenment, which during Norris's career was in process of finding its ideals mirrored in the works of John Locke, was not likely to encourage Locke's paradigmatic opposite in thought, the man who penned the first printed critique of the *Essay Concerning Human Understanding*. Feeling his own centrality (could a diplomat and eighteenth-century man of affairs yield to a recluse pastor?) Locke himself could afford to be casually dismissive of the curious challenge delivered to him by the 'obscure enthusiastic man'[5] from Bemerton.

In short, Locke and Norris saw in each other a commitment to opposite views of the world, and Locke's was in the ascendant. Ever since, Norris has seemed as one gone off on a wrong track, and those most interested in him have been aware of exploring a byway, a run-off which settles in a quiet pond, pleasant but with limited perspective.

Still, an egress for these waters may well come by way of the twists and turns of the mainstream itself, which in doubling back may enable a fresh view on this recluse oddly motivated to write a great system of ideas linking the method of Descartes to the religion of Augustine, and may even make of him a useful tributary rather than a curious digression. The opportunity for such a fresh view I believe is provided by the history of the movement in European thought mustered in France by the Capucins, which I have described in an earlier chapter. John Norris too is part of this story, and although his solutions, like Crashaw's, did not meet with general acceptance, they are not insignificant. We do not today imagine modern man developed from Neanderthal, but now that we are modern men and know about Neanderthal, it is unwise to ignore what that may tell us about where we might have gone, and also where we *have* gone.

JOHN NORRIS: POETRY AND AUTHORITY

John Norris was born in 1657, and entered Winchester in 1671.[6] He was resident at Oxford, 1676–89, and then spent two years at Newton St Loe before becoming rector of Bemerton in 1691. He married a woman called Elizabeth, and probably had children for whom he wrote a manual of spiritual advice. He corresponded with the elderly Cambridge Platonist Henry More, fell under the influence of Nicolas Malebranche and engaged in minor skirmishes with Quakers and with Locke, who more or less dismissed him. In 1711, in the parish of Bemerton, he died, having 'exhausted his strength by intense application and by habits of severe reasoning'[7] according to one assessor, and 'Bene latuit', well-hidden, according to another. There are no portraits, and only a single passing reference in a flightly letter from one society lady to another touches on a physical description. We learn that Norris was 'a little man of pale complexion'[8] and that he was sweet, good humoured, and humble.

Yet the virtues so casually passed off here as gifts of nature, like his complexion, seem to have come hard to this little recluse who continued all his life to emulate the solitude and retirement which he so admired in his mentor Malebranche. Unlike Malebranche, however, Norris remained strangely discomposed in his search for composure, always chafing and uneasy in the pursuit of an ideal philosophy, and he cannot keep the worried quality out of his writings. The causes are at least partly psychological, for it seems that Norris had a special need for authority which he found particularly difficult of gratification in the unsettled times in which he lived. For instance, the vision of a strong constitutional order to which he could submit in an act of obeisance, exerted a powerful influence on his imagination, and he professed an uncompromising royalism. As a young man, he wrote an elegy on Charles II which, conventional though it is, caused Norris's liberal nineteenth-century editor to blench at the King thus 'canonized to the verge of blasphemy'.[9] Clearly, Norris's royalism has little to do with the bestial life of Charles II among his harlots as Grosart imagines, but with the principles of order and harmony in nature and in human society. These are represented in the poem by nature's response to the death of Pan, and by the solicitude of the higher powers in re-instating the bond which links man to the heavens in the new Pan, King James II. The poem, spoken by four shepherds, and with all the props of pathetic fallacy and nature deities, is a conventional piece of pastoral and also an elaborate compliment rather than a lament. But if we look elsewhere in Norris, it is soon clear that the characteristic style of his address to authority remains close to the kind of rhapsodic idealism which so clearly does mark the tone of the elegy. As Powicke says, Norris in his life never ceased to be enamoured of authority and to show undue deference to it.

The lesson seems to have been learned early. Norris was probably a bright enough youth, but he was not exceptional, and failed his exam for a scholarship to New College, entering Exeter instead as a sojourner and graduating B.A. in 1680. The next step is a puzzle, for also in 1680 Norris became a fellow of All Souls—a prestigious position, not open to him by regular channels. One explanation is the practice of 'corrupt resignation', whereby the sponsorship of a resigning fellow secured his position for a particular favourite, and it seems likely that Norris entered into his career in Holy Orders through such a back door.[10] At the same time, he was busy with idealising poems about solitude and retirement from the vanities of position and worldly glory. But he was not to forget the means of his preferment, and even when he sought the obscurity of a small parish, he did it by pulling more strings in high places.[11]

This consistent approach to what Norris no doubt thought the practical facts of life finds expression also in his opinions on other matters. Undue respect for authority on his part is the main cause of his attacks on the Quakers, with whose ideals he otherwise had sympathy. Quaker spirituality is not in question: the breach with established authority is. Only 'if they had just cause for their separation, then they would be excused from Schism without a Toleration'.[12] Conversely, Norris sought in his own writings to place himself under the aegis of authoritative figures whenever possible, and to work from within the security they offered him. Not surprisingly, he writes a great deal in the scholastic manner (despite vigorous repudiations of scholastic thought) and his ambition is to complete a systematic philosophy. His style characteristically is direct and assertive, with a ring suggesting the pleasure he found in being right. But most importantly, Norris fell under the influence of Malebranche, or rather he subordinated himself almost totally to Malebranche's authority. The *Recherche de la Verité*, explains Norris, is among the best books in the world, and in many subsequent years of study which may have given him opportunity to modify this opinion, Norris was not to change his mind: 'If you would have a Book that is alone a *Library*, and an ever-rising and flowing Spring of Knowledge . . . let me recommend to you *M. Malebranche de la Recherche de la Verité* . . . . For indeed, to speak out freely what I think . . . I take it to be upon all accounts one of the best Books that is in the World.'[13]

The biography outlined here is odd and paradoxical. We observe a recluse writing about the virtues of retirement and the vanities of the world, who also courts the favours of the powerful; a philosopher of illumination who writes against Quakers; a Cartesian admirer of clear ideas who is full of scholastic terminology; a man of puritan upbringing who embraces the thought of a leading French Oratorian; and an individual strongly concerned to submit to authority who finds in himself also a bewildering array of self-assertive impulses. This last, most general, point in a way contains the others, and in Norris it is also the most central of those many human preoccupations which may inspire poets. He knew that a high degree of individual self-consciousness is not readily compatible with submission to authority, but he found himself fostering a good deal of the first while he also needed, it seems more than most men, the security of the second.

Norris's poetry reflects this predicament in interesting ways. It is, first of all, an uneasy amalgam of Metaphysical and Augustan; in Norris's day the metaphysical conceit was out of date (bizarre to the Cartesian mind) but the compact clarity of the couplet had not yet come into its own.[14] Norris therefore looks to the Pindaric Ode as one way of amalgamating sublimity and order with freedom to extemporise, but despite his movements of departure from the Metaphysicals, his debt to them is unmistakable. There are hints of Herbert and Vaughan and Crashaw everywhere, and also of Cowley, who provided inspiration for the Pindarics. George Herbert's homely familiarity is clear, for example, in lines like, 'Well, I have thought on't, and I find/This busie world is nonsense all' ('The Retirement', 65), and Vaughan's more rarefied voice with its language of occult sympathies is not far absent from 'The Aspiration':

> How cold this clime! and yet my sense
> Perceives even here thy influence.
> Even here, thy strong magnetic charms I feel,
> And pant and tremble like the amorous steel   (174)

Crashaw also may influence Norris's imagery of hard and fluid substances combining to describe Christ's wounds:

> His tortured body weeps all-o're
>   And out of every pore
> Buds forth a precious gem of purple gore.
>   ('The Passion of Our Blessed Saviour', 38)[15]

But more important than particular borrowings is the general technique, for in spirit as well as in letter, Norris is often clearly in the line of his Metaphysical forebears. He favours direct personal openings which exploit the dramatic qualities of the speaking voice:

> Not yet convinc'd? why wilt thou still pursue
> Through nature's field delusive bliss?

('To Himself', 76)

And he is willing to torment even the most abstract technical language to an expression of emotion. A poem which nicely exemplifies this is 'The Infidel' (66–7). I quote it in full, because Norris' writings are hard to come by, and there are no modern editions.

> Farewel fruition, thou grand cruel cheat
> Which first our hopes does raise and then defeat.
> Farewel thou midwife to abortive bliss,
>   Thou mystery of fallacies
>   Distance presents the object fair,
> With charming features and a graceful air,
> But when we come to seize th' inviting prey,
> Like a shy ghost, it vanishes away.
>
> So to th' unthinking boy the distant sky
> Seems on some mountain's surface to rely;
> He with ambitious haste climbs the ascent,
>   Curious to touch the firmament:
>   But when with an unweary'd pace
> Arriv'd he is at the long-wish'd-for place,
> With sighs the sad defeat he does deplore,
> His heaven is still as distant as before.
>
> And yet 'twas long e're I could thoroughly see
> This grand impostor's frequent treachery.
> Tho often fool'd, yet I should still dream on
>   Of pleasure in reversion.
>   Tho still he did my hopes deceive,
> His fair pretensions I would still believe.
> Such was my charity, that tho I knew
> And found him false, yet I would think him true.
>
> But now he shall no more with shews deceive,
> I will no more enjoy, no more believe.
> Th' unwary jugler has so often shewn
>   His fallacies, that now they'r known,
>   Shall I trust on? the cheat is plain,

I will not be impos'd upon again.
I'll view the bright appearance from afar,
But never try to catch the falling star.

The decisive tone establishes a speaking voice from the opening
line ('Farewel, fruition . . .') and sustains it through the ensuing
persuasive rhetoric as the main parts of the poem exploit the
connections of logical argument—'So to . . .' and 'And yet
. . .', 'But now . . . '. The sense of debate is maintained by
self-questioning ('Shall I trust on?'), the assertive anaphora
('no more', 'no more', 'no more') and conceits which combine
the abstract language of false logic and the allusion to abortion
to suggest how physically and intellectually frustrating is the
search for happiness in this world:

Farewel thou midwife of abortive bliss,
Thou mystery of fallacies.

The conceptual compression gains vigour from the contemptuous
and dismissive sounds of the second line, where 'mystery' means
both mumbo-jumbo (false and confusing chicanery, the opposite
of the truly mysterious) and also the false skill (mystery as
trade or craft) of the midwife. All this has the true Metaphysical
tang about it, as does the image of the 'unwary jugler' of
the last stanza, and the reference to the 'shy ghost' which
vanishes just when you think you have got hold of it.

Still, if we look again, 'The Infidel' appears both typically
Metaphysical and not, for the dramatisations are not quite
as full-blooded as I have suggested. They are really shadows
of anger, a kind of indignation in retrospect. The 'I' of Norris's
poem, we discover, has already solved the problem, and has
achieved a perspective outside the struggle even before the
poem begins. The most telling modification of the Metaphysical
manner lies in the fact that nothing changes, from beginning
to end, in what the speaker realises. If Donne had used that
'Farewel, fruition . . .' with such confidence, it would have
been to make the poem turn the tables on him, either by
revealing the careless confidence as thinly masked bitterness
(if it is a love poem), or by showing that the easily assumed
autonomy and self-determination is after all a gift of grace
(if it is a divine poem). But Norris means it simply as it
stands. 'Fruition' is 'a grand cruel cheat' in line one, and
in the concluding lines he re-affirms 'the cheat is plain'. Because
nothing changes there can be, of course, little drama, and

the conceits and scornful lines lose a good deal of energy because they do not describe a present perplexity at all, but at best recall something of what that perplexity meant before the cheat became plain. Norris's speaker is secure as the speaker of no good Metaphysical poem is. Indeed the image of the boy climbing the mountain in order to touch the sky fails just because there is no way we can join in the boy's illusion: the foolishness is revealed by the very terms of the quest, as both Norris's speaker and we readers watch from a secure perspective outside the process of the action.

Accompanying this less personal and more public point of view in 'The Infidel' is a certain coolness and neatness in the tone and design of the verse:

> Distance presents the object fair,
> With charming features and a graceful air.

This is closer to the Augustans than to Donne, and if Norris affects the metaphysics he also refines them;[16] the 'bright appearances' are kept distant and judged 'from afar'. So, the smooth cadence and directness of 'The Infidel' already offer a touch of Neo-Classical grace, and not surprisingly Norris early in his career admired the Cartesian ideal of 'clear and distinct thought'.[17] Indeed the claims of Cartesian method (with) its objective and rational observer) and of Christian devotion on the Augustinian model (with its personal participation in meditation) are the horns of a dilemma on which Norris was to develop his entire career. His poems, although he abandoned them early, therefore make a useful introduction to the later strenuous philosophic activity, for the conflict between Descartes and St Augustine is in a way already there in the mixture of Metaphysical and eighteenth-century verse styles.

JOHN NORRIS: THE OBSERVERS IN THE POEM

To embody the point of view of his detached observer, Norris often deploys in his poems the language and insights of Platonism,[18] describing worldly vanity through the vision of angels and powers and disembodied spirits. There are angels in the arbour to advise on bliss (84), angels stand trembling at the crucifixion (99), angels direct the Blessed Virgin and sustain the suffering Christ (40, 148), angels see 'with steddy and

attentive eyes' (136), and clearly understand the vision of divine
Ideas. The poems are cluttered with angels presumably because
Norris himself yearns after what he imagines to be their point
of view. He even writes a poem, 'The Impatient' (128), to
say that he cannot wait to become (almost) an angel himself,
to know intuitively, and not by the discursive process of dialecti-
cal argument. Even his preface has something to say on angelic
and human knowledge, with a wry glance at the poems to
follow: 'were angels to write, I fancy we should have but
few folio's' (35).

Angelic joy and harmony, in short, eclipse for Norris the
concerns of the individual human self, and in evoking the
splendours of angelic vision, he tries to release the tension
between self and world by transcending both. 'The Retirement',
for example, opens in a typically Metaphysical manner:

Well, I have thought on't, and I find
    This busie world is nonsense all;
    I here despair to please my mind,
Her sweetest honey is so mixt with gall. (65)

But the intimations of conflict between honey and gall go unde-
veloped. As in 'The Infidel', the poet has already set himself
safely apart, with one eye on the angels:

No tumults can my close apartment find,
Calm as those seats above, which know no storm nor wind.
    (65)

Similarly, in 'The Advice' (74) we are urged to assume a
calm and providential view of time and fortune, and in 'To
Himself' (76) the 'short-sighted souls' who engage in the affai
of the world are pitied: 'The world is best enjoy'd when 'tis
best understood' (78), and you do not understand it while
you are in it.

Throughout his poetry, Norris's technique remains consistent:
he uses the Metaphysical manner to invite us to share in the
speaker's spiritual conflicts, and then shifts the point of view
to a transcendent perspective from where the conflict disappears.
Even the Pindaric ode on the passion, a theme which confronts
us with human suffering before which we especially acknowledge
our own guilt and recalcitrance, yields to Norris's special treatment. The sublimity of the Pindaric form itself distances us
from the human subject, and Norris makes Christ the 'great
hero' (37) and 'champion' (41), rather than a suffering man.

Yet the poem does, for a moment, invite us to meditate on the human element by composing the place: 'Lo, in Gethsemane, I see him prostrate lye/Press'd with the weight of His great agony' (38), and the tortured body weeps gems of blood. But no sooner are we faced with this spectacle of woe than it is removed from us. Christ sees God frown, sees the whole 'dismal scroll' (39) of human sin, and his fortitude wavers. But immediately a ministering angel confronts him with 'cordials of light refin'd' (40), shows him 'Types, figures, and mysteries' (41), and with an Ideal discourse sustains the languishing hero. Heaven and hell then join in a drama of cosmic dimensions as Christ endures 'the great hyperoble of pain' (45). Caught in the balance between warring opposites of such great magnitude, man the observer is reduced to inconsequence, indeed almost annihilated. The line that best describes the speaker's eventual position is 'Fear on, 'tis wondrous all, and new' (44), and Norris clearly wishes to create here a sense of the theocentric mystery rather than its immediate, anthropocentric challenge to faith.

Possibly, there is an irony in all this: the poem could really be a superlative rebuke of human sinfulness, implying that the huge series of events was sparked off, caused even, by human vanity which seems in the end so mean and trivial. But if this meaning is implied, it is sufficiently tacit to cause doubt that Norris fully intended it, or that the poem bears it out. My main point therefore remains that the theocentric impulse is central to Norris's verse, and lies behind his various depictions of the detached speaker, whether the Horatian *beatus ille* who watches from the shade, the hierophant who sings in Pindarics of high subjects, the pastoral elegist, the Platonic idealist, or the angelic observer. All reach towards a 'new scene of things', the vision of 'pure forms' where knowledge transcends poetry itself:

I cannot here sing more exalted layes,
But what's defective now I will supply
  When I enjoy Thy deity,
  Then may'st thou sleep my lyre,
I shall not then thy help require,
Diviner thoughts will then me fire
Than thou, tho' play'd on by an angel's hand, canst raise.   (140)

So far I seem to be suggesting that Norris employs his Metaphysical persona mainly to express the experience of human vanity and frustration, and his detached observer to describe the joys which await the soul freed from the ego. There seems no reason, in theory, why a poem should not successfully combine these two elements, and yet for the most part Norris's poems do not. The claims of the Metaphysical speaker with his agonised, guilty, time-bound ego stand consistently divorced from the angelic observer. They share no common ground though they must often inhabit the same poem, and the result is uncertainty rather than provocative ambiguity. There are some exceptions, such as 'The Conquest', which is entirely in the Metaphysical manner, and exploits the cut and thrust of the mind's self-defeating intentions. But poems like 'The Conquest' are rare in Norris, and appear but sporadically in a collection which seems on first view a mixed bag of moderately talented versifications: an assortment of panegyrics, elegies, paraphrases of the psalms, pastorals, Platonic contemplations, Horatian retreat poems, devotional meditations, and Pindaric sallies. Certainly in the first two-thirds there is little to dispel the impression that the collection is random.

But then occurs a group centered on the death of the poet's niece, and following them a poem called 'The Retraction', wherein Norris laments the callowness of his earlier practice. In light of 'The Retraction' the remaining one-third of the volume frequently seems intent on correcting imbalances evident earlier. The first two-thirds are marked by a conviction that the world is a hindrance to happiness, and that the solitary contemplative enjoys superior wisdom in detachment. The main point in 'To Himself' is the 'delusive bliss' (76) of seeking nature's secrets, as it is in 'The Infidel', 'The Chase', 'The Refusal', and 'Against Knowledge', where all learning gained from the world is 'false and vain' (130), depending merely on tricks and cheats and 'Fancy's happy imagery.' In general, such poems underestimate the contribution of the world, with its joys and sufferings, to the development of human destiny towards God: 'How should that empty thing deserve my care,/ Which Virtue does not need, and Vice can never bear?' ('The Refusal', 79).

If the collected poems tell us anything autobiographical at all, we may hazard that Norris encountered, at the death of his niece, one limitation in his theory of detachment from the passions. The poems which deal with the event are tightly grouped, and reveal a man touched and disturbed by a normal human grief. They include 'To The Memory of my Dear Neece M.C.', 'The Resignation', 'To My Good Angel', 'The Defiance', 'Superstition', 'The Complaint of Adam Turn'd out of Paradise', 'To Sleep', 'The Grant', and perhaps 'The Aspiration', a poem which, after the wrestlings with grief, attempts to set the soul again calmly heavenwards.

As with many poems in the 'Anniversary' tradition, Norris's laments for the dead 'she' seem extravagant, but when the bitter occasion of the loss is seen symbolically, the poems become a lament for the conditions of human fallenness itself. They describe also a kind of Boethian curve as the speaker is unable first to find consolation in philosophy ('By tears to ease my grief I've try'd/And philosophick med'cins have applied' (156)), then swallows his bitter draught ('Thy med'cine puts me to great smart' (162)), returns to the comforts of philosophy while denouncing fortune ('I'll shew thee Fortune ... / ... /Clad in the armour of philosophy' (165)), and in the end returns to God and, though still imprisoned ('How long great God, how long must I/Immur'd in this dark prison lye',)[18] is filled with reconciliation and divine love ('The Aspiration', 173).[19] The consolation and the accompanying wisdom of the beautiful, stern lady are acquired here with as much difficulty as for Boethius himself, because Norris does not now simplify the problems of the world's joys and sufferings. The irrational usurpation by grief of the axioms of good sense is, at last, acknowledged with a disturbed but honest directness (161). There is genuine hurt bewilderment in lines like these:

Is she then dead, and can it be
That I can live to write her elegy?
I hoped, since 'twas not to my soul deny'd
To sympathise in all the pain
Which she, tho long, did well sustain,
T'have carried on the sympathy and dy'd. (157)

Although the dead girl does become an occasion for large reflections on the destruction of nature's perfection (159), the basic personal sorrow is never eclipsed, and for the first time Norris's poetry registers a note of nostalgia as his voice accompanies Adam's—'O whither now, whither shall I repair ...'

(169). The note recurs, particularly in the poems on dreams where 'kind Fancy' brings the image of the dead girl to mind, and then it is dispelled on waking, with a complex residue of happiness and grief and bitterness:

What bliss do we oft to delusion owe!
Who would not still be cheated so!   (173).

The simple disdain of the tricks of fancy in 'Against Knowledge' is now quite gone, and in 'The Retraction', Norris openly acknowledges his earlier naïveté:

I've often charg'd all sublunary bliss,
    With vanity and emptiness:

. . . .

But now great Preacher pardon me.   (175-6)

Coming as it does after the poems of lament, and casting a retrospective view upon Norris's earlier writing, 'The Retraction' can indicate that Norris had learned something important about poetry from this experience of death. But, paradoxically, the experience of death and the consequent re-estimation of the world in relation to his theocentric themes may well have tipped the balance for Norris against poetry itself. The self-eclipsing which every man needs in order to achieve submission of the ego to God's supreme authority is not, Norris finally sees, to be found in poetry which at best expresses, rather than annihilates, the self in relation to the world. The detached observer of self-evident principles cannot also be the Augustinian meditator, for the images in which the individual dwells in his peculiar and personal complexities, and in which poetry has its being, are replaced and not simply modified by the Cartesian clear ideas which are the patrimony of all men without distinction. In the end, the lure of that realm of Ideas and immutable truths was stronger for Norris than the dramatic brilliance of poetry. Although in his fairwell verse 'To his Muse' (201) he acknowledges the power and value of poetry and the insights to the world which it provides, he is careful to point out the one thing of special significance to himself, which poems cannot supply, namely 'security'. The word occurs twice in the last stanza, and offers the key to the quest that absorbed Norris during the rest of his writing career, for the task of reconciling Augustine and Descartes moves now to a new phase precipitated by those yearnings for authoritative order which so motivated Norris in his own personal dealings with the world. First he had questioned the images themselves in his poetry, and his earliest attitude saw mainly a discontinuity between images of things and intuitions of Ideas which transcend them. Then, in the spirit of his 'Retraction', he had granted to the world a real value as a declaration of God's love. But the critical question was upon him, and poetry could not solve it. Norris in consequence sought a theoretical solution elsewhere, and at last in Nicolas Malebranche, the French Cartesian and Oratorian Father, thought he had found a mature answer to the challenge of releasing the tensions between self and world by transcending both, to dwell in an angelic vision of divine Ideas.

THE ORATORIAN SOLUTION

Why Norris chose Malebranche and what exactly he found there makes a complex question. Certainly Malebranche's vocation as an Oratorian is important, for Norris became heir not only to a system of thought but also to a type of spirituality nurtured half a century earlier and handed on to Malebranche by the peculiar genius of Pierre de Bérulle (1575—1629), founder of the French Oratorians, confessor of Descartes, devotee of St Augustine, and disciple of Benet of Canfield. In broad terms, the type of influence which reaches Crashaw through the Capucins comes also to Norris through the kindred spiritual programme of the French Oratory. Oratorians and Capucins together had visited England as chaplains to Henrietta Maria, and although there were some real differences between the two groups, they shared common aims and ideals. Bérulle had found a lifelong friend in the daunting Grey Eminence, the Capucin Joseph du Tremblay, and both men in turn found inspiration in the work of Father Benet, just as both were stimulated and directed by the cultural climate which was to produce Descartes and the achievements of French rationalism.

As we have seen, Benet's *Rule of Perfection* represents a powerful attempt to fix the will on God in a world fast relinquishing the old, unselfconscious assumption that in the physical universe around us God's design lies immanent. Benet takes up the challenge presented by the new science to ecclesiastical authority on the question of discernment of spirits, and his answer involves an exploitation of the physical world which mechanical determinism itself had brought to light, namely the realm of pure extension. By reaction from its horrifying impersonality we are moved, in Benet's devotional practice, to reaffirm the more comforting notion that things signify Ideas they embody. But Benet has to force us to this reaffirmation, for already a wedge has been driven between material object and divine Idea by the fast-growing popularity of materialist theories. Benet assumes these theories to exploit them for devotional ends.

With Crashaw I have suggested that Benet's devotional style finds a way into English poetry. This is not to say that Crashaw theorised about the relationship between material substance and imagery, but in adapting French Capucin spirituality to his poetry he helps to educate and enliven devout sensibilities to problems engaged by the culture at large on the questions of bodies, images, and Ideas. Now, with Norris, I can suggest a continuation of the same kind of French influence, except that Norris, unlike Crashaw, does theorise. His acknowledged aim is to reconcile Descartes and St Augustine, and his explicitness helps to make plain the line of transmission I seek to establish. Norris stops writing poetry not to denounce it, but in order to define, theoretically, the ground on which it could be written at all in Augustinian terms in the new age of Descartes. But first, to chart the curve of this development, a word about Cardinal de Bérulle and the type of thought and devotion which he helped to promulgate.

PIERRE DE BÉRULLE

Pierre de Bérulle (1575–1629)[20] was born of noble parentage at the Château de Serilly near Troyes. He received his early education from the Jesuits at Clermont, where he showed himself an intellectually precocious and spiritually sophisticated child. When still a young man, he was exposed in his own home to the influence of Mme Acarie, who was related to the Bérulles and sought refuge with them after the political decline of her husband's fortunes. A hasty and ill-advised adventurer, Pierre Acarie had thrown in his fortunes with the League against

Henri IV, and had suffered in consequence. But political fortune was never really to affect because it did not really touch the sublime spirit of his wife, and her biographer tells us of the trances and ecstacies into which she passed with a frequency embarrassing even to herself.[21] Yet Mme Acarie was an effective organiser too: her caritable enterprises were renowned, and she managed to gather about her a circle comprising some of the most gifted minds of her day. Her influence on the young Pierre de Bérulle was profound, and the spirit of the Hotel d'Acarie, with its adviser Benet of Canfield and its following of fervent and dedicated disciples of the new devotion left a mark on all his written work.

Certainly from the example of Benet of Canfield, St François de Sales, and Mme Acarie, the young Bérulle must have learned the signal importance for the spiritual life of subordinating and conforming the will to God. He becomes in consequence a chief exponent of what Brémond calls the 'culte du non-moi'[22] in seventeenth-century French devotion, and the necessity of self-abnegation remains basic to his thought: 'nous nous devons entièrement dépouiller de tout usage et disposition de nous-mêmes' (col. 1292). The austere directives of the *Bref discours de l'abnegation interieure* (1597), which Bérulle wrote when he was 22 years old, are always assumed, even though more graciously extrapolated, by his later work. With his remorseless denial of the ego goes an adhesion to God's will, and to describe it, Bérulle embraces the Dionysian vocabulary and high example of the Flemish mystics, as Benet had before him.[23] The spiritual sacrifices of the negative way become necessary prologues to the soul's absorption in wordless communion with the divine splendour: 'Selon S. Denys, *toutes choses sont sorties de l'Vnité par la nature,* et elles recherchent cette Vnité par vn secret instinct de la nature; elles y rentrent par la grace; elles s'y abismět par la gloire' (col. 205).[24] On the way back to this glorious secret centre where 'chaque poinct est vn abysme' (col. 208) the soul must especially acknowledge its own nothingness as it waits on grace: 'c'est à l'ame de se perdre en son neant, et à Dieu seul de la conuertir à son tout' (col. 904).

Upon the basis of this kind of sublime transcendence made to serve the doctrine of self-abnegation and total recreation by grace, Bérulle's distinctive thought has a footing. Yet his special quality is more difficult to describe, for its effect lies largely in the intensity and brilliance of his imagination and language in making familiar ideas new. Although Christian writers had always insisted on the principle of all things for God, none before Bérulle had been able with such ingenuity to take a perspective on human affairs from God down to man. For Bérulle, every meaningful human act seemed to conform to a divine mystery, revealing not the virtuous attainment of the doer but the degree to which he has the capacity to be like God.[25] Such a 'capacité' (it is a special word of Bérulle's) when brought into action reveals an 'état', a 'state' or present disposition, a way in which a small humanity can participate in the divine essence. All acts are thus exemplary, and Bérulle's ideal is to make human discourse transparent to a transcendental significance by seeing it symbolically. But first one must 'se rendre', give oneself over entirely in 'adhérence' to God. To do this, all attachments to nature and ego are relinquished and annihiliated, for self-will above all stands between us and the supernatural divine life that is in us. The self, Bérulle insists, is nothing:

> L'Abnegation est fondée en la Grandeur de Dieu, et en l'estat de la creature tirée du néant, et tendante au néant par sa condition propre. (col. 1167)

The emphasis here on inner disposition is similar to that of Benet of Canfield, and like him, to avoid quietism, Bérulle insists that man must co-operate in the process of regeneration, at least by desiring it and by willing himself over to it. Yet Bérulle carries further the insights of these earlier writers by developing their theocentricism in a vocabulary peculiar to himself and in an especially direct relation to the challenge presented by the modern climate of scientific thought. In a famous passage, Bérulle compares himself to Copernicus and claims that the new theocentric spirituality with its language of 'états', 'capacité', and 'adhérence' is to the history of devotion what Copernicus is to science:

> Vn excellent Esprit de ce siecle [the margin has Nicolaus Copernicus] a voulu maintenir que le Soleil est au Centre du Monde, et non pas la Terre. . . . Cette opinion nouvelle, peu suivie en la science des Astres, est vtile, et doit estre suivie en la science de Salut. (col. 161)

The comparison is not merely an engaging analogy: historians agree that the movement begun by Benet of Canfield and brought to fulfilment by Bérulle was indeed revolutionary.[26] In Bérulle's Copernican claim he is thus fully conscious of attempting to define a viable spirituality for an age of scientific enquiry and rationalism, and his awareness of the problem and of the implications for Christian devotion of Enlightenment thought are also indicated by his close personal relationship with Descartes.[27]

Bérulle had encouraged the young Descartes to pursue the new method of philosophical enquiry which Bérulle had found promising and exciting. Descartes in turn was deeply affected by the qualities of mind he found in Bérulle, whom he took as his confessor. When Bérulle died, Descartes remained faithful to the Oratorians in whom he saw promulgated the Cardinal's thought and insight. The admiration, while Bérulle was alive, was mutual, and among the Oratorians a tradition of Cartesian studies grew up and continued in high repute, culminating in Malebranche. It is difficult to determine exactly how much Bérulle and Descartes contributed to each other, but there was cross-fertilisation,[28] even to the point of providing for Bérulle special insight to the possible spiritual dangers of Cartesian thought. Certainly, a number of points basic to Descartes' method carry over into Oratorian tradition. For instance, Descartes had vigorously criticised the language of scholastic philosophy, with its fanciful theories of substances and accidents and naïve inability to distinguish primary from secondary qualities. To imagine colour was actually *in* the object in the same way as, say, length or weight was to confuse the real thing with modifications of our perceiving minds. Consequently, elaborate discursive proofs of God's existence from the design of such imagined substances and accidents in nature are a waste of time. We can prove that God exists, but it is more adequately done by considering the thinking mind itself. Descartes abandons the old deductive proofs of God's existence from the world of bodies for proofs based on intuition, and on our ability to recognise the necessary truth of self-evident principles.[29] Having thus separated the realm of extension (bodies and their modifications) from the realm of thought (which intuits the existence of God, *sui generis*), Descartes goes on to stress the transcendence of the creator, who encompasses our finite minds. For Descartes, though God creates truth, he does so arbitrarily: $2 + 2$ could have made something other than 4.[30]

Bérulle's thought addresses precisely this kind of rationalist theory. His theocentricism insists everywhere on the mystery of divine transcendence. The work of God, like His transcendent unity, is a secret: 'cet oeuvre est vn oeuvre et vn Mystere d'Vnité, lequel part d'vn sacré conseil, d'vn conseil adorable et admirable, d'vn conseil secret d'Vnité' (col. 195). So also is the approach of God to us in his Son 'fondé sur vn grand secret' (col. 196). And even when we devote ourselves to worshipping and dwelling in the secret unity of God we do not understand the real depth of our dependence or the nature of our union. The mystery must be admired and reverenced, for the experience of our participation in it is self-evident only when we annihilate the selfish screen of our egotism, and for this we need the gift of divine grace.

Bérulle also attacks the futility of scholastic attempts to reason deductively on such matters, and replaces them simply with the prayer of assent. Argument becomes adoration: 'Il est donc superflu d'en alleguer des textes et des raisons, et il nous doit suffire de supposer cette verité, d'adorer cette Vnité . . .' (col. 130). We are faced with the mystery of annihilating love, which justifies itself by blinding self-evidence, and much of Bérulle's writing is devoted to the evocation of the grandeur of such a mystery. The characteristic note of the French school is both sublime and abstract:

> Amour aneantissant, et aneantissement d'Amour, que je reuere et adore, comme donnant existence et subsistence à une nature humaine en la grandeur d'vne Personne diuine, et comme ayant son origine dans l'excez d'un Amour increé et infiny! (col. 162).

It was for Bérulle's follower Gibieuf to make explicit in a systematic Cartesian way the principle that God's transcendence implies God's liberty from the causality of creation itself,[31] and to reaffirm the insignificance of secondary causes for approaching divine mysteries. But he does not have to develop Bérulle very far in order to do so.

Bérulle thus combines a Cartesian scepticism about natural knowledge in relation to divine truth with an Augustinian insistence on self-mortification as the channel whereby divine grace may totally replace natural knowledge by supernatural illumination. Such a process, Bérulle was quick to recognise, must not now lead to a Manichaean rejection of the material creation:

Christ himself had not despised the flesh, and the sublime grandeur of the Godhead must somehow be made compatible with the everyday facts of mundane and material existence. Thus, when Urban VIII gave Bérulle a cardinal's hat, he gave him also an honorary title, 'Apostle of the Incarnate Word', to acknowledge how intense was Bérulle's preoccupation with the doctrine of the Incarnation, and how ingenious his interpretation of it as a means of making available to men the secret mysteries of God in a manner compatible with an orthodox attitude to the physical world.

First, the union of Christ to God is, as we have seen, a 'secret', and the doctrine of the Trinity represents the mystery of God's transcendent unity. But Christ as God is also life in us, and the verse of St Paul from Galatians I remains a favourite of Bérulle's—'*Viuo ego, iam non ego, viuit verò in me Christus*' (col. 181). Jesus is the actual root of our being, 'celui qui est le fond de notre être' (col. 1181), and as such is our 'capacité' for life in the body, hindered only by the shield of our ego. We are conformed to God in the degree to which it is open for our everyday lives to be Christ-like, and this in each of us is according to particular vocations, gifts, and aptitudes. These 'capacities' should be raised up in selfless adoration, and in becoming permanent dispositions for the praise of God, they are elevated from mere capacities to enduring 'états'. Only in the life of Christ is every human capacity in fact raised in this way to adore God; so Christ is unique because his adoration is complete. Perfectly human and perfectly Godlike, he is the sole infinite adorer of the Father:

> De toute eternité il y a auoit bien vn Dieu infiniment adorable: mais il n'y auoit pas encore un Adorateur infiny; . . . Vous estes maintenant, ô IESVS! cét Adorateur, cét homme, ce Seruiteur, infiny . . . (col. 183)

We should therefore study the life of Christ to find how it speaks to the 'state' of our particular natures. In Bérulle's language, an initial 'admiration' of the divine mystery in Christ becomes 'adoration' by our 'adhérence' to the 'états' of the incarnate word. The emphasis throughout is, however, on our intuitive recognition of the relevance to ourselves of Christ's example. Bérulle's view of the Incarnation, while acknowledging the importance of God's assuming material flesh, is also exemplary, as Bourgoing points out; Christ is 'comme nostre exemplaire;

en dépendant de luy, comme de nostre principe; et en tendant
à luy, comme à nostre fin' (col. 87). Still, Bérulle has worked
hard to make the traditional Augustinian devotion to the physical facts of the life of Christ important, and the line of continuity
through the Franciscan Father Benet to the wellsprings of Western Catholic devotion is kept open[32] as Bérulle furthers his
Copernican revolution by way of the strongly stressed exemplarism and arguments from intuition. Bérulle therefore manages
to deploy traditional meditation techniques, but he does so
to claim that the physical must be stripped of all appurtenances
of naturalism in order to reveal the pure 'état' of the soul
conforming to God, a knowledge which comes to us altogether
without physical sentiments or experience. Bérulle's combination
of exemplarism and intense abnegation thus ends up confirming
the Cartesian divorce between physical and spiritual knowledge.
The images of rhetoric consequently do not mediate mysteries
in the traditional manner, but Bérulle's work is full of what
he calls 'élevations', or prayer-like rhapsodies of devotion written
to move us by inspiring and inflaming the spiritual affections:

> quelles éleuations! quels abbaissemens! quelles loüanges! quel
> hommage! quels remerciemens! & quel amour d'vne Ame
> tirée du neant, comblée de gloire, & en vn moment éleuée
> par dessus tout ce qui peut estre creé, & iointe à Dieu
> mesme personnellement! O Vie! ô Puissance! ô Majesté sor-
> tante d'vne Diuinité viuante & subsistente en cette nature
> creée! ô Splendeur de l'eternelle lumiere! ô Roy de gloire!
> ô Soleil de Iustice! (col. 174)

Here are all the Bérullian marks—the pure and sublime transcendence, the focus on the mystery of Incarnation, on the
'néant' of human nature, and the characteristic vocabulary,
'état', 'élevation', 'adorer'. The peculiar tone of 'élevation'
resides in the combination of high formality and breathless
rhapsody in the lists of expostulating 'o's', the exclamations,
incantatory clauses, and the use of present participles, a technique by which Bérulle consistently attempts to give a sense
of 'état' as not merely an action but a disposition, or 'durée'.

Bérulle's originality is formed partly by such a style and
novel vocabulary, but partly also by the cultural situation to
which he addressed himself. As a modern he has recognised
the redundancy of scholastic theology and epistemology, and
the attempt to effect a Copernican revolution in devotion

remains, as Bérulle himself recognised, the most significant single feature of his thought. Nonetheless, as an Augustinian, Bérulle was alive to some spiritual limitations of the new method, and he felt acutely some dangers which Descartes seems to have cared little about. For example, the relegation, on Cartesian terms, of an inscrutable God to his Heaven, together with an intense concern for the operational principles of an inert, mechanical nature, constituted a strong temptation to displace God almost entirely from the realm of the extended universe of objects. Consequently, Bérulle insists on self-annihilation to enforce the lesson that without God's continued creation in the roots of our physical being we would lapse immediately into the nonentity from which we are drawn. Humility, Bérulle insists, is the best (and only) antidote to the pride of human self-sufficiency. So, while Bérulle accepts from the new science that God's purposes can no longer be well perceived in the images of material nature, he believes also that the mysteries are intuited, through introspection and self-mortification, as revelations to the spiritual faculty. The truth of such revelations is self-evident, and depends upon supernatural grace rather than a deliberate questioning of the natural images of the book of the world. Where or how, then, the physical world relates to our images of it is a question Bérulle does not attempt to answer, for his main aim is devotional. But for Nicolas Malebranche, heir to Bérulle's thought, this question becomes of paramount importance.

NICOLAS MALEBRANCHE

Like Bérulle, Malebranche early in life fell under the influence of a saintly woman who confirmed him in the pursuit of sanctity and the practice of the devout life. A spinal disorder, resulting in physical malfunction, discouraged him, likewise early, from the world of affairs, and Malebranche became an Oratorian. His scholarly abilities and zealous devotion soon impressed his superiors, and, as his talents matured, he became an ardent student of Descartes, complementing this interest with an almost total immersion in the writings of St Augustine. In these scholarly pursuits Malebranche confirms the patrimony of Bérulle, but he was to examine much more rigorously than Bérulle the spiritual implications of Cartesian methodology. The result is a complex and rich philosophy, written in a gracious, individual style, and presenting an original synthesis of the materials which inform it.

In assessing Malebranche in relation to his antecedents, critics have concentrated on two main points. First, they have taken account of the Bérullian component and have pointed out that Malebranche modifies what he receives, by addition as well as omission. Second, they have suggested that despite the obvious indebtedness to Descartes, an anti-Cartesian attitude also informs Malebranche's writings.[33] From what I have said on Bérulle it is possible to see these two points merge, for among Oratorians from the inception a respect for Cartesian method is mixed with a suspicion of it, and certainly Malebranche remains Bérullian in many important ways. He insists, for example, on a similar theocentricism, over and against which man in himself is nothing: 'I derive nothing whatever from my own nature, nothing from the nature derived from the philosophers—all comes from God and His decrees.'[34] Like everything else in nature, man exists in a state of total dependency: 'the conservation of created things being on the part of God merely a continuous creation, merely an act of volition which persists and operates without ceasing' (189). For the creature the way to God is thus by self-abnegation, and by removing from the ego every motion of self-determination: 'Of ourselves we can do nothing, hence of ourselves we ought to will nothing' (196). Like Bérulle, Malebranche also attacks the scholastic attitude to language. On Cartesian grounds, he argues that qualities like colour and taste do not inhere in bodies as the scholastics suggest, but are modifications of our perceiving selves. The realms of thought and extension are, therefore, distinct, and Malebranche goes further even than Descartes in stressing that they cannot act on one another in any circumstances.[35] The world of bodies cannot mediate in any active sense the contents of our ideas or sensations or imaginations. Images are not caused by bodies, and Malebranche, like Descartes, argues for God's existence not from bodies and images but from the idea of God perceived as a self-evident truth:

> By the Divine we understand the Infinite, the Being without restriction, Being infinitely perfect. But nothing finite can represent the Infinite. Hence it is enough to think of God to know that He exists.   (203)

The ontological argument, based here both on the mind's power and the otherness of physical nature further divorces the world of secondary causes from that of theology. Consequently Malebranche, like Gibieuf and Descartes, thinks that talk of final causality is a presumptuous encroachment on divine liberty and transcendence: 'Do you not see, Aristes, that to look for the motives and ends of His actions outside Himself means to anthropomorphise God? (229).[36] But Malebranche fears, with Bérulle, that the scientist whose concerns are thus liberated from final causes can too readily fall foul of the errors of self-sufficiency. So, in the characteristic style of the Oratory he engages a passionate self-abnegation to instil the lesson that humility is the only means to the kind of love that redeems.

Like Bérulle, Malebranche also sees the Incarnation as the highest exemplar of redeeming humility and of all the other acts of devotion that may bring men to God. We belong in Christ, Malebranche goes on, in proportion to what in us is worthy of love, and God has ordained his son's mission 'in order to receive from Him, and through Him from us, the adoration which is His due' (236). By living in Christ, we therefore also adore the Father, and though Malebranche emphasises more than Bérulle the philosophic and exemplarist elements of the Incarnation, the thought of both men interpreting Jesus in the context of Descartes is marked by a similarity of conception and expression. In Malebranche the result is a peculiarly theological mysticism and a chastely abstract rhetoric evoking the mystery to which we are drawn by our own hidden depths.[37]

Bérulle's rhapsodic 'élevations' have their counterpart in the similar but more reserved Malebranchiste 'considerations'.[38] Here, for instance, is a passage which marks both the Bérullian influence and Malebranche's personal quality of restraint and limpid beauty:

Man is made to adore God in the wisdom of His action. Let us try to lose ourselves happily in its depths. The human mind is never better occupied than when in enforced silence it adores the divine perfections. But this silence of the soul can come to us only after contemplating what is beyond us. Courage then, Aristes! Contemplate, admire the general providence of the Creator. I have placed you at a point of view from which you ought to discover an incomprehensible wisdom. (272)

This recalls the Bérullian self-abnegation and adoration as we move towards the silence of the transcendent secret, though Malebranche renders the thought of the master in a style of his own.

The question now arises, if the world of extension is totally separate from the world of thought and if we ourselves are nothing, how exactly do we know God or the world? Malebranche here takes his leave both from Bérulle, who had not given this question serious philosophical consideration, and from Descartes who had offered a fairly trite answer. Descartes simply does not believe that man is as much a nothing as Malebranche's Bérullian tradition demands, and claims instead that man has an idea of himself, and because he knows himself clearly he can argue (Descartes thinks, clearly) about other things, for instance God and the world.[39] But this is precisely the kind of autonomy which both Bérulle and Malebranche abhor. Both insist that because we are nothing we have no idea of ourselves at all,[40] and so no autonomous basis for arguing clearly about anything. Our lack of self-knowledge is a direct consequence of our depths being hidden in Christ, and Malebranche goes on to single out the illusions of self-sufficiency which scientists in particular can fall into by following alternative solutions:

> I could, by considering my own modifications attentively, become acquainted with physics and several sciences which consist only in the knowledge of the relations of extension, as you know quite well. In a word, I should be a light unto myself, and I cannot think of that without a kind of horror.   (147)

Since we have no ideas of our own, scientific or otherwise, how then do we know? Malebranche introduces three main and original suggestions. First, the theory of images and ideas as *vision in God*; second, the doctrine of *occasionalism*; and third, the notion of *intelligible extension*. In each he attempts to adapt the Bérullian teachings on self-abnegation and theocentricism to a Cartesian view of the physical world as extended substance.

Malebranche begins,[41] somewhat paradoxically, by arguing that although we have only confused sensations of our selves we can have a clear idea of body. We can, for instance, reason clearly that the secondary qualities of bodies are partly modifications of ourselves, experienced as sensations, but that they must be caused by something external to ourselves, and we then can posit an underlying material substance. We thus arrive, says Malebranche, at a clear idea of extension—'intelligible extension'—even though we do not ever experience *actual* extension directly. We have, in short, a sensation but no idea of ourselves, and an idea but no sensation of bodies. Whence, then, our idea of bodies if not from ourselves, and if there is no interaction between body and spirit? Malebranche answers without hesitation, 'From God'.

Taking Bérulle's exemplarist theocentricism to heart, Malebranche claims we have all our images, sensations and ideas 'in God' because they cannot come from bodies, or from our dependent and confused selves. But Malebranche also pulls back from Bishop Berkeley's line of argument at this point and refuses to doubt the existence of material substance. It exists all right, and affects us not as the cause but as the *occasion* of our images and ideas. God, the only source of ideas, and of our souls's activity in sensing and forming images, has established in nature a law of psycho-physical parallelism: physical objects do not cause images but images are made by God to correspond to physical objects insofar as these objects represent the pure idea of the thing in God. But when he claims that we therefore have our ideas in God, Malebranche does not imply that we know God's essence. He avoids the pitfall of ontologism by saying that we perceive an idea as it relates to material creatures, insofar as they can embody it. We cannot, by this account, know the material world in itself, for what we know are ideas, and matter is antagonistic to idea. What we ordinarily take to be bodies are, therefore, really images occasioned by things participating in the general idea we have of extension, and embodying to some degree the pure Idea of the species in God.

In this context Malebranche is forced to encounter head on the problem of how we know there are actual material bodies and what is their relation to intelligible extension or their use in creation. At this end of the scale Malebranche's thought is weak. He concedes that, strictly speaking, on his terms we cannot prove that bodies actually exist and we must take it on faith (from Genesis) that they do. And as to the relation of this imperceptible materiality to intelligible extension, Malebranche, like many a Platonist before him, simply gives up. It is a mystery. So, faced with the challenge of a scientific and rationalist view of material nature, Malebranche ends up emphasising sharply one pole of the old Augustinian theory of spiritual vision. Our images are from God, and the world of bodies becomes a more opaque, remote, unknowable element than it had ever been before Descartes so firmly distinguished 'extension' from 'thought'. But the curious extremes to which Malebranche pushes language in his attempt to vindicate his views should not deflect our attention from the major spiritual affirmations, the inheritance of Benet of Canfield and Pierre de Bérulle, which likewise underlie his writing, or from the profound problems to which he addressed himself. The doctrines of occasionalism and of vision in God are really a means of asserting the irreducible activity and importance of the spirit in an increasingly reified world where the goals of clear-thinking men are increasingly pursued without reference to God. The devotional practice which Bérulle had developed to offset the potential spiritual hazards of Cartesian methodology and materialist doctrine are carried a step further by Malebranche into the realm of fully-fledged philosophy. Bérulle and Malebranche both accept the challenge of the new science while defending the traditional Augustinian theory of spiritual vision. But in Malebranche the rationalist's awareness of the subjective nature of images is highly developed, and he is faced with the problem of bridging the gulf between his intimations of God's transcendent wisdom, and knowledge of the inert otherness of material things. The best means, Malebranche thought, for keeping God and the world of the atomists together, was to describe bodies as real but in fact unknowable. So he attempts to encourage the scientific assumption that there is a world of matter which influences us and which we should investigate, and also to insist that all the scientists know as a result is known in God. For Malebranche, knowledge of God has the clarity of self-evidence, while the world of bodies becomes an object of faith.

JOHN NORRIS: ORATORIAN PROSE

To make John Norris the English representative of this European effort to meet the challenge of the new science is to make no small claim for him. Towards the end of the seventeenth century, leadership in the new philosophy had shifted from

Descartes to Locke and Newton, and it is no accident that at the height of his career Norris should square off against Locke, and that the issues should be those which we find developing from the complex relationships between Descartes and Malebranche—What is the basis of human perception? What is the relationship between sense and body? Between God and the material universe? Whereas Malebranche had claimed that images are not caused by bodies but by God, and the existence of bodies was a matter of faith rather than self-evidence, Locke was to claim just the opposite: images *are* caused by bodies, the existence of which *is* self-evident, while God is the object of faith. That Locke's view sounds more modern is less a matter of commonsense than the fact that his explanation was so widely accepted by his own and subsequent times, for the flaws in it seem plain enough today. Yet to posterity this confrontation between Locke and Norris has also seemed an unfair match, and in a way it was. Norris simply did not have the intellectual fire power to match Locke, and in following Descartes as closely as he did, was already behind the times. Still, he was of them too, and in his poems the search for authority, the theocentric impulse, the temptations to autonomy and the clash between dramatic and detached speakers are preoccupations rooted in his Metaphysical antecedents. We can appreciate also how they might well produce a mentality especially open to influence by Malebranche's kind of philosophy.[42] And from Malebranche Norris received, besides a conceptual framework, the spirituality of the French Oratorians. His attempt to adapt the Oratory to England is therefore essential not only for understanding the unity of his own thought, but for understanding his place in the continuity of English devotional traditions which link the Metaphysicals to the Enlightenment.

The most interesting book which Norris wrote between the early *Miscellanies* and his main work, the *Theory of the Ideal World*, is *Reason and Religion, or the Grounds and Measures of Devotion* (1693). It stands as a compact summary of Norris's main positions and is the best example of his mature writing. The style is clear, straightforward, sometimes logic-chopping but without undue entanglements of the main line of argument. The book is divided into two parts, the first considering the nature of God, and the second dealing with man as a creature. The subdivisions consist of *contemplations* which lead to considerations

of the *devotional uses* of the argument, and which end with
an *aspiration*. In the second part Norris offers an extended
summary of Malebranche's theory as the best means of carrying
on his own argument.[43] But the debt to Malebranche involves
more than theory, for the major Oratorian devotional themes
and practices are also present.

The main two-part division is itself significant. Norris works
from 'Of the general Idea of God' at the beginning of Part
I to 'Of Man consider'd as a Creature' at the beginning of
Part II, and his detailed development of the argument thus
taken from God down to man underscores an intense theocentric
emphasis: '*My Lord and my God*, with what awful apprehensions
do I *contemplate* thy Perfections! How am I struck, dazled,
and confounded with the light of thy Glories!' (40). Like Malebranche, Norris insists on 'vision in God' to confirm the theocentric perspective: we only know ideas, and these have their
source not in ourselves or in bodies, but in God alone. 'First',
Norris argues, 'those Objects which are without the Soul, cannot
be perceiv'd by themselves, but by the Mediation of *Ideas*'
(186–7). And, since 'God has in himself the Ideas of all things',
we '*see all things in God*' (194). From here Norris proceeds
easily to Malebranche's occasional causality, explaining it in
a passage on how a child learns to recognise ideas. The account
seems naïve beside Locke's version of the same process, as
Norris tells us that when the child hears a word, God 'by
exhibiting such a part of the *Ideal World*, to the mind of the
Child, as is signified by such an arbitrary sign' (213), brings
the child to the idea. The word is thus the occasion, but
God the cause of understanding, and the world of bodies has
no active part in the process. In consequence of this kind
of thought, Norris also stresses the function of Christ as logos
and 'eternal Exemplar', and resorts to the favourite Oratorian
text, that in Christ we live and move and have our being
(29) to clarify how we see all things 'in the Ideal World,
or Divine λογος' (222).

In the foregoing argument Norris also maintains Malebranche's Cartesian distinction between thought and extension:
because the two do not interact it seems obvious that we cannot
derive ideas from the senses, never mind the idea of God (3).
And yet God as the source of ideas is eminently intelligible:
'God is the most knowable Object in himself' (4), even too

intelligible for us to bear (5). From here, Norris mounts the predictable Cartesian attack on the Scholastics, alleging that their theory of perception confuses what is in the object with what is in the mind. By arguing that species is inherent in bodies they make objects themselves the cause of ideas, and bodies perfective of minds, which to Norris is absurd and abhorrent (188 ff.). Instead Norris argues about God and the Ideas not from sense but by way of the mind's capacity for self-reflection:

> For 'tis plain that we *perceive* Infinite, though we do not *comprehend* it, and that our mind has a very Distinct Idea of God, which it could not have but by its union *with* God. Since 'tis absurd to suppose that the Idea of God should be from anything that is *Created*.   (198)

Although the insights of true philosophy can dispel the superstition that ideas inhere in bodies, this does not mean for Norris that ideas do not exist, or that images do not embody them, for otherwise there would be no science at all, and no apprehension of enduring truth. There would not even be human thought. The Ideas, however, merely are made present to the human mind on the occasion of our senses being exposed to objects, and to the extent only that God permits the image occasioned by the object to participate in the idea of the species in His own mind. By this elaborate indirection Norris essentially follows Malebranche's 'occasionalism' and 'vision in God' in order, again, to assert allegiance to the New Philosophy and at the same time confirm adherence to the theocentricism of the French School. This 'Copernican' emphasis moreover is developed in conjunction with the typical Oratorian preoccupation with the creature's nothingness and the necessity of self-abnegation for true devotion. The 'root of all evil', says Norris, is '*self-love*' (153) and in exhorting us to mortifications he often catches the characteristic tones of Bérulle in a language filled also with sublime aspiration:

> O Soverign greatnes, how am I *impoverish'd*, how am I *contracted*, how am I annihilated in thy Presence! .... O *Being it self*, 'tis in thee that I *live*, *move*, and *have my being*. Out of thee I *am* nothing, I *have* nothing, I can *do* nothing. ... To thee therefore I devote and dedicate my whole self, for I am wholly thine.   (29)

Many passages throughout *Reason and Religion* combine this

kind of high tone, abstract vocabulary and expostulation, and are often reinforced by the further Bérullian idea of continued creation: 'Created Minds', writes Norris, 'are placed in the *greatest dependence* upon God that can possibly be' (196), and their preservation depends on a 'Continued Creation' without which they would disintegrate entirely (143). From such persuasions on the illusion of autonomous selfhood it is a small step, and one at which Norris does not hesitate, to the Malebranchiste idea that we cannot have a clear idea of ourselves at all, because we are founded so mysteriously in God. Our self-abnegation is at best a faithful dedication of our nothingness to our Creator in hope that our capacities for being will be fulfilled by him as he chooses. The realms of nature and grace therefore remain as firmly divided in Norris as in Bérulle.

The main lines of Norris's argument reproduce faithfully the philosophy of Malebranche, but they do not merely conform to Malebranche's major theories (indeed the question of intelligible extension is largely ignored in *Reason and Religion*), for they also reproduce the distinctive devotional emphases of the Bérullian and Oratorian spirit. Norris freely employs the characteristic terminology—'adhérence' ('an embracing of, and an adhesion to Truth' (183)), 'admiration' ('I can *admire* nothing but thee' (41)), 'adoration' ('in the first place to admire and adore' (63)), and the Bérullian 'élevation', referred to by Norris in the Malebranchiste term as 'consideration', but essentially the same prayerful outpouring which evokes the mystery through a rapturous prayer of the affections, rather than a meditation through the senses.

Yet the entire programme seems also to point towards the particular danger to which Norris, like his French forebears, felt the age particularly prone, and against which Norris's ingenuity and Malebranchiste theory combine forces. Man is not self-sufficient, and the danger of Cartesian methodology is to encourage the scientist in the illusion that he is. Norris is explicit on the problems of an epistemology which tries to argue that bodies cause sensations, images, or ideas:

> that the Mind needs no other thing but *it self* for the Perception of Objects, and that by Contemplating it self and her own Perfections, She can perceive all *External* Objects. This is the boldest Assertion of all, and is full of *Impiety* as well as *Absurdity*. (193)

God alone 'sees by his *own Light*' (194) and to usurp this function and claim it for the self under the guise of empiricism or rationalism is impious and idolatrous.

Norris's other prose works in general demonstrate the same congeries of elements as *Reason and Religion* but they all prepare for the greatest labour of his life, if not the most memorable or enduring of his writings. It is difficult to assess why Norris expended and exhausted himself on the two massive volumes of the *Theory of the Ideal World*, for the task seems plainly to have defeated him. There are theoretical problems unanswered in *Reason and Religion*, but the lively and flexible devotion is not disturbed: it remains the work of a refined contemplative who wishes to acknowledge the achievements of science while presenting his witness to the spirit. But in the *Ideal World* a good deal of this life and flexibility is extinguished.

A division into two books confirms Norris's determination to adapt a theocentric perspective from God to man, and Book I is the 'Absolute Part' (I, 1), with man the dependent subject of Book II. In neither part does Norris relax this theocentricism, and he stresses how Malebranche's theory underlies his own procedure. Norris also seems aware of the originality of his French materials, at one point comparing Malebranche to Galileo—'He is indeed the great Gallileo of the Intellectual World' (I, 4)—in a manner which recalls Bérulle's claim to spiritual Copernicanism. Following such inspiration, Norris prefaces his work with an undaunted commitment to the principle, '*Exemplaria rerum in mente Divinae*' (I, 139): the primary fact about creation and human thought is that they are most real, not when centered on man, but when most in accord with the divine Ideas, immutable and perfect in the mind of God (I, 164). Norris then attempts to argue his case first by demonstrating in a Cartesian manner a clear distinction between thought and extension (II, 15), and then, like the Oratorians, by criticising the Scholastics for inventing 'material Species' (II, 312) to promulgate the impossible notion that there is interaction between body, image, and idea (I, 157 ff.). The essences of things, Norris argues, are not *in* things in any respect (I, 411), and by claiming otherwise the Scholastics are 'very confused and perplex'd' (I, 411), simply falling prey to their own imaginations of '*Impres'd* Species, Images, or Phantasms' (II, 349). They are not, therefore, philosophers at all, but poets, and this to their perpetual undoing, for "'Tis a sign Philosophers are hard put to't when they must intrench upon the Province of *Poets*, and use *Fiction* for the support of an Hypothesis' (II, 351).

Here we can see one sense in which Descartes, as Boileau claimed, had indeed cut the throat of poetry, for when images are no longer believed to mediate truth, as we see in Norris, the claims of poetry against abstract reason weigh light in the balance. For Norris, as for Descartes and Malebranche, the mind's power of reason and self-reflection is the only basis for human certainty, and knowledge by intuition alone is truly scientific: 'if any Knowledge should be call'd by way of Eminence by the Name of *Science*, methinks it ought to have been that of *Intuition*' (II, 149). Consequently even the existence of God is most certain from a consideration of the power of our minds and from the fact that we think about God at all (II, 295). So, if God exists, and in Him the Ideas, and if the realms of ideas and bodies are utterly separate, it follows again that our knowledge, whether by sensation, image, or idea is somehow *in* God, for bodies cannot cause knowledge or any spiritual affect, such as sensation or imagination (II, 224). In all this Norris repeats at length the Occasionalist theory with its main adjuncts, the *vision in God* and *intellectual extension*, explaining at one point, however unconvincingly, that when we observe a coloured object, 'we see in God the intelligible Extension, and feel in ourselves the Colour' (II, 501). But the Malebranchiste themes are not thus scrutinised in the *Ideal World* without the difficulties emerging ever more brightly as the author searches ever more closely: his microscope enlarges.

However, before looking at some of these problematic developments, I should say that all this philosophic speculation is developed still recognisably in terms of the other main Oratorian emphases. There is, for example, a consistent and fervent stress on man's dependency on God and on continuing creation: 'O Lord, what is Man, that thou should'st have such respect unto him . . .' (II, 303). We are exhorted repeatedly to humility (II, 168), and are assured, in Malebranchiste terms, that we can have no idea of ourselves, 'A Consideration certainly that ought to humble us in the height of our intellectual Attainments' (II, 111). Also, there are plenty of Bérullian 'élevations' even though their presence in the midst of vast tracts of abstract reasoning often seems to mark a disjunction between argument and inspiration, rather than the opposite, as is sometimes evident even to the author himself. After one such heightened passage, Norris self-consciously gets back to his spade work: 'But to unstring my Instrument for a while, and reprosecute our Theory, wherein after this little devotional Interlude my refresh'd Reader may perhaps accompany me with new Vigour' (I, 175). Still, there are two good poems which are worth unearthing, and several striking passages on the mystery of silence. Here for instance is a passage where theocentricism, abstract vocabulary, expostulation, admonishment to humility, and preoccupation with nothingness call Bérulle to mind and indicate that even through the intellectual perplexities of the *Ideal World* Norris preserves a sense of devotional purpose.

> All that is good or Excellent in the farthest extent of Nature is in thee, and all that the fruitful Womb even of Possibility it self can ever bring forth is also in thee. Thou art the Center of Being, whence all the Rays of Perfection rise, and where again they meet, and as there is nothing but what is *from* thee, so there is nothing but what is *in* thee. And where in such an Infinite Circle of Glories shall I begin, or rather where shall I leave off to Adore, Admire, and Love thee!   (I, 170–71)

Nevertheless, the *Ideal World* is a work in many ways flawed, and not least by a final impression it leaves of incompleteness. There is a feeling, hard exactly to demonstrate, that Norris almost discovers too late that Malebranche's brand of Cartesianism is already *passé*, containing too many problems for eighteenth-century tastes, and the degree to which Norris has moved away from his earlier flexible synthesis of devotion and speculation is also the degree to which he is worried about the technical consistency of his system. The endless pages of distinctions and discriminations, divisions and categories, are not really the expression of a mind optimistically developing a harmonious vision. The disjunction between spirit and theory rather betokens an unease which becomes acute when we consider the arguments dealing with the material world. If we do not sense bodies directly, as Norris contends, how do we know that they exist, and what are they good for? Norris agrees that it is indeed possible to doubt the existence of bodies (II, 210) but he refrains from doing so, partly because it is not commonsensical ('I am well enough satisfy'd', he says, about 'the meer *Existence* of things', and it is 'an Extravagance' seriously to doubt of it (I, 188)), and partly because we have it from revelation that God made bodies. Yet the argument from revelation does not rest easy with Norris's proposal of systematic rigour based on clear and distinct ideas. In other places, he is quick enough to advise us to follow reason even when the conclusions seem to confound everyday experience (II, 80). A vigorous pursuit of clear thought is, after all, the best way to avoid the pitfalls of an imagination (II, 242) which causes us 'Naturally' to make mistakes. Still, on the question of bodies Norris simply balks at drawing the logical conclusions which his system entails.

The problem persists in other dimensions of the *Ideal World* as well. For instance, if what God knows are Ideas, and there are no sensible appearances in him (I, 253), the question arises of how God knows his own material creation. Norris struggles with this and around it, but twice when the issue comes to a head he admits himself beaten: 'I must confess my self unable to explain the very precise manner of it' (I, 296). And in Part II, more breezily, 'I shall therefore leave every one to conceive of this Matter as he pleases, or as he can' (II, 512). Such paradoxes are not so important (what philosopher does not face them somewhere?) as the general and less precise sense which accompanies them of not having given a plausible answer to questions which, for Norris's times, were crucial. The irresolution becomes especially plain when the argument, in pursuing the elusive dimensions of intellegible extension, gets so bogged down that it collapses at last into a barrage of 'authorities', pages simply of citations a-critically selected from St Augustine, which Norris uses at last to shore up his failing case.

The deficiencies of these positive arguments are offset throughout the *Ideal World* by attempts at negative persuasion. In this respect Norris rings some interesting changes on the Oratorian theme of man as nothing with a capacity for God, and his favourite argument is that if man ignores the fundamental fact that he is founded in God, he will soon destroy himself. Without the 'Ideal Hypothesis', the 'Foundations of Truth' itself are undermined (I, 74), and science becomes mere 'Relations of *Nothing*' (I, 74), having no certainty. The choice is quite simple—God or nothing, for 'The Relation of things

. . . must be Absolute and Actual, or none' (I, 97). To Norris the answer seems obvious: the entire 'Basis and Foundation' (I, 133) the 'root' (I, 137) and 'Bottom' (II, 557) of ourselves and what we know is God. The alternative, 'impossible to be Conceiv'd' (I, 141) is a world determined by '*Chaos* or *Nothing*' (I, 134), which is for Norris an absurdity. Especially in Part I, this concern for 'foundations' or 'roots' is pervasive. 'God' and 'nothing' are repeatedly presented as exclusive radical alternatives, for man's pride, despite his reason, leads him all too easily to think his foundations are not on God but on himself. This single fact is at the heart of all human delusion and suffering, and for Norris the danger can come in many guises. Certainly it is one direct consequence of an epistemology like Locke's, which suggests that our images and our ideas are derived from sense impressions caused by bodies, for this is essentially to transplant the ground of man's spirit from God to the natural world. It is plain, says Norris, that bodies 'have no such Power' (II, 240), any more than man himself has the power to produce images or conceive ideas (II, 217). Such theories are merely 'bold and forward offers . . . towards the setting up the Creature upon a bottom of its own' (II, 557), and by ignoring the fact that we are 'placed in the greatest and most immediate dependence upon God' (II, 557) they lead straight to atheism. Man on a 'bottom of his own' is without God, and, says Norris bluntly, with a stagey side-glance at Locke, 'It is, I confes, no small Prejudice with me against the other Accounts of Humane Understanding, that they are all of them (except one) consistent with *Atheism*' (II, 553). The one exception is presumably Malebranche, and among the unfortunate 'other Accounts' Norris includes not only the scholastic philosophers and Locke, but also Descartes. Briefly, as we have seen, Descartes claimed that God was free to create truth as He willed, and the gesture of deference to divine omnipotence was really a handy way of divorcing final causality from the concerns of science. But for Malebranche and Norris alike, to base science on anything other than eternal and unalterable truth is to shake its foundations by once more threatening the ontological security of knowledge with the hammer of chaos. Norris is vehement in his attack on Descartes on this question. It is 'A most monstrous Doctrin', he declares, the worst thing in Descartes' whole philosophy, and 'fatal' for '*Religion, Morality,* and even *Natural Science*' (I, 340). However subtly and indirectly, by distinguishing the inscrutable truths in God from the more manageable and not necessarily related truths of science, Descartes has forced human knowledge again to stand on its own foundations—'a very fair step', says Norris, 'towards *Atheism* itself' (I, 347).

Such warnings against self-sufficiency grow noticeably in frequency and vigour in the second part of the *Ideal World* and their main point is again that we 'are not a Light to our selves' (II, 409). The ubiquitous temptations to think otherwise, so energetically opposed by Norris through the reaches of his massive work, he now brands openly and simply as '*Luciferian* Ambition' (II, 396). A world dominated by such Luciferian principles is for Norris alien and scarcely imaginable, though perhaps less so for us. Basically, it is a secular society, practically atheistical, and dominated by a science founded on probability rather than the certainty of Divine Ideas.

The *Ideal World* is thus a complex book, and the problems which we have found central to Norris's early poems remain with him as he examines again, late in life, the urges of the clever and ingeniously self-sufficient ego in relation to the clear light of the detached idealist. And once more Norris is tempted to underestimate the passionate and image-making ego in his yearning for security and rest in some authoritative certainties. As an inheritor of the traditions of English meditative poetry he had attempted to bring the images of the old devotion into the world of new ideas, but the muse he felt early on could not supply the authority he desired in order to set his perspectives adequately in a demanding and critical eighteenth-century world. Then, in discovering Malebranche, Norris encountered a systematic philosophy dedicated to solving the same problems by conforming St Augustine to Descartes.

Malebranche, far from seeming an exotic importation to English thought, must have spoken directly to it, and the rich amalgam of speculation and devotion in *Reason and Religion* shows that Norris had discovered a happy blend of native inspiration and continental thought. But, as Norris increasingly came to realise, the conspiracy of civilised fashion in Western Europe was determined to take Descartes not in the direction of theocentric exemplarism, but in the direction of Locke. The subsequent pressures on Norris to examine in depth the coherency and persuasive power of his own increasingly unfashionable Malebranchiste theory were thus very much increased. The result is, in part, a failure, but I have discussed Norris's writings here because his is a significant failure, and because through it I can reconstruct an untold chapter in the history of French rationalist thought in England during the seventeenth century. I have summarised the main ideas of Bérulle, Malebranche, and the *Ideal World* partly because they will be unfamiliar to most English readers, and because, when interpreted in conjunction, they throw fresh light on the history of English empirical philosophy itself. As we have seen, the problems Norris addresses through Malebranche and St Augustine have to do with the conflict between a scientifically described world of objects founded in God, and an empirical epistemology grounded on the senses, according to which it becomes legitimate to pursue knowledge without reference to a divine source. Norris's theory led him by way of Descartes to attack images as a valid means of attaining certain truth about the world, and although Norris did manage to redeem for the images some participation in the transcendent Ideas, he sacrificed their real relationship to material things. But in losing the capacity to discover his certainties in and through the images of bodies, Norris lost touch also with the traditions of Christian devotion which he sought so earnestly to present to the modern world.

In John Norris we therefore observe first a poet whose concern for the new ideas caused him to mistrust the traditional function of images. Subsequently, the pressure of a modern, critical attack on the old theory of spiritual vision turned him away from literature to wrestle with problems of how, on the old model, poems could continue to be written at all. His work thus offers, for this study, a clear example of how change in the climate of ideas could directly affect poetic practice.

7 Conclusion. John Norris and Mr Locke: bodies and the uses of imagination

THE QUESTION OF BODIES

Despite their mutual antagonisms and rebuttals, John Norris and John Locke have a surprising amount in common, and their theories constantly overlap. Yet when they do, we have an uneasy feeling that the view typical of one of them has been somehow altered in the other, like the slide of a familiar landscape being projected the wrong way round. Because of Locke's wide reception (the *Essay* became so popular that he thought there must be a conspiracy) and our consequent familiarity with his way of looking at things, most readers will feel it was Norris who got the picture backwards, particularly in dealing with images and the material world.

When Norris and Locke face the question of matter, they do so first as Cartesians. Both assume a world of bodies which is solid, measurable, and really existing outside the mind, and both deploy Descartes' distinction between primary and secondary qualities to establish the necessity of clear and distinct ideas for genuine progress in intellectual enquiry. Also, both inherit from Descartes a similar residual Scholastic notion about substance. Descartes, despite his demonstration that the perceiving subject is the source of many impressions which cannot be 'in' the object, as is often assumed, still argued that they must be 'in' something.[1] He therefore posited, in the Scholastic manner, two basic substances, namely extension (fundamental to the object) and spirit (fundamental to the subject), and he argued that we have a clear idea of both.

Though Norris and Locke both modified Descartes' views on substance, they could not in the end shake free from his basic Scholastic assumptions and vocabulary. As we have seen, Norris takes Malebranche's view, and Malebranche had striven as hard as he could to explain the relationship between the substances while maintaining their clear separation, concluding that God alone causes modifications of spirit on the occasion of certain material conditions. From this basis, Malebranche and Norris find they can agree with Descartes that the realm of extension is grasped by its idea but they reject Descartes' clear idea of the spiritual substance, for we have only a confused sensation of ourselves. As I have suggested, the intense humility, self-abnegation, and Copernican theocentricism of the Oratory caused Malebranche formally to offset Descartes' anthropocentric pride by rejecting on philosophical grounds a clear idea of self. By this means, paradoxically, the unsearchably transcendent God remains intimately but secretly present as well as necessary to every human act. Here, however, the other horn of the dilemma of substances becomes acutely uncomfortable: we may know bodies in their idea, but if we do not know them directly, how do we know they exist? Neither Malebranche nor Norris has a satisfactory answer.

To a surprising degree, Locke follows this same path of development, but with modifications which produce, in the long run, considerable divergences. Locke, like Malebranche, received his first 'relish'[2] for philosophy from Descartes. There must be some basic material thing, Locke argues, in which the qualities of bodies inhere, and so also there must be a spiritual entity in which, likewise, inhere the subject's perceptions. Locke also agrees with Malebranche and Norris against Descartes that we do not have a clear idea of this spiritual substance though we can know of its existence immediately and intuitively by self-consciousness. But Locke departs from his predecessors altogether by saying that we have no idea of the material substance either. We may infer, having considered the question, that such a substance probably exists, but that is all.[3] The main problem which Malebranche and Norris encounter is now for Locke even more acute: how do we know that objects exist if we do not experience them directly *and* have no idea of their substance? Like the others, Locke does not have a convincing answer, and appeals simply to common-sense against solipsism (there is a difference between thinking about pain and experiencing it, therefore some external thing must cause it in us [IV, 11, 8]), and he argues then to the underlying substance in which the 'powers' of the body (which for example cause pain) inhere. Such arguments, says Locke, should certainly put us past doubting, though they are not as conclusive as intuitive knowledge, being based rather on a high degree of probability.

In constricting the reach of human thought even more tightly than Norris, Locke would seem to be underlining the very humility which the Oratorian spirit demanded. And the *Essay*, like all of Locke's writings, is indeed full of warnings against human presumption, repeatedly exhorting us to observe the limits of what the mind can certainly attain: always, Locke holds, a great deal less than we would like. But an important shift of emphasis begins to become evident. The idea of intelligible extension in Norris is really the guarantee that man can know nothing at all in the material world without the intervention of God who is directly present in every act of perception. For Locke, duly observant of the orthodox pieties, God is also important as the initiator of all things, but Locke argues that God has made us with certain limited but real powers of our own, and through these we have our own ideas. As is well enough known, the *Essay* is largely devoted to demonstrating that these ideas (by 'idea' Locke means simply the object of understanding, whatever the mind can be employed about in thinking [*Intro.*, 8]) are founded in sense impressions. He does not say that sense stimuli are all we know, for ideas are formed by sense plus reflection (II, 1, 2); yet our ideas are always based on sense (II, 1, 23). This is true even of our idea of God, a complex idea, says Locke, made up of other simple ideas (II, 23, 25), so that although we may be able to demonstrate with certainty that God exists (IV, 10, 1 ff.), our idea of him will still remain imperfect because it is derived from a mere laborious 'enlarging' (II, 23, 34) of the basic simple components. The idea of God therefore is not innate (I, 3, 8) and Locke criticises Descartes' ontological argument which claims to prove God from intuition alone. To move, as Descartes does, from the idea of God to his existence, says Locke, is to presuppose the existence but no whit to prove it: no idea can prove existence, which can only be proved by existence itself.[4] Such self-evidence Locke finds only in the conscious self (IV, 9, 3) which becomes conscious, once more, through the power of reflection upon sense impressions. Locke therefore has managed nicely to cut man off at both ends of the vertical axis—his idea of God is slight and by no means self-evident at the one end, and there is no idea of material substance at the other, from which we could argue to a realm of essences or divine ideas. All we have are the images and ideas in ourselves, and the notion that these put us in touch with anything like the Platonist world of essences or the Scholastic world of forms and *prima materia*, is for Locke merely fanciful. It is one more example of human readiness to mistake words, especially abstract words, for things, whereas the only significance of such words lies in the fact that men have agreed on them to indicate a certain combination of ideas (II, 32, 1 ff.). Complex ideas have thus no reference outside themselves, and are their own essence (III, 3, 11). Certainly they do not refer to or figure forth by some mystique of participation a higher ontological realm of any sort, and belief that they do is erroneous and dangerous.

Locke therefore takes the whole paraphernalia of transcendental Ideas and reduces it remorselessly by grounding it upon images of sense engendered by bodies. The resultant ideas, the psychological contents of our individual minds, are their own validation, and the conclusions we can draw with certainty from the fact that we have them, Locke warns, are very limited. But where Locke has effectively de-emphasised the vertical axis, he enormously expands the horizontal, for his curiosity is mainly devoted to carefully examining the contents of ideas, always with a shrewd empirical eye to their humdrum earthbound origins and the means by which they can be most effectively and simply combined, especially in service of the ultimate human science of morality (IV, 12, 11). The feeling that Locke everywhere gives of having his feet on the ground is confirmed by his refusal to allow images to mediate, on the old model, between the realm of matter and any hypothetical transcendental world, and by his confident attitude towards his inferred material world itself, which he thinks of as solid, definite, and consisting of minute particles (II, 4, 4; II, 21, 75; II, 23,

8; II, 23, 29; IV, 3, 21). It is something pre-eminently real and measurable and quite unlike the fluid and elusive prime matter of the traditional theory which derives from St Augustine and the schools. It provides a solid footing for an empirical approach to human psychology, and for a confident exploration of the physical laws of nature.

Both Locke and Norris therefore argue alike from Cartesian premises, and both assume the reality of physical and spiritual substances which in some sense bespeak a divine creator. But for Norris the critical wedge has gone in mainly between material substance and image, and for Locke between image and Idea. The contents of the old 'spiritual vision' in a sense remain central to their deliberations, for despite the importance they give to the new method, both expend great pains to explicate the relationship between images and substance, and for each the question of imagination remains crucial.

THE QUESTION OF IMAGINATION

Just as Locke was concerned to reduce ideas to images in order to show that the roots of ideas are in the senses, so Norris, to preserve the immateriality of the spiritual (something Locke's theory does not necessarily do),[5] insists on the difference between pure thought and thinking in images, even though he admits a continuity between them. For Malebranche, on whom Norris bases his theory, the imagination is the power of recalling to mind, through traces left on the brain, the images of past sense impressions.[6] Sense impressions themselves, as modifications of the soul caused by God on occasion of our contact with bodies, indeed represent their idea truly, but only partially and obscurely. They are necessary, Malebranche tells us, for the preservation of our bodies in a physical world (*Dialogues*, 70), but they are, in the end, an impediment to clear thought. In this respect, imagination is even more remiss: it is 'a fool that likes to play the fool' and its 'phantasms', based on these impressions, easily distract us from clear ideas. 'Indeed, reason is silent and escapes us ever, when imagination comes in the way' (70). From this standpoint Malebranche naturally holds rhetoric in grave suspicion, for imagination is the foundation of figurative speech and the images of poetry which can seduce us so readily to dangerous errors.

Norris, reproducing the main lines of this theory, is a good deal preoccupied by imagination throughout the *Ideal World*. He agrees with Malebranche that sense knowledge and pure thought are both spiritual and 'in God', but, despite the continuity, that the first is much less clear and altogether less desirable than the second. Ideas, he insists, are imageless (I, 231) and are not to be conceived as actually existing as the senses represent them to us, that is, by images or according to their 'pictures' (I, 252–3). This is not to say that the senses misinform. They do not. Only our judgement can make errors, but our senses are designed to preserve our bodies through the hazards of material existence, and we should not expect from them the untrammelled clarity of reason. In a chapter devoted to the differences between the intellect and the imagination, Norris makes his point clear:

> the difference between imagination, and intellect strictly and properly so call'd, that in the former, the immediate Object of Thought is an Idea that is representatively material, and that in the latter the immediate Object of Thought is an Idea that is representatively immaterial. And therefore it is that it may with just propriety be call'd *pure Intellect*, as being a Perception purely Spiritual, or as we say *Intellectual*, because without any corporeal Image. (II, 187)

The imagination, in other words, is limited by the degree to which the individual bodies it encounters are themselves capable of representing their species or idea. Since the images are always partial, the sheer multiplicity is liable to induce error by way of confusion. But if we strip body of 'all those false Ornaments' which are non-essential and cease attending to our 'prejudic'd Imagination' (II, 257) we will soon see that bodies have little power to rouse us. Likewise, by depending largely on metaphorical allusions and figures based on images, rhetoric can also constitute a dangerous distraction from ideal clarity (II, 110, 117), and we should learn to resist its blandishments. Indeed, those who, like the schoolmen, think that they need images to know, become merely poets, not philosophers at all, and are victims of their own imaginations (II, 349–50). Norris then goes on especially to criticise attempts to conduct philosophic discourse by basing it on such volatile images of sense, and warns against those who, like Locke, would 'explain the manner of Human Understanding by material Effluvia's and Emanations from Bodies', thus leaving 'no room for any distinction between *Intellection* and *Imagination*' (II, 183). By attempting to reduce Ideas to images, Locke and his followers base themselves not only on unreliable foundations, but by cutting themselves off from the realm of divine Ideas they imply human self-sufficiency. With a certain perspicacity about the direction the Lockean type of theory was to take towards Romanticism, Norris also suggests that the imagination allied with such a theory of self-sufficiency will soon produce delusions about personal creativity. 'And therefore unles we will be so impiously vain in our Imaginations, as to assume to ourselves a *Creative* Power, we must not pretend to an Ability of producing our Ideas' (II, 380). To avoid indulging such illusions himself, Norris has stressed the differences between images and Ideas even while admitting the likeness between them is more real than that between images and material substances. This part of his theory therefore reproduces the Augustinian teaching on images and intellectual vision, while subjecting to critical scrutiny the older assumptions that images are caused to some degree by bodies.

For Locke, as we have seen, an idea has no reality whatever when it is not in our conscious minds, '*having ideas*, and *perception*, being the same thing' (I, 127). But Locke, no less than Norris, is well aware also that people are easily deceived in judgements about their perceptions, and a great deal of the *Essay* is devoted to demonstrating the need for basing judgements as far as possible on clear ideas. Like Norris, Locke stresses the great variety of our ideas, which can be real or fantastical, adequate or inadequate, true or false (II, 30, 1ff.). He also warns against the deceptive imagination which he associates with the mind's proclivity for presenting fantastical, inadequate, and false pictures of things as true. For Locke, the most insidious trick of imagination is to have us take names for actual things (III, 10, 14). He consistently warns against this, and in consequence finds reason to attack rhetoric no less vehemently than Norris, for in poetry we are swayed by associations of images, so that the conformity between our resultant ideas and the real nature of things is very likely to be much distorted:

But yet if we would speak of things as they are, we must

allow that all the art of rhetoric, besides order and clearness; all the artificial and figurative applications of words eloquence hath invented, are for nothing else but to insinuate wrong ideas, move the passions, and thereby mislead the judgement; and so indeed are perfect cheats. (III, 10, 34)

How seriously Locke took such arguments is indicated by his definition of madness as a too lively imagination (II, 11, 13).

So far I have discussed imagination in Locke not in terms of a difference in kind between images and ideas, but a difference in degree, with imagination linked to rhetoric, wit, fancy and metaphor and having a power to distract from simplicity and clarity. All this would be agreeable to Norris, except that Locke interprets the difference between ideas and imagination in a different sense. All our knowledge, in Lockean terms, is in images because knowledge is rooted in the senses. Our simple ideas are not any Forms in God, but the basic irreducible images of colour, shape, and so on, which we put together in complex ideas. So although he does not say much in the *Essay* directly about imagination, it is everywhere indirectly the subject of discussion because for Locke it is the medium of all thought.[7] In thus combining images and ideas to root them in physical reality, Locke denies the relevance to human knowledge of transcendent Ideas and assumes instead, because it seems the best hypothesis, that God has created us able to make the ideas which each of us experiences: 'We are like God in our understandings; he sees what he sees, by ideas in his mind; therefore we see what we see, by ideas that are in our own minds.'[8] Man is therefore the autonomous agent of his ideas, experienced as images uniquely his own, and shaped by him into patterns which he must judge adequate or not for explaining the silent world of material and spiritual substance.

Norris therefore mistrusts imagination because it is 'representatively material', and insofar as God causes an image to be occasioned by a material thing, he causes it to be unclear. In terms of the Augustinian 'spiritual vision' Norris stresses the continuity upwards rather than downwards: we do not know real corporeal substance in images, but we may reason through our 'material representation' to the transcendent Ideas. Locke mistrusts imagination, not because it impedes our knowledge of Ideas, but because it is often ill-used to convince us that we can know Ideas at all. Locke stresses rather the continuity downwards: we cannot know Ideas, but our images are rooted in corporeal things.

MUTUAL ASSESSMENT, SEPARATE COMMITMENT

A direct confrontation between these opposing but curiously inter-related theories of imagination occurs in an exchange of documents wherein Locke and Norris directly assess each other. Indeed, Norris's *Cursory Reflections Upon a Book Call'd An Essay Concerning Human Understanding (1690)*[9] was the first critique of the *Essay* in print, and Locke in turn composed a series of *Remarks upon some of Mr. Norris's Books, wherein he asserts P. Malebranche's Opinion of our seeing all things in God*, as well as a longer, unpublished essay entitled *An Examination of P. Malebranche's Opinion of Seeing all things in God*.[10]

In *Cursory Reflections* Norris begins by professing himself a great admirer of Locke, 'and would not part with his Book for half a *Vatican*' (43). Nevertheless, Norris finds some basic flaws in the *Essay*, and in describing them is not unperceptive. He accuses Locke of giving no satisfactory definition of ideas (3), and suggests that the arguments against innate ideas do not prove their point. 'If there may be Impressions made on the Mind, whereof we are not conscious, or which we do not perceive' (7) then there may be innate ideas also affecting the subconscious (7–8). Locke's theory of memory itself demonstrates this, says Norris, for according to it we have dormant ideas, present but not attended to. Norris here is content to show the deficiencies of Locke's arguments, for he does not believe there are innate ideas either, although he proposes 'something of near Analogy' (21) in his theory of vision in God. Norris then accuses Locke of making no sense in describing the effects of body upon sense, for 'Corporeal Effluvias' (25) cannot by definition modify spiritual substances. Predictably, Norris appeals to the distinction between '*Pure Intellection*' and '*Imagination*' (27) to confirm his point, arguing that sense cannot give rise to ideas and objecting to Locke's appeal to occult 'powers' in bodies as an explanation (32). Norris also takes exception to the idea of God arising from bodies alone (27–8). Here, although he is restrained no doubt by personal considerations, we can see the outline of his more explicit accusation in the *Ideal World* that the Lockean theory which founds ideas on sense leads straight to materialism and atheism.

Locke's remarks upon Norris are also brief, and, as with the *Examination* on Malebranche, dismissive. To say that we see Ideas in God, he suggests, is nothing more than to assume we understand 'what ideas in the understanding of God are, better than when they are in our own understandings' (247), which is plainly absurd. As to Norris's accusation that the *Essay* does not define ideas—well, that is because, says Locke, I don't know what ideas are, nor does anybody. The important fact is that we have perceptions, even though we must realise we can never ascertain exactly how we have them (248). Certainly if we look at the accounts Malebranche and Norris give of how they think we have ideas, they are quite obviously an elaborate subterfuge which hides a similar ignorance and engenders a number of absurdities to boot. For instance, Malebranche argues that God operates in the most direct and simplest ways, but if bodies do not directly cause our ideas or sensations the curious structure of the eye and the ear remains to be explained. Why all that intricacy, if the sound vibration does not cause us to hear? Moreover, the notion of seeing all things in God, like the assertion that we know universals before we know particulars (250) refutes common experience—'for this I must appeal to common experience, whether every one, as often as he sees any thing else, sees and perceives God in the case' (251). Also, to claim that the ideas of bodies are perceived in God's essence will lead directly to pantheism (253) on the one hand and, by preventing the mind from doing anything for itself, to determinism on the other (255). In short, all this 'brings us at last to the religion of Hobbes and Spinosa' (255).

The *Examination* of Malebranche repeats several of these arguments and adds a few more. Locke turns about-face, for example, Norris's objection that it is inconceivable how body could produce an image on the mind by saying it is equally inconceivable how an unextended substance should represent an extended figure to the mind (219). Neither way do we have a satisfactory explanation. He objects too that on Malebranche's principles we cannot ever know external reality (221) which seems to have no use in the creation at all. Also, if sensations and ideas are distinct, as Malebranche suggests, how is it that I have as clear an idea of a smell as of a figure (233) and why is colour not an idea as clear and actual as any other (236)? Furthermore, we surely have no idea of body as Malebranche claims (244), for if we did there would not be such vigorous disagreement about it, and certainly Locke himself has quite a different theory from Malebranche, though just as plausible (244).

Refinements of arguments such as these fill out the *Examination*, but Locke's objections centre on a small number of general attitudes towards the kind of theory which Norris and Malebranche espouse. First, he believes they are asking questions to which they cannot possibly give definitive answers. Second, they are presumptuous to assume they have given such answers and their arrogance is expressed in elaborate but empty language which merely conceals their ignorance. Third, faced with the limitations of human knowledge, the hypothesis which works best in relation to the facts of experience should be adopted.

In both his brief essays, Locke uses a style carefully calculated to reinforce his arguments, and assumes consistently a tone between contempt and bemusement which he then turns easily to irony by taking samples of Malebranche's abstract language and reducing them to plain words which make the author of the original look pedantic while revealing also the obviousness or absurdity of his meaning. On the theory of occasional causes, for instance, Locke summarises Malebranche's elaborate indirections and then concludes flatly that such a theory 'seems to me to say only thus much, that when we have these ideas, we have them, and we owe the having of them to our Maker; which is to say no more than I do with my ignorance' (229). Locke is relentless in this kind of reductive application of plain language because he believes he is dealing with nothing more than presumptuous 'metaphorical expression' (230). All theories which describe the basic 'how' of perception, he maintains, are in the end 'equally incomprehensible' (238) and we should therefore be content with the simpler hypothesis rather than dupe ourselves with pleasant but aberrant gestures at profundity in language.

Locke's reply to the accusations of atheism and materialism is again skilful, and depends most simply on the direct assertion that Norris and Malebranche are themselves full of ungodly pride, and that their own theories end up in determinism. The best means of defence, Locke sees, is attack, and in this connection he never tires of finding ways to intimate his own humility and stress God's omnipotence. Both essays are full of avowals of their author's small wit: 'have but humility enough to allow, that there may be many things which we cannot fully comprehend' (212); 'ingenuously own the shortness of our sight where we do not see' (215); 'I frankly avow my ignorance' (219). Such dissimulation, Locke claims, is merely appropriate when we encounter a greatness and power which we cannot hope to understand (256). The speculations of Norris and Malebranche become a kind of blasphemy because they assume that God *should* be comprehensible (250), and Locke's half-ironical deference to Malebranche's jargon becomes an elegant affirmation of orthodoxy. What more pious (and at the same time amusing) than to demonstrate that Malebranche reduces to what Locke has already believed: 'that I have those ideas that it pleases God I should have, but by ways that I know not' (223)? The inaccessability of God's purposes and procedures thus remains fundamental to Locke: 'how he knows, or how he makes, I do not conceive' (255). We have our own ideas to consider, so let us remain satisfied with what seems equally obvious: 'God has given me an understanding of my own' (251).

This comes close to the crucial point, for Locke's argument makes of God the inscrutable designer of a magnificent machine, a creator who remains aloof while providing man with autonomous power and movement. Man, according to this approach, enjoys an independence to which the bounds are set mainly by his limitations in making and judging images. In a way, the whole drift of Bérulle's Copernican revolution had been towards the opposite point, making of God's transcendence the mysterious ground of our intimacy with him (even in a post-Cartesian world without the old hierarchies and intermediaries to help establish the links) and giving man no autonomy at all in the formation of images. Such a desire to have God intimately present in every human act is noticed by Locke when he presents us, in the *Remarks*, with his own quite different watchmaker image, objecting that, on Norris's grounds, God's power is bound within the compass of human operations: 'This is to set very narrow bounds to the power of God, and, by pretending to extend it, takes it away' (255). Instead, Locke pays tribute to the 'infinite eternal God', the 'fountain of all being and power' (255), and argues that it is more in keeping with such a power to make a world like a watch with man in it as a free agent:

> For which (I beseech you, as we can comprehend) is the perfectest power; to make a machine, a watch, for example, that when the watch-maker has withdrawn his hands, shall go and strike by the fit contrivance of the parts; or else requires that whenever the hand, by pointing to the hours, minds him of it, he should strike twelve upon the bell?   (255)

In the end, the victory of the Lockean view owes a good deal to the criteria Locke himself established for it: it is more coherent and less rash than the theory of Norris. Yet, up to a point Norris was fighting without his potentially strongest weapons. He was temperamentally drawn to poetry, but by a deep paradox was attracted also to a theory which, to accommodate the quantitative view of bodies, denigrated the imagination. In so doing he deprived himself of the opportunity of promulgating, as he desired, the old insights of St Augustine, whereby images signify the meaning of material things with actual reference also to transcendent reality. Norris's awareness of the critical questions on images, Ideas, and bodies, in short, led him to sacrifice images as real representations of material things. John Locke, on the other hand, took a position sceptically critical of belief in images on the old model by allowing them no capacity whatsoever to mediate transcendent realities, and Locke was no poet at all. Accordingly, 'disbelief' can be used more accurately to describe Locke's position than Norris's, if the word is interpreted consistently with my general usage whereby belief entails a transcendent object. There is a sense of course in which Locke does trust his images, simply because he regards them as the basic data of knowledge. But the primary object of Locke's attention is the *sensory* image, and here 'belief' shifts towards the kind of trust or commitment which is a precondition of organised thinking about the ordinary world, rather than belief in a transcendent reality. Locke insists repeatedly that we should not pry into whatever transcendent intimations seem to attend our image-making, for we can learn nothing real or useful from that kind of enquiry. Yet the mind's powers, as Locke acknowledges, are God-given, and insofar as Locke allows us on this basis the ability to relate and judge images, he is not expressing a radical hostility to the old picture, for the mind can indeed detect God's design in nature. Nonetheless, by concentrating so heavily on his sensory image grounded on material substance, Locke is able to condemn the fictive images of poetry because they are so uselessly uncritical in presuming misleading correspondences to transcendent truths. My main point about Locke is therefore not to deny his connectedness to the past, but to suggest a powerful drift in him, based on his critical approach to images and bodies, against the habit of mind which found in the effortless pursuit of analogies a real evidence of divine Ideas.

CODA

The application of all this to the authors considered in the present study can now, in conclusion, be stated fairly simply. In the period between Spenser and Locke I have described a change in received attitudes towards the nature and hence the theological significance of the material world. I have suggested that a qualitative view of matter accompanies a tendency to 'believe in images', meaning by this to describe a powerful if philosophically uncritical sense of continuity between material object, mental image, and eternal species or Idea. Analogies discovered among nature's multiplicity by the image-making of the Augustinian 'spiritual vision' are referred confidently in praise to their divine source, for the transcendent mystery (the object of belief) is represented truly if partially in images. Rhetorical theory in this tradition is consistent with epistemology, and the practice of mediaeval poets by and large reflects the prevailing criteriology of images.

The quantitative view of matter that grows up with empirical science imposes a hard rein on the old habits of mind mainly because, by insisting on the real and pre-eminently measurable identity of matter, the new theory entails also a separation of our mental images from material substance and transcendent Ideas. The critical mind formed by the new method is aware of discontinuities where the mediaeval mind had not been concerned to find any, and the truth-telling of images is consequently subjected to sceptical scrutiny. Yet the new men did continue to believe. Locke was not an atheist, despite accusations to the contrary, and in his influential thought we find an empiricism more paradoxical than thoroughgoing.

As we have seen, Locke argues that man is psychologically cut off from reality above and below him. All he knows are images, but these tell him nothing reliable about the constitution of spirit or matter. The contents of 'spiritual vision' are therefore divorced from the 'intellectual' and 'corporeal' elements which had given Augustine confidence that our images communicate the true meaning of things. In Locke, an older, poetic sense of a universe fraught with symbolic meaning collapses before an empirical theory confining man's knowledge to configurations of his brain, rather than abstraction of nature's God-ordained essences.

The paradox comes when Locke as philosopher, not psychologist, argues for the commonsense theory that material and spiritual substances exist. His empirical approach to images, strictly applied, could never justify such a conclusion, but Locke knew the dangers involved in abandoning teachings men had found valuable in the long process of founding a humane civilisation. Man without a sense of transcendence could find no cause for moral restraint but in himself, and that would be insufficient. Locke the philosopher therefore affirmed the traditional pieties, while he helped, as psychologist, to introduce an empirical, materialist theory which made such traditional affirmations increasingly difficult to accept.

The transformation I have described from Augustine to Locke represents a broader, complex movement in the history of ideas which occurred throughout the Renaissance in England, and most vigorously in the seventeenth century. Such a development does not of course prescribe for literary men the kinds of poems they should write, though it is not surprising that literature should discover fit subject matter in problems posed by such developments. I have selected examples which show this process at work, from the traditional and philosophically unreflective Spenser to the highly reflective Norris, whose poetic talents were eventually overwhelmed by the weight of philosophical problems.

Among my authors, Spenser remains closest to the old Augustinian model. He feels by second nature a correspondence between the meaning of his images and the things they depict.

His poetry encourages our free-ranging pursuit of analogies, confident that images will disclose truly, though never perfectly, the mysteries to which the poem directs us. There is some critical self-consciousness in Spenser too, some Protestant scepticism about the usefulness of images for belief, evident in his wariness about using the sign of the cross overtly in the traditional Catholic manner. But the philosophical problem is not taken up seriously by him, and our central experience remains fixed in the sense that his imagery yields effortlessly to allegory and then to imageless mystery. He leads us through a continuity of corporeal and spiritual visions towards the silence of contemplation and enduring beauty, which also hauntingly draws us through the trials of faith described in the journey of Red Cross Knight.

With Shakespeare the new critical interest in the relationship of language to things is more clearly a pre-occupation. The traditional values and great images which embody them, he seems to say in *The Tempest*, cannot be done without, for they are part of the process of civilisation by which Miranda is nurtured and protected. But in *The Tempest* man is no longer just the interpreter and promulgator of the God-given meanings of nature's book, and Shakespeare says that man's configurations and language to some degree also create the values he serves. As magus or scientist or absolute monarch, man manipulates the spirits, 'materialising' and directing them to private ends. He is not only the servant and contemplator, but the inventor and enforcer of his own ideals.

Shakespeare therefore makes the subject of his drama 'spiritual vision' itself. He shows us his characters 'believing in' their separate patterns of images, and he is able to stand outside, critically observing this process, as Spenser could not. Yet *The Tempest* is not coldly sceptical, and Shakespeare's art deploys, throughout, an interplay of traditional values nostalgically evoked, with those which result from masterful ingenuities of a challenging, empirical enterprise.

We can see Crashaw and Milton, each in his own way, as a kind of manipulating Prospero. Both remain sharply aware of problems presented for poetry by the discontinuity between private images and traditional ideals, and they toy consciously with images in order to vindicate the assertions of orthodox belief.

Crashaw's extraordinary and tangibly obtrusive imagery I have suggested owes much to contemporary Capucin prescription, and exploits the material *en soi* of the new philosophy to reaffirm the 'vertical' spiritual meaning of the conventional emblems. From the Capucins, Crashaw learned a devotional technique which assumes the vision of materialistic atomism and the separation it involves of corporeal from spiritual reality. Then, using this division, he forces us to see how repugnant is the physical component of traditional images (such as the cross) if deprived of spiritual significance. The challenge presented to traditional piety by rationalist thought has, in this case, certain consequences for artistic practice.

Milton, like Crashaw, struggles also in new ways with the relationship between images and bodies, but counters the claims of the old Augustinian realism by his stance against mystery and by stressing instead a 'horizontal' sameness, not difference, between spiritual and material realities. In his treatment of time and eternity in *Paradise Regained*, Milton eschews the notion that time somehow reflects a higher, changeless world. His images do not embody a transcendent Ideal reality, but suggest that human fulfilment lies ahead, in a world sufficiently progressive to merit the second coming and to stand as a new heaven on a new earth. As politician, historian, and man of affairs, Milton had felt the impact of the new philosophy in a number of ways. It contributed to his opinions on mortalism, to his progressive social ideals (both secularist and millennial), and, finally, to his incapacity to deploy the images of poetry in the old way, according to the dynamics of spiritual vision.

In John Norris, the split we see in Crashaw between image and object is again the preoccupation of a poetic sensibility convinced of the importance of real human contact with transcendent Ideas. But in attempting to save the direct participation of his images in Ideas, Norris sacrificed the material world. Scrambling then to redress the balance, he chose to denigrate imagination, the incapacities of which become indirect evidence of the material universe we can never know immediately, though we must live (as the weakness of our imagination shows) in some close relationship to it.

John Locke on the other hand chose to affirm not the continuity between Idea and image, but (like Milton) that between body and image. Correspondingly, he faced the prospect of cutting off his images from transcendent truths altogether, a conclusion which might encourage atheism and self-sufficiency, as Norris saw. But although Locke held back from this conclusion, he, in turn, protected his epistemology by denigrating imagination, which, according to his empirical theory, blurs our clear perception of things.

Norris, first of all a poet, therefore found himself overwhelmed by problems attendant upon the relationship of images to the world, so that he ceased writing poetry in order to understand what exactly the images of poetry could say. But his philosophy is deficient because he does not move us by his intimations of the enduring beauty of his Ideal realm. His failure is of imagination, which cannot bridge the gap his thought has opened between heaven and earth. Locke, whose logic dispensed with the transcendent Ideas Norris held so dear, seems to have allowed his imagination to interfere and check instead his empirical theory. His appreciation of the value of traditional ideals and spiritual wisdom deflects him from the severely materialist conclusions on which he often seems set. His failure, as generations of his perplexed students have found, is one of logic.

The discussion of Norris and Locke shows, finally, a direct confrontation between philosophy and poetic practice. Yet all the authors I have chosen to some degree felt themselves living in a world of verbal discourse profoundly in process of change as a result of a new critical interest in the relationship between language and the nature of reality. The works I have discussed are some of their responses to this situation, not of course exhaustive of the interest shown throughout the period by literary men in a philosophical question of special significance to the culture at large. Their writings, nonetheless, reveal something of a new area of concern in English letters, and in addressing it, none of these authors wished to abandon God or the world. Yet they found themselves faced alike by a dwindling, mediaeval vision of nature as symbol, and in consequence they sought, in their various ways, after images to show God's truth afresh in a less enchanted, if no less challenging, new world of empirical materialism.

Notes

ABBREVIATIONS

EETS	Early English Text Society
ELH	*Journal of English Literary History*
JEGP	*Journal of English and Germanic Philology*
JHI	*Journal of the History of Ideas*
PQ	*Philological Quarterly*
SEL	*Studies in English Literature, 1500–1900*
UTQ	*University of Toronto Quarterly*

CHAPTER I

1. See M. H. Abrams, *A Glossary of Literary Terms* (New York: Holt, Rinehart and Winston, Inc., 3rd ed., 1971), pp. 76–7, for the source of this broad definition of a term which has much currency but little precision in literary criticism. This wide sense accords well with St Augustine's 'spiritual and corporeal vision', below. See also *Encyclopedia of Poetry and Poetics*, ed. Alex Preminger (New Jersey: Princeton University Press, 1965), p. 363 ff.: 'An image is the reproduction in the mind of a sensation produced by a physical perception. . . . More specifically in literary usage, *imagery* refers to images produced in the mind by language, whose words and statements may refer either to experiences which could produce physical perceptions were the reader actually to have those experiences, or to the sense impressions themselves.' The relationship between mental and literary images is very perplexed. See for instance P. N. Furbank, *Reflections on the Word 'Image'* (London: Secker and Warburg, 1970). I have avoided entering this debate not because I think it is unimportant, but because the main concern of this study is what the seventeenth-century authors themselves thought images were.
2. See F. R. Tennant, *The Sources of the Doctrines of the Fall and Original Sin* (Cambridge: Cambridge University Press, 1903).

3. See Vernon T. Bourke, *Augustine's View of Reality* (Villanova, Pa.: Villanova University Press, 1964), p. 15.
4. See *Confessions*, I, xiii, 20: 'I was forced to learn the wanderings of one Aeneas, forgetful of my own', trans. E. B. Pusey (London: Everyman's Library, 1907), p. 13.
5. *De natura boni*, c. 19, trans. Pusey, *Confessions*, p. 135, n. 3.
6. See *De gen. ad litt.*, Bk I; Ronald H. Nash, *The Light of the Mind: St Augustine's Theory of Knowledge* (Lexington: The University Press of Kentucky, 1969), p. 6.
7. *Confessions*, XI, xi, 13, trans. Pusey, p. 260.
8. Ibid., XI, xxix, 39, trans. Pusey, p. 275.
9. Ibid., XI, xi, 13, trans. Pusey, p. 260.
10. Ibid.
11. *Answer to Sceptics*, III, 17, 37, trans. Denis J. Kavanagh, O.S.A., S.T.M., *The Writings of Saint Augustine*, I, 213, in *The Fathers of the Church*, Vol. 5 (New York: Cima Publishing Co., Inc., 1948).
12. *Confessions*, I, vi, 7, trans. Pusey, p. 4.
13. Ibid., XII, xvi, 23, trans. Pusey, p. 291.
14. Robert J. O'Connell, *St Augustine's Confessions. The Odyssey of Soul* (Cambridge, Mass.: Harvard University Press, 1969), pp. 11–12, stresses the pilgrimage motif; Marcia L. Colish, *The Mirror of Language: A Study in the Medieval Theory of Knowledge* (New Haven and London: Yale University Press, 1968) p. 19 ff., concentrates on Augustine's theory of 'redeemed rhetoric; John J. O'Meara, *The Young Augustine: The Growth of St Augustine's Mind up to his Conversion* (London and New York: Longmans, Green, and Co., 1954), pp. 2–3, suggests that the verb 'confiteri' provides the clue; M. Wundt, 'Augustins konfessionen', in *Zeitschrift für die heutestamentliche Wissenschaft*, XII (1923), 185, suggests that Augustine is adapting a catechetical method outlined in *On Catechising the Uninstructed*: cf. P. Courcelle, *Recherches sur les Confessions de Saint Augustin* (Paris: 1950), pp. 20–26, who develops this idea, and thinks the most important part of the *Confessions* was the commentary on Genesis, that the autobiographical section ran away with the author, and that Bk X was inserted at a later date at the request of readers. Perhaps it is just a badly made book: see O'Meara, *The Young Augustine*, p. 13.
15. *In Ps. 8*, V, trans. Pusey, *Confessions*, p. 229, n. 2. The following account of the *Confessions* uses Pusey's translation: references are in the text.
16. On faith passing see *Enchiridion* I, 5. See also Marcia L. Colish, *The Mirror of Language*, p. 35, and chapter I, *Passim*, for a discussion of Augustine's theory of language as signs through which we know God by faith in this life, *per speculum in aenigmate*.
17. See Nash, *The Light of the Mind*, p. 24 ff.
18. See *De Ordine*, I, ii, 51.
19. See *Sermo* 43, i, 1.
20. See *De gen. ad litt.* for the fullest account of Augustine's main divisions. Also, Bourke, *Augustine's View of Reality*, p. 7 ff.; Nash, *The Light of the Mind* p. 1 ff., *et passim*.
21. See *De gen. ad litt.*, XII, 24, and Bourke, *Augustine's View of Reality*, p. 10, for the imageless vision; *Epist.* LV, vii, 13; *De civitate Dei*, XI,

18; *De Magistro*, III, 5–6 for the silence of God's creative voice; and especially J. A. Mazzeo, *Renaissance and Seventeenth Century Studies* (New York: Columbia University Press; London: Routledge and Kegan Paul, 1964), chapter 1, 'St Augustine's Rhetoric of Silence: Truth vs. Eloquence and Things vs. Signs', pp. 1–28.

22. See *De Civitate Dei*, X, 7, and XI, 9.

23. On intellectual vision being necessary for spiritual vision while the reverse is not true, see Bourke, *Augustine's View of Reality*, p. 10. In *De Musica*, VI, v, 8, Augustine finds it a detestable thought that the soul can be modified by the body. See Nash, *The Light of The Mind*, p. 45.

24. *De gen. ad litt.* VI, v, 10, and Nash, *The Light of The Mind*, p. 44.

25. *De gen. ad litt.*, XII, 24.

26. As Frederick Copleston points out, *A History of Philosophy*, *II. Mediaeval philosophy*, *Augustine to Scotus* (London: Burns and Oates, 1950), p. 56, the question of whether the external world exists or not did not preoccupy Augustine's mind.

27. Nash, *The Light of the Mind*, p. 55.

28. *De doctrina Christiana*, I, ii, ff.

29. *De civitate Dei*, XI, 18. See Mazzeo, 'Rhetoric of Silence', p. 25.

30. *De doctrina*, IV, xxix, 61, trans. D. W. Robertson, Jr., *On Christian Doctrine* (New York: Bobbs-Merrill Co., Inc., 1958), p. 166.

31. Ibid., II, vi, 7.

32. Ibid., IV, viii, 22.

33. This pleasure is not explained further: it is connate with illumination. See *De doctrina*, II, vi, 7–8. See Marcia L. Colish *The Mirror of Language*, p. 71: through the medium of language the faithful are brought to a 'shared joy in the vision of God'.

34. *Boccaccio on. Poetry: Being a Preface to the Fourteenth and Fifteenth Books of Boccaccio's 'Genealogia Deorum Gentilium'*, trans. and ed. Charles G. Osgood (New York: Bobbs-Merrill Co., Inc., 1951), p. 39.

35. Ibid., p. 44.

36. Ibid., p. 46.

37. Ibid.

38. Ibid., p. 41.

39. Mazzeo, 'Rhetoric of Silence', pp. 2–5, sees this as revolutionary.

40. *Confessions*, VIII, xii, 29. On the symbolic dimensions of the childhood motif, see Courcelle, *Recherches*, p. 190 ff; O'Meara, *The Young Augustine*, p. 182 ff.

41. *De civitate Dei*, XII, 4–5, trans. Gerald G. Walsh, S.J., and Grace Manahan, O.S.U., *The Fathers of the Church* (Washington: Catholic University of America Press, 1954), pp. 250–52.

42. See *De div. quaest. LXXIII*, q. 46, 1–2.

43. Ibid., q. 46.

44. *Timaeus*, 52, trans. H. D. P. Lee, *Plato*, *Timaeus* (Middlesex: Penguin Books, 1971), p. 70.

45. *Confessions*, XII, v, 5, trans. Pusey, p. 280.

46. Ibid., XII, vi, 6, Pusey, p. 280.

47. Ibid., XII, iii, 3.

48. Ibid., XII, viii, 8, Pusey, p. 282.

49. See Bourke, *Augustine's View of Reality*, p. 19.
50. There was a reaction by Franciscan 'murmurantes' which led to the condemnation of Aristotle in 1277. See Thomas Aquinas, Siger of Brabant, St Bonaventure, *On the Eternity of the World*, trans. Cyril Vollert, Lottie H. Kendzierski, Paul M. Byrne (Milwaukee, Wis.: Marquette University Press, 1964), preface, p. ix: the 'murmurantes' are those addressed in the title of Aquinas's *De Aeternitate Mundi, contra murmurantes*. For Bonaventure and Aquinas, see especially John Francis Quinn, *The Historical Constitution of St Bonaventure's Philosophy* (Toronto: Pontifical Institute of Mediaeval Studies, 1973).
51. Not to be over-simplified either: see G. F. L. Owen, 'The Platonism of Aristotle', in *Proceedings of the British Academy*, LI (London: Oxford University Press, 1965), which notices what a 'slippery term' (150) Platonism is, while describing Aristotle's relation to it.
52. Marcia L. Colish, *The Mirror of Language*, p. 222.
53. See *Metaphysics*, A, 9, 990b, ff.
54. Ibid., Z, 1, 1028a, ff.
55. John Herman Randall, Jr., *Aristotle* (New York and London: Columbia University Press, 1960), p. 118.
56. The *Metaphysics* is a complex, many-layered book. See Werner Jaeger, *Aristotle: Fundamentals of the History of his Development*, trans. Richard Robinson (Oxford: Clarendon Press, 2nd ed., 1948), pp. 167–227; Randall, *Aristotle*, p. 116 ff.; W. D. Ross, *Aristotle* (London: Methuen and Co. Ltd., 1923; 2nd ed., 1930), p. 159.
57. *Ethica Nicomachea*, X, 7, 1177a, ff.
58. *Metaphysics*, H, 2, 1042b, ff.; θ, 1, 1046a, ff.
59. Ibid., Λ, 6, 1071b, ff., and Λ, 9, 1074b, ff.
60. See F. E. Peters, *Aristotle and the Arabs: The Aristotelian Tradition in Islam* (New York: New York University Press; London: University of London Press, Ltd., 1968), p. 231 ff; E. Gilson, *History of Christian Philosophy in the Middle Ages* (New York: Random House, 1955), pp. 387, 402 ff., 410 ff.; *Philosophy in the Middle Ages: The Christian, Islamic, and Jewish Traditions*, ed. Arthur Hyman and James J. Walsh (New York: Harper and Row, 1967), p. 285.
61. *On the Immortality of the Soul*, trans. William Henry Hay II, revised by John Herman Randall Jr., and annotated by Paul Oskar Kristeller, in *The Renaissance Philosophy of Man*, ed. Ernst Cassirer, Paul Oskar Kristeller, John Hermann Randall Jr. (Chicago and London: University of Chicago Press, 1948), p. 255 ff.
62. See *On the Eternity of the World*, p. xi.
63. Ibid., p. 103.
64. *Summa Theologica*, I, 15, 2–3.
65. See *Summa Contra Gentiles*, 2, 54; *ST* 1, 66, 2; Etienne Gilson, *The Christian Philosophy of St Thomas Aquinas*, trans. L. K. Shook, C.S.B. (New York: Random House, 1956), pp. 32 and 177, for explication of matter as potency and as concreated with form.
66. *ST*, I, 44–5. On the principle that *fines primorum conjuguntur principiis secundorum*, see Gilson, *St Thomas*, pp. 211, 240, 440, n. 7.
67. Gilson, *St Thomas*, p. 232.

68. Ibid., p. 184.
69. *In II de Anima*, 1, 1; *ST*, 1, 75, 1; *CG*, II, 65; Gilson, *St Thomas*, pp. 187; 469, n. 3, on the soul inferring and affirming by judgement.
70. *CG*, II, 77, cited in Gilson, *St Thomas*, p. 220.
71. *CG*, III, 40.
72. For a careful account of Aquinas on art and beauty see Jacques Maritain, *Art and Scholasticism. With Other Essays*, trans. J. F. Scanlon (London: Sheed and Ward, 1930). See p. 28, n.1. The following summary derives from Maritain's work, to which page references are given in the text.
73. *ST*, I, 2, 3.
74. For the analogy between *summa* and Gothic cathedral see Erwin Panofsky, *Gothic Architecture and Scholasticism* (Cleveland: Meridian Books, 1957); Frances Yates, *The Art of Memory* (London: Routledge and Kegan Paul, 1966), who suggests that the *Summa* can be 'corporealised in memory' (p. 79); A. D. Nuttall, *Two Concepts of Allegory: A Study of Shakespeare's 'The Tempest' and the Logic of Allegorical Expression* (London: Routledge and Kegan Paul, 1967), pp. 90–91, argues further for the possibility that the *Summa* is 'iconic' (90). Marcia L. Colish, *The Mirror of Language*, p. 191, argues that Aquinas regards the proofs of God as 'inadequate signs'.
75. 'Mihi videtur ut palea.' See Maritain, *Art and Scholasticism*, p. 36.
76. See D. W. Robertson, Jr., *A Preface to Chaucer* (New Jersey: Princeton University Press, 1962), p. 354.
77. *Familiari*, 10, 4.
78. For a concise account of what the transition involved in broad terms appropriate to this study, see Richard A. Watson, *The Downfall of Cartesianism 1673–1712: A Study of Epistemological Issues in Late 17th Century Cartesianism* (The Hague: Martinus Nijhoff, 1966), pp. 1–12.
79. For a still excellent account, see E. A. Burtt, *The Metaphysical Foundations of Modern Physical Science* (London: Routledge and Kegan Paul, rev. ed., 1932), esp. ch. I–V.
80. *Meditations*, 4, trans. Arthur Wollaston (Middlesex, Penguin Books, 1960), pp. 136–7.
81. Images in words and painted or graven images were distinguished: Puritans were not anti-literature. See William Madsen, *From Shadowy Types to Truth: Studies in Milton's Symbolism* (New Haven and London: Yale University Press, 1968), esp. ch. 5, 'The Eye and the Ear', p. 145 ff., which discusses differences in these types of images.
82. See Samuel I. Mintz, *The Hunting of Leviathan* (Cambridge: Cambridge University Press, 1962), which gives an account of reactions to Hobbes between 1650 and 1700.
83. *Leviathan*, I, 4, in *The English Works of Thomas Hobbes of Malmesbury*, 11 vols. (London: John Bohn, 1839–45), III, 21. This edition is hereafter cited as *EW*. See Richard Peters, *Hobbes*, (Middlesex: Penguin Books, 1956), p. 120 ff., 'The Theory of Universals'.
84. *Leviathan*, 4, 46 (*EW*, III, 674): 'this doctrine of *separated essences* . . . would fright them from obeying the laws of their country with empty names.' See J. G. A. Pocock, 'Time, History and Eschatology in the Thought of Thomas Hobbes', in *The Diversity of History: Essays in Honour*

of Sir Herbert Butterfield, ed. J. H. Elliott and H. G. Koenigsberger (London: Routledge and Kegan Paul, 1970), pp. 149–98. Pocock examines Hobbes' fear that universals allow the intrusion of false authority in the state, e.g., pp. 179, 186, 197, etc.

85. See Burtt, *Metaphysical Foundations,* pp. 62, 118.
86. *Leviathan,* I, 2 (*EW,* III, 4).
87. Ibid., I, 11 (*EW,* III, 93).
88. Ibid., IV, 45 (*EW,* III, 657): the following account is from *Leviathan* IV, 45, and page numbers to *EW* are cited in the text.
89. Ibid., IV, 46 (*EW,* III, 676–7); *Of Liberty and Necessity* (*EW,* IV, 271); *Answer to Bishop Bramhall* (*EW,* IV, 298–300).
90. *Leviathan,* III, 38, (*EW,* III, 441).
91. See *De Rerum Naturae.*
92. See Burtt, *Metaphysical Foundations,* ch. I–IV; Frederick Albert Lange, *History of Materialism and Criticism of its Present Importance,* 3 vols. in one, trans. Ernest Chester Thomas (London: Routledge and Kegan Paul, 1925), I, 2, 3: 'The Return of Materialistic Theories with the Regeneration of the Sciences', p. 215 ff.
93. See Francis Bacon, *The Masculine Birth of Time, or Three Books on the Interpretation of Nature,* trans. Benjamin Farrington (Chicago: Phoenix Books, 1964), pp. 71, 80; for Descartes, see L. J. Beck, *The Method of Descartes. A Study of the 'Regulae'* (Oxford: Clarendon Press, 1952), pp. 29; Kuno Fischer, *History of Modern Philosophy. Descartes and his School,* trans. J. P. Gordy, ed. Noah Porter (London: T. Fisher Unwin, 1887), pp. 382, 397; Frederick Copleston, *A History of Philosophy, vol IV. Descartes to Leibniz* (London: Burns and Oates, 1960), p. 125 ff.
94. See Lange, *Materialism,* p. 143; Watson, *The Downfall of Cartesianism,* p. 31 ff; Burtt, *Metaphysical Foundations,* p. 102 ff.
95. Julien Offray de la Mettrie, *L'Homme Machine* (Leyden: 1748).
96. Flora Isabel Mackinnon, ed., *The Philosophical Writings of Henry More* (New York: Oxford University Press, 1925), p. xviii, ff., *et passim.*
97. See A. D. Nuttall, *A Common Sky: Philosophy and the Literary Imagination* (London: Chatto and Windus for Sussex University Press, 1974), ch. I, 'The Sealing of the Doors' p. 13 ff., for a discussion of problems implicit in Locke, and for suggestions on how they reflect in literature.
98. *An Essay Concerning Human Understanding,* II, 23, 29–30, ed. Alexander Campbell Fraser, 2 vols. (New York: Dover Publications, 1959), I, 414–15.
99. See *The Works of John Locke,* new ed., corrected, in 10 vols. (London: Thomas Tegg, 1823), X, 255.
100. See R. R. Palmer, *A History of the Modern World* (New York: Alfred A. Knopf, rev. ed., 1960), pp. 290–91, pointing out that in the Enlightment the favourite symbol is not the cross but the watch.
101. See *An Essay Concerning Human Understanding,* II, xi, 2; II, xi, 13; II, xiii, 25; II, xiii, 28; II, xxx.
102. For the development from Locke's theory of the very serious-minded and image-orientated aesthetics of Romanticism, see Ernest Lee Tuveson, *The Imagination as a Means of Grace: Locke and the Aesthetics of Romanticism* (Berkeley and Los Angeles: University of California Press, 1960).

103. 'A Letter concerning Toleration', *Works*, VI, 11.
104. See the interesting theory of 'moral inversion' argued on these grounds by Michael Polanyi, *Personal Knowledge: Towards a Post-Critical Philosophy* (New York: Harper Torchbooks, 1964), pp. 231–5.

CHAPTER 2

1. Most of the poems in the *Complaints* (1591) are early works (1570–80), but *Muiopotmos* is a more sophisticated poem, and has a title-page dated 1590. See *Edmund Spenser. Books I and II of 'The Faerie Queene', 'The Mutability Cantos' and Selections from The Minor Poetry*, ed. Robert Kellogg and Oliver Steele (New York: The Odyssey Press, Inc., 1965), p. 525. For a discussion of the date, see *The Works of Edmund Spenser. A Variorum Edition*, ed. Edwin Greenlaw, Charles Grosvener Osgood, Frederick Morgan Padelford, Ray Hefner (Baltimore: The Johns Hopkins Press, 1932–49), vol. II, *The Minor Poems*, special eds. Charles Grosvener Osgood, Henry Gibbons Lotspeich, assisted by Dorothy E. Mason (1947), pp. 598–9. All quotations from Spenser are from this edition, and are indicated in the text.

2. For the political allegory, see *Variorum*, II, 599 ff.; also Franklin E. Court, 'The Theme and Structure of Spenser's *Muiopotmos*', *SEL*, 10 (1970), 1–15, which stresses the poem's mood of disillusionment.

3. See Don Cameron Allen, 'On Spenser's Muiopotmos', *SP*, 53 (1956), p. 146 ff., for the Psyche analogy; p. 150 for the Scapula reference. For the funerary art, see Edgar Wind, *Pagan Mysteries of the Renaissance* (Middlesex: Peregrine Books, 1967), p. 160 ff.

4. E.g. Sir Philip Sidney, for whom in the *Apology for Poetry*, the 'infallible grounds of wisdom' are 'figured forth by the speaking picture of poesy', ed. Roy Lamson and Hallet Smith, *The Golden Hind* (New York: W. W. Norton & Co., rev. ed. 1956), p. 281. Poetry is thus the monarch of the sciences. Also see Rosemond Tuve, *Elizabethan and Metaphysical Imagery* (Chicago: The University of Chicago Press, 1947) pp. 33–6, *et passim*, on the imitation of the intelligible world by the images of poetry in Elizabethan literature.

5. See Thomas P. Roche, *The Kindly Flame: A Study of the Third and Fourth Books of Spenser's 'Faerie Queene'* (New Jersey: Princeton University Press, 1964), pp. 72 ff., 116 ff.: Kathleen Williams, *Spenser's World of Glass: A Reading of The Faerie Queene* (Berkeley and Los Angeles: University of California Press, 1966), p. 107. C. S. Lewis, *Spenser's Images of Life*, ed. Alastair Fowler (Cambridge: Cambridge University Press, 1967), p. 60 ff.

6. See *Edmund Spenser's Poetry. Authoritative Texts and Criticism*, selected and ed. Hugh Maclean (New York: W. W. Norton & Co., Inc., 1968), p. 333.

7. The mythographers agree that the basic truths are veiled: see Boccaccio, *Boccaccio on Poetry*, trans. Osgood, pp. 39, 44. For the importance of 'veiled mysteries' and *natura unialis* see Lewis, *Spenser's Images of Life*, p. 42 ff.

8. See Allen, 'On Spenser's Muiopotmos', p. 146 ff:; Wind, *Pagan Mysteries*, p. 59.
9. *Mythologiae*, III, 6. See *Fulgentius the Mythographer*, trans. Leslie George Whitbread (Columbus: Ohio State University Press, 1971), p. 88 ff.
10. Wind, *Pagan Mysteries*, p. 59.
11. See C. S. Lewis, *The Allegory of Love: A Study in Mediaeval Tradition* (New York: Galaxy Books, 1958), p. 324 ff., on the opposition of artifice to nature in the Bower of Bliss, and R. Nevo, 'Spenser's "Bower of Bliss" and a Key Metaphor from Renaissance Poetic', reprinted from *Studies in Western Literature* vol. 10, ed. D. A. Fineman (Jerusalem: 1962), pp. 20–31, in *Essential Articles for the Study of Edmund Spenser*, ed. A. C. Hamilton (Connecticut: Archon Books, 1972), pp. 29–39, who answers Lewis and suggests that the problem really is that art contends with nature.
12. See Roche, *The Kindly Flame*, p. 3 ff. for a discussion of the mediaeval 'realism' of Spenser's language; and Nuttall, *Two Concepts of Allegory*, p. 30 ff., for remarks on the haunting quality of true allegory.
13. See Allen, 'On Spenser's Muiopotmos', p. 151.
14. There are the many standard acknowledgements that the arms of the Red Cross Knight relate to Ephesians 6: 10–22 which discusses the breastplate of righteousness and the shield of faith, and also on the relation of Christ's death on the cross to these theological concepts. Vergil Whitaker, *The Religious Basis of Spenser's Thought* (Stanford, Cal.: Stanford University Press, 1950), Stanford University Publications, University Series, Language and Literature, Vol. VII, no. 3, p. 29ff., has most to say on this point. But there is no study of the sort which I propose here, and which suggests how the structure of Book I may relate to a particular iconographic programme for representing the crucifixion.
15. I allude here to the important point which Spenser takes care to establish in Bk I that the Red Cross Knight is not an elf: he does not represent holiness, but is on the way to achieving it. See M. Pauline Parker, *The Allegory of the 'Faerie Queene'* (Oxford: Clarendon Press, 1960), p. 67 ff., on Holiness not being a virtue; Georgia Ronan Crampton, *The Condition of Creatures: Suffering and Action in Chaucer and Spenser* (New Haven and London: Yale University Press, 1974), p. 116 ff., on the ambiguous and open-ended nature of Red Cross Knight's pilgrimage; Angus Fletcher, *The Prophetic Moment: An Essay on Spenser* (Chicago and London: The University of Chicago Press, 1971), p. 88, on George's 'intermediary' status in Faeryland, and Isabel E. Rathborne, *The Meaning of Spenser's Fairyland* (New York: Columbia University Press, 1937; reprint, New York: Russell and Russell, 1965), p. 201 ff., on the same point.
16. *Spenser's World of Glass*, pp. 5–6.
17. See Davies, *Worship and Theology in England, From Cranmer to Hooker, 1534–1603* (New Jersey: Princeton University Press, 1970), p. 354, from *Visitation Articles and Injunctions*, ed. W. H. Frere and W. H. Kennedy, 3 vols (1910), II, 126. The following summary derives from Davies.
18. Ibid., *A Necessarie Doctrine and erudition for any chrysten man, set furth by the Kynges maiesty of Englande, Ec.* (1534), is the full title of a work popularly known as *The King's Book*.

19. William Wood Seymour, *The Cross in Tradition, History and Art* (New York and London: The Knickerbocker Press, 1898), p. 444. See John Jewel, *An Apologie of the Church of England*, ed. J. E. Booty (New York: Cornell University Press, 1963), pp. ix–x, which gives a concise summary: John Jewel described the cross to Peter Martyr in *The Zurich Letters*, ed. Hastings Robinson, 1st ser. (Cambridge: Parker Society, 1842), p. 55; Nicholas Throckmorton, English ambassador to Paris thought the Queen's behaviour was adversely affecting foreign policy, *Calendar of State Papers* (1562), no. 618, p. 370; Recusants saw it as a sign of hope, e.g. John Martiall, *Treatyse of the Cross* (Antwerp: 1564), sig. A.2 verso; Thomas Harding, *A Confutation of a Booke intituled An Apologie of the Church of England* (Antwerp: 1565), sig. 2 verso.

20. *The Religious Basis*, p. 29 ff. See also Beatrice Ricks, 'Catholic Sacramentals and Symbolism in Spenser's *Faerie Queene*', *JEGP*, LII (1953), 322–31, which likewise sees the second cross as a protection; and Roland M. Smith, 'Origines Arthurianae: The Two Crosses of Red Cross Knight', *JEGP* LIV (1955), 670–83, which gives an occasional explanation of the two crosses, which Spenser combines with Arthurian materials.

21. 'Spenser and Some Pictorial Conventions, with particular reference to illuminated manuscripts', ed. Thomas P. Roche, Jr., *Essays By Rosemond Tuve: Spenser, Herbert, Milton* (New Jersey: Princeton University Press, 1970), p. 112. See John B. Bender, *Spenser and Literary Pictorialism* (New Jersey: Princeton University Press, 1972), p. 3 ff., which offers a subtle reading of Spenser's pictorial imagery, stressing the non-decorative but essential contribution of the 'visual' component. Bender agrees substantially with Tuve, but cautions against her tendency to oppose 'word painting' to images based on other kinds of experience. See also Rudolf B. Gottfried, 'The Pictorial Element in Spenser's Poetry', *ELH*, XIX (1952), 203–13; Carl Robinson Sonn, 'Spenser's Imagery', *ELH*, XXVI, (1959), 156–70 for arguments against the older view of Spenser's imagery as decorative illustration of moral precept.

22. For instance those of John Dee or John Lord Lumley, of Henry Fitzalen, Earl of Arundel and his uncle the fifth earl of Northumberland. See Tuve, 'Pictorial Conventions', p. 116, C. B. Millican, *Spenser and the Table Round* (Cambridge, Mass.: Harvard University Press, 1932), p. 42 ff.

23. See especially Robert L. Füglister, *Das Lebende Kreuz: Iconographisch-ikonologische Untersuchung der Herkunft und Entwicklung einer spätmittelalterlichen Bildidee und ihrer Verwurzelung im Wort* (Zurich: Benziger Verlag, 1964), and the materials collected in Appendix I.

24. Seymour, *The Cross*, p. 355.

25. See plate 1.

26. See Erasmus, *The Enchiridion*, trans. and ed. Raymond Himelick (Bloomington: Indiana University Press, 1963), p. 171: 'The seventeenth rule (The Mystery of the Cross)', describes how 'against every kind of adversity or temptation the cross of Christ is by far the one most potent.'

27. See plate 1. King James, 'I will even betroth thee unto me in faithfulness.'

28. *On Christian Doctrine*, II, xli, 62, trans Robertson, p. 77.

29. Letter 140, ch. 26, trans. Sister Wilfrid Parsons, S.N.D., *Letters, Vol. III (131–164)*, The Fathers of the Church. A New Translation, vol. 20 (Washington: The Catholic University of America Press, 1953), pp. 113–14.
30. Letter 147, ch. 34–5, trans. Sister Wilfrid Parsons, p. 202.
31. Letter 55, in *Letters, Vol. I (1–82)* trans. Sister Wilfrid Parsons (1957), pp. 262–3. Page numbers to the following account of this letter are given in the text.
32. For example, Rabanus Maurus, *De laudibus S. Crucis*, lib. 1 (*PL*, 72, 829); *En. in Epp. S. Pauli*, lib 18 (*PL*, 112, 423 ff.); Walafrid Strabo, *Glossa Ordinaria* (*PL*, 114, 594); Hugh of St Victor, *Miscell.* lib. 1, tit. 50 (*PL*, 177, 499); Bernard of Clairvaux, *Sermo in die S. Paschae* (*PL*, 183, 275); Alanus de Insulis, *Sermo 2, De S. Cruce* (*PL*, 210, 223 ff.), Thomas Aquinas, *Comment in Ep. ad Eph.*, cap. III, lec. v.
33. See 'In Exaltatione Sanctae Crucis', in *Analecta Hymnica Medii Aevi*, ed. Guido M. Dreves, S.J., and Clemens Blume, S.J., 55 vols (Leipzig: O. R. Reisland, 1886–1922), 8, 23, no. 17, st. 1a ff. (Hereafter cited as *AH*.)
34. 'De Christo Domino Psalterium Triplex', II, 6, Quinquagena I, 23, *AH*, 38, 88: 'Ave, clavis reserans . . . .'
35. 'Super Ave Maria', *AH*, 30, 260, no. 143, st. 13.
36. 'In Festo Exaltationis S. Crucis', *AH*, 8, 24, no. 18, st. 7a. For other hymns on the cross which are full of typological material, see *AH*, 8, 18 ff, nos. 11–28.
37. See for instance Rosemond Tuve, *A Reading of George Herbert* (Chicago: University of Chicago Press, 1952), *passim*; Emile Male, *The Gothic Image. Religious Art in France of the Thirteenth Century*, trans. Dora Nussey (London: J. M. Dent and Sons, 1913).
38. 'The Second Homilie concerning the death and Passion of our Saviour Christ', in *Certaine Sermons or Homilies Appointed to be Read in Churches in the Time of Queen Elizabeth I (1547–1571)*, a facsimile reproduction of the edition of 1673, with an introduction by Mary Ellen Rickey and Thomas B. Stroup (Gainesville, Florida: Scholars Facsimiles and Reprints, 1968), p. 186.
39. See Rosemond Tuve, 'Pictorial Conventions', p. 112; Bender, *Spenser and Literary Pictorialism*, p. 21, n. 30.
40. *New Catholic Encyclopaedia* (New York: McGraw Hill, 1967), VI, 354.
41. See Peter Heylyn, *The Historie of St George* (1631), which is wholly concerned with the relation between event and symbol: cf. Mantuan, *The Life of St George* (1509), trans. Alexander Barclay (1515). Mantuan omits incidents he thought too fanciful and extends the symbolic significance by introducing numerous classical references. Barclay's epistle to Nicholas West concerning the translation defends the historical truth of the legend. See William Nelson, *EETS* O.S. 230 (London: Oxford University Press, 1955), pp. xxi–xxiii. Calvin simply sees St George as a spectre whose intercession is an erroneous superstition (*Institutes*, III, xx, 27). Also, Tristram White, *The Martyrdome of Saint George of Cappadocia* (1614), in a preface assures us that the pictures of St George and dragon are 'but Symbolicall and figurative.'

42. Ed. William Nelson, *EETS*, OS 230 (London: Oxford University Press, 1960). Line numbers in the following account are to this edition.
43. Published in an appendix to the *EETS* edition of Mantuan's *Life*, p. 112 ff. Page numbers refer to this edition.
44. Aelfric's *Lives of the Saints*, ed. Walter W. Skeat, *EETS*, O.S. 76 and 82 as one volume (London: Oxford University Press, 1966), 11, 21 and 114.
45. *Mirk's Festial: a Collection of Homilies*, part I ed. Theodor Erbe, *EETS* Extra Series, 96 (London: Kegan Paul, Trench, Trübner, and Co., Ltd., 1905), pp. 132–5.
46. *The Historie of St George*, p. 86. In the following account page numbers are given in the text.
47. See Kellogg and Steele, eds., *Edmund Spenser Books I and II* p. 10 ff, who give an account of this painting in relation to Bk I.
48. See, for example, St Augustine, *Sermo XXV*, i, on the words of Matt. 14: 'But the ship was in the midst of the sea, tossed with waves', where ship and cross are compared. The 'navis' and 'clavis' rhyme led to ready association between ship and key as signs of the cross:

    Regnum quaeritis?
    Non intrabitis
    Sine crucis clavi
    Partum petetis?
    Non transibitis
    Sine crucis navi.   (*AH*, 8, 18, no. 11, st. 7a–b)

49. The insistence that Spenser's allegory is more concerned with the reader's psychology than with other kinds of consistent correspondence within the poem is argued by Paul J. Alpers, *The Poetry of the Faerie Queene* (New Jersey: Princeton University Press, 1967). See also Harry Berger Jr., 'At Home and Abroad with Spenser', *MLQ*, 25 (1964), 106: many of Spenser's characters have double lives determined by the allegory wherein the reference is primarily psychological; the characters live both in and out of the hero's mind.
50. See *Spenser's Images of Life*, p. 112. Donald Cheyney, *Spenser's Image of Nature: Wild Man and Shepherd in ' The Faerie Queene'* (New Haven: Yale University Press, 1966), p. 35, stresses the knight's naïveté in the first half.
51. For examples from the *Biblia Pauperum*, the *Specula*, and *Horae*, see Tuve, *A Reading of George Herbert*, p. 32 ff. On the cross in this episode, see Kellogg and Steele, *Edmund Spenser Books I and II*, pp. 31 ff., 167–8. For an account of the full complexity of Orgoglio, including the redemption theme, see S. K. Heninger, Jr., 'The Orgoglio Episode in *The Faerie Queene*', *ELH*, 26 (1959), 171–87.
52. *On Christian Doctrine*, II, xii, 62, trans. Robertson, p. 77.
53. Sinai, Olives, and Parnassus are all mentioned. See Carol V. Kaske, 'Spenser's Pluralistic Universe: The View from the Mount of Contemplation (*F.Q.* I, X.)', in *Contemporary Thought on Edmund Spenser, With a Bibliography of Criticism of ' The Faerie Queene', 1900–1970*, ed. with an introduction by Richard C. Frushell and Bernard J. Vondersmith (Carbondale and Edwardsville: Southern Illinois University Press, 1975), p. 147,

for a suggestion that the three mountains represent the three dispensations, Nature, Law, and Grace.

54. See *Symbols of the Church*, ed. Carroll E. Whittemore (Boston, Mass.: Whittemore Associates Inc., 1960), p. 33; cf. John 3: 14 on the serpent lifted up in the wilderness as a type of Christ on the cross. As I have mentioned, the emblem appears on Melanchthon's coat of arms.

55. cf. Roche, *The Kindly Flame*, p. 59. Carol V. Kaske's excellent study, 'The Dragon's Spark and Sting and the Structure of Red Cross's Dragon-fight: *The Faerie Queene*, I, xi–xii', *SP*, 66 (1969), 609–38, makes clear how the Red Cross Knight gradually becomes Christ-like, and how the identity with Christ culminates on the third day in the image of the cross. See also D. Douglas Waters, 'Spenser's "Well of Life" and "Tree of Life" Once More', *MP*, 67 (1969–70), 67–8, which sees the well as washing by grace, and the tree as the Lord's Supper.

56. See Crampton, *The Condition of Creatures*, p. 179 ff.: there is a larger circle, the poet intimates, which is communicated in gleams and fragments though we address it mainly in faith.

57. *Of the Imitation of Christ*, II, 12, 4, trans. Abbot Justin McCann (New York: Mentor Books, 1957), p. 69.

58. See *Variorum*, p. 436; Graham Hough, *A Preface to 'The Faerie Queene'* (London: Gerald Duckworth and Co., 1962), p. 150.

59. Application of traditional mediaeval and Catholic materials to anti-Catholic satire was familiar practice among Protestant apologists. See Josephine Waters Bennett, *The Evolution of 'The Faerie Queene'* (Chicago: University of Chicago Press, 1942), p. 108 ff., and John Erskine Hankins, *Source and Meaning in Spenser's Allegory* (Oxford: Clarendon Press, 1971), p. 99 ff., who show that Spenser adapts the technique of Protestant commentators on the apocalypse who use mediaeval Catholic satire against the Catholic Church itself. An example in relation to the St George legend occurs in Tristram White's *Martyrdome*, where the description of the idolatrous emperor seems to suggest Roman Catholic worship, sig. B.

60. See esp. Guillaume De Guileville, *The Booke of the Pylgremage of the Sowle*, ed. Katherine Isabella Cust (London: Basil Montagu Pickering, 1859), I, xxiii–xxvii, where the balance of Justice is righted by Christ's merits and the allegory is sustained by our appreciation that the balance is a type of the cross. BM Yates Thompson 13 fol. 151r, has a nice illumination which conflates the figure of a balance and the redeeming efficacy of the cross.

61. Kellogg and Steele note in *Edmund Spenser Books I and II*, p. 186 (note to 47. 3–4) that the implied answer to Despair's question is 'a resounding "yes," for Christ did take upon himself the sins of all men. His death on the cross was the atonement for the sin of mankind.'

62. See Cheyney, *Spenser's Image of Nature*, p. 37 ff.

63. Spenser borrows here from Ariosto. See *Variorum*, p. 202 ff.

64. E.g., see Augustine, *In epist. ad Parthos.*, 3, 1; *Serm.* 216, 7.

65. Cheyney, *Spenser's Image of Nature*, p. 27 argues that Error is here a parody of Christ as the self-wounding pelican.

66. See Kellogg and Steele, *Edmund Spenser Books I and II*, p. 105.

67. The lion is emblem of St Mark: winged, it represents Mark's account

of Christ's royal dignity. See W. Ellwood Post, *Saints, Signs and Symbols* (New York: Morehouse-Barlow and Co., 1962), p. 11.

68. See I, iii, 39, 4; I, iv, 41, 2; I, vi, 42, 8.
69. See Kellogg and Steele, *Edmund Spenser Books I and II*, p. 36.
70. Northrop Frye's observation here is sound: 'One cannot begin to discuss the allegory without using the imagery, but one could work out an exhaustive analysis of the imagery without ever mentioning the allegory,' In 'The Structure of Imagery in *The Faerie Queene*,' in *Essential Articles*, ed. Hamilton, p. 156.

CHAPTER 3

1. See Jackson I. Cope, *The Theater and the Dream: From Metaphor to Form in Renaissance Drama* (Baltimore and London: Johns Hopkins Press, 1973), p. 241, who argues that the central theme of *The Tempest* is isolation.
2. See Howard Felperin, *Shakespearean Romance* (New Jersey: Princeton Universty Press, 1972), p. 249; A. D. Nuttall, *Two Concepts of Allegory*, pp. 1–14.
3. Nuttall, *Two Concepts of Allegory*, pp. 159–60: this is the most philosophical and persuasively argued assessment of Shakespeare's imagery in relation to metaphysics, and I am indebted to it especially in the following account of 'placing' Shakespeare's images between percept and allegory, on the haunting suggestiveness of the higher meanings, and on the dramatising of the mind configurating.
4. Ibid., p. 157: '*The Tempest* is, for much of its length, *about* people configurating, imagining without actualising, and so on.' Quotations are from *The Tempest*, ed. Robert Langbaum, *The Complete Signet Classic Shakespeare* (New York: Harcourt Brace Jovanovich, Inc., 1972).
5. See Jackson I. Cope, *The Theater and the Dream*, p. 236: that *The Tempest* 'is insistent upon specific christian patterns for a principal sounding board seems clear', and Northrop Frye, 'Introduction' to *The Tempest* (Baltimore: Penguin Books Inc., 1959), pp. 15–26, on patterns of fall, illusion, and redemption.
6. The interpretations of Prospero as a white or natural magician are manifold. See Frances A. Yates, *Shakespeare's Last Plays: A New Approach* (London: Routledge and Kegan Paul, 1975), ch. 4, 'Magic in the Last Plays: *The Tempest*', pp. 85–106; D. G. James, *The Dream of Prospero* (Oxford: Clarendon Press, 1967), ch. III 'The Magician', pp. 45–71; D'Orsay W. Pearson, '"Unless I be Reliev'd by Prayer" *The Tempest* in Perspective', *Shakespeare Studies* VII (1974), 253–82, challenges the reading of Prospero as a beneficent natural magician. He is convincing on the idea that Prospero has something important to learn, but omits discussion of the masque elements of the play.
7. See Frank Kermode, ed. *The Tempest* (London: Methuen and Co. Ltd., 6th ed., reprinted, 1961), p. li ff.
8. See F. H. Anderson, *Francis Bacon: His Career and His Thought* (Los Angeles: University of Southern California Press, 1962), p. 125.
9. See Frances A. Yates, *Theatre of the World* (London: Routledge and Kegan Paul, 1969), p. 11.

10. Ibid., esp. ch. V, 'Inigo Jones in a New Perspective', pp. 80–81.
11. See D. P. Walker, *Spiritual and Demonic Magic from Ficino to Campanella* (London: Warburg Institute, 1958), p. 51; Peter J. French, *John Dee: The World of an Elizabethan Magus* (London: Routledge and Kegan Paul, 1972), p. 81 ff.
12. *Autobiographical Tracts of Dr John Dee, Warden of the College of Manchester*, ed. James Crossley, The Chetham Society, vol. XXIV (Manchester: 1851), p. 5.
13. French, *John Dee*, p. 81: 'The Fact that John Dee was essentially a secretive man can hardly be over-emphasized.' See p. 64 for an account of Dee's pride, also Yates, *Theatre*, p. 18.
14. *A True and Faithful Relation of what passed for many years Between Dr: John Dee ... and Some Spirits*, ed. Meric Casaubon (London: 1659), p. 231.
15. See Yates, *Theatre*, pp. 88–9.
16. See C. S. Lewis, *English Literature in the Sixteenth Century, Excluding Drama* (Oxford: Clarendon Press, 1954), p. 49. My summary account derives from Lewis, p. 46 ff.
17. *Basilikon Doron*, ed. Charles Howard McIlwain, *The Political Works of James I* (Cambridge, Mass.: Harvard University Press, 1918; New York: Russell and Russell, 1965), p. 3 ff.
18. *Advancement of Learning*, ed. G. W. Kitchin (London: Everyman, 1915), p. 3.
19. 'Image, Form and Theme in *A Mask*', ed. John S. Diekhoff, *A Maske at Ludlow: Essays on Milton's 'Comus'* (Cleveland: Case Western Reserve University Press, 1968), pp. 163, 150.
20. Enid Welsford, *The Court Masque: A Study in the Relationship Between Poetry and the Revels* (Cambridge: Cambridge University Press, 1927), Part III, 'The Significance of the Revels', pp. 353–407. See also C. L. Barber, 'A Mask Presented at Ludlow Castle: The Masque as a Masque', ed. Diekhoff, *A Maske at Ludlow*, p. 191: 'The court masque was only possible so long as there was majesty to realize', *et passim*. Stephen Orgel, *The Illusion of Power: Political Theatre in the English Renaissance*, (Berkeley: University of California Press, 1975), *passim*.
21. Yates, *Theatre*, p. 86.
22. Ibid., p. 171; see *Shakespeare's Last Plays*, ch. 4, *passim*; cf. French, *John Dee*, p. 19.
23. *Institutes of the Christian Religion*, 4, 14, 4 and 14, ed. John T. McNeill, trans. and indexed Ford Lewis Battles (Philadelphia: Westminster Press, 1960). All references to *The Institutes* are from this edition, and are cited in the text.
24. *The History and Antiquities of the University of Oxford*, ed. J. Gutch (Oxford: Clarendon Press, 1780–90), ed. II; part I, pp. 107–8.
25. John Ferrar, *A Life of Nicholas Ferrar*, ed. B. Blackstone, *The Ferrar Papers* (Cambridge University Press, 1938), p. 60.
26. *Daemonologie* (1597), ed. G. B. Harrison (Edinburgh: Edinburgh University Press, 1966), p. 18. The following references are to this edition, and are cited in the text.
27. McIlwain, *Political Works*, p. 26 ff.

28. For Bacon's Calvinism, see Paolo Rossi, *Francis Bacon: From Magic to Science*, trans. Sacha Rabinovitch (London: Routledge and Kegan Paul, 1968), p. 164.
29. Ibid., esp. ch. I, 'The Mechanical Arts, Magic, and Science', pp. 1–35.
30. See Frances A. Yates 'The Hermetic Tradition in Renaissance Science', ed. Charles S. Singleton *Art, Science, and History in the Renaissance* (Baltimore: Johns Hopkins Press, 1967), p. 270.
31. *The Masculine Birth of Time*, ed. Benjamin Farrington, *The Philosophy of Francis Bacon* (Chicago: Phoenix Books, 1964), p. 70. The works quoted in the following account were all written between 1603 and 1613.
32. Ibid., p. 63.
33. *Thoughts and Conclusions on The Interpretation of Nature or a Science Productive of Works*, ed. Farrington, *The Philosophy*, p. 73.
34. *The Masculine Birth of Time*, p. 65.
35. *The Refutation of Philosophies*, ed. Farrington, *The Philosophy*, p. 123.
36. Ibid., p. 122.
37. Ibid., p. 129.
38. Ibid., p. 120.
39. *The Masculine Birth of Time*, p. 64.
40. *The Refutation of Philosophies*, p. 107.
41. Ibid., p. 118.
42. Ibid., p. 119.
43. *Advancement of Learning*, ed. Kitchen, p. 132.
44. *Sermon VII*, 11.
45. *De Dignitate et augmentis scientarum*, ed. James Spedding, Robert Leslie Ellis, Douglas Denon Heath, *The Works of Francis Bacon* (Cambridge, Mass.: Riverside Press, 1863), II, 456–57.
46. *Thoughts and Conclusions*, p. 75.
47. cf. A. C. Bradley, *Shakespearean Tragedy* (London: Macmillan, 1960), p. 263 ff.
48. See Sears Jayne, 'The Subject of Milton's Ludlow *Mask*', ed. Diekhoff, *A Maske at Ludlow*, p. 168.
49. Ibid., p. 158 ff.; Tuve, 'Image, Form and Meaning', p. 154.
50. *Confessions*, VIII, iii, 7, trans. Pusey, p. 154–5.
51. trans. Abbot Justin McCann (New York: Mentor Books, 1957), pp. 77, 160, 158.
52. ed. Helen Gardner (Oxford: Clarendon Press, 1964), p. 9–10.
53. *Pagan Mysteries of the Renaissance* (London: Peregrine Books, 1967), p. 146 ff.
54. *The Enchiridion on Faith, Hope and Love*, ed. Henry Paolucci (New York: Henry Regnery Co., 1961), p. 86.
55. See French, *John Dee*, p. 118.
56. *Autobiographical Tracts*, p. 71.
57. Ibid., p. 80.
58. Ibid., p. 79.
59. Ibid., p. 53.
60. *Mathematicall Preface*, Sigs, A. iiii, r–v.
61. *Autobiographical Tracts*, p. 83.
62. *Advancement of Learning*, II, 15, ed. Kitchin, p. 177.

63. *Valerius Terminus*, ed. Spedding, VI, 34.
64. *Advancement of Learning*, II, 15, ed. Kitchin, p. 177.

CHAPTER 4

1. See Marc F. Bertonasco, *Crashaw and the Baroque* (Alabama: University of Alabama Press, 1971), pp. 9, 21, 38, *et passim*.
2. Julius D. Locke, 'Images and Image Symbolised in Metaphysical Poetry with Special Reference to Otherworldliness', Diss. University of Florida, 1958, cited in Bertonasco, *Crashaw and the Baroque*, p. 139.
3. See Bertonasco, *Crashaw and the Baroque*, p. 71.
4. Ibid., p. 143.
5. *John Donne, the Divine Poems*, ed. Helen Gardner(Oxford: Clarendon Press, 1964), p. 16.
6. *The Poems English, Latin and Greek of Richard Crashaw*, ed. L. C. Martin (Oxford: Clarendon Press, 2nd ed., 1957), p. 99. All quotations from Crashaw are from this edition, hereafter cited in the text.
7. *On Christian Doctrine*, I, 32, trans. Robertson, p. 27.
8. Ibid., II, 20, Robertson, p. 55.
9. *The Works of George Herbert*, ed. F. E. Hutchinson (Oxford: Clarendon Press, 1941), p. 74.
10. See *The Transformation of Sin* (Amherst, Montreal, and London: University of Massachusetts Press and McGill-Queen's University Press, 1974).
11. See also the deep admiration expressed in 'On Mr. G. Herberts booke intituled the Temple of Sacred Poems, sent to a Gentlewoman', *Works*, p. 130.
12. See Austin Warren, *Richard Crashaw: A Study in Baroque Sensibility* (Ann Arbor: University of Michigan Press, 1939), p. 42. Also *Works*, xxiii, ff., for Crashaw's relation to the Ferrars.
13. See my *Transformation of Sin*, ch. 4.
14. E.g. A. Alvarez, *The School of Donne* (London: Chatto and Windus, 1962), p. 92 ff.
15. See *Catholic Encyclopaedia* (New York: Encyclopaedia Press, 1913), 3, 325.
16. See P. Hildebrand d'Hooglede, O.F.M. Cap., 'Deux Poètes peu connus: Les Capucins Remi de Beauvais (1568–1622) et Jean Evangéliste d'Arras (1654)', *Collectanea Franciscana*, 24 (1954), 160.
17. See *Works*, p. xxxv.
18. Within the 'historical' camp I can also suggest a means of reconciling the broad view of Warren who draws from the Baroque as a general style, with the specific view of Bertonasco who claims the main influence is St François de Sales. Both studies are excellent. As Bertonasco suggests in summary (p. 129), Warren's book stresses the sensual elements of the Baroque; although highly suggestive, I find it not firmly enough centered in the native traditions from which Crashaw's art also develops. Bertonasco's specific suggestion, St François de Sales, is illuminating but perhaps overly reductive. The uniqueness of St François is much stressed (e.g. pp. 59, 63, 67, 69), and I believe that the salesian spirit is more typical, in broad outline, of the counter-Reformation spirit which helped

bring it to birth. Though Brémond points out St François' uniqueness (see Bertonasco, p. 69), see Julien-Eymard D'Angers, O.F.M. Cap., *L'Humanisme Chrétien au XVIIe Siècle: St François de Sales et Yves de Paris* (The Hague: Martinus Nijhoff, 1970), which challenges this point in my favour.

19. See Father Cuthbert, O.S.F.C. *The Capucins: A Contribution to the History of the Counter-Reformation*, 2 vols. (London: Sheed and Ward, 1928); Godefroy de Paris, *Les Frères mineurs capucins en France. Histoire de la province de Paris*, t. 1, en 2 fasc. (Paris: 1937–9; t. 2, 1950); Optat de Veghel, O.F.M. Cap., 'La Réforme des Frères Mineurs Capucins dans l'Ordre Franciscaine et dans l'Eglise' *Collectanea Franciscana*, 35 (1965), 5–108. The following account is summarised from these sources.

20. See Cuthbert, *Capucins*, I, 121, ff.

21. Ibid., I, 99 ff., 126 ff; Optatus, 'La Réforme', p. 31 ff.

22. *The Catholic Encyclopaedia*, 3, 323.

23. See Henri Brémond, *Histoire Littéraire du Sentiment Religieux en France, Depuis la Fin des Guerres de Religion Jusqu'à nos Jours*, (Paris: Bloud et Gay, 1916–71), II, 140.

24. L. Hertling, 'Spiritualité Franciscaine: 16e–17e siècles', in *Dictionnaire de Spiritualité*, vol. V, col. 1367: 'L'influence des capucins sur la spiritualité d'une époque ou d'un pays ne fut peut-être jamais aussi grande qu'au siècle d'or français.'

25. Cuthbert, *Capucins*, II, 255.

26. Ibid.

27. For a fascinating account of Père Ange, and especially of Joseph du Tremblay, see Aldous Huxley, *Grey Eminence: A Study in Religion and Politics* (London: Chatto and Windus, 1944).

28. For the complexities of such interrelationships see Anthony Levi, S.J., *French Moralists: The Theory of the Passions, 1585 to 1649* (Oxford: Clarendon Press, 1964).

29. *Histoire*, II, 156: 'Maître des maîtres eux-mêmes'; Cuthbert, *Capucins*, II, 267, gives a similar witness of extensive influence. Paul Renaudin, *Un maître de la mystique française: Benoît de Canfield* (Paris, 1956); Optat de Veghel, *Benoît de Canfield (1562–1610), sa vie, sa doctrine et son influence* (Rome: Institutum Historicum Ord. Fr. Min. Cap., 1949); Etta Gullick, 'The Life of Father Benet of Canfield', *Collectanea Franciscana* 42 (1972), 39–67, all give accounts of Benet's extensive influence.

30. The following biographical account is summarised from the above sources, especially Gullick, 'The Life'.

31. Even before the publication of *The Rule of Perfection* (1609), which went through many editions and was widely translated. See 'Benoît de Canfield', *Dictionnaire de Théologie Catholique*, 2ⁱ, 718–19 for a list of translations.

32. See Brémond, *Histoire*, II, 193 ff.; 'Madame Acarie et le Carmel'; A. Duval, *La vie admirable de la Bienheureuse Sœur Marie de l'Incarnation* (Paris: 1893; 1st ed., Paris: 1621).

33. Duval, *La vie admirable*, pp. 25–6, trans. Gullick, 'The Life', p. 59.

34. See Gullick, 'The Life', p. 61.

35. See Paul Renaudin, *Un maître*, p. 224; Michael de la Bedoyère, *François de Sales* (London: Collins, 1960), p. 95 ff.

36. See Brémond, *Histoire*, II, 135 ff., 'Benoît de Canfeld, Le Père Joseph

et la Tradition Séraphique'; Huxley, *Grey Eminence*, p. 47 ff., 'The Religious Background'.

37. See Cuthbert, *The Capucins*, II, 261.

38. Optat de Veghel, *Benoît de Canfield*, pp. 328 ff.; 359 ff.; *Dictionnaire de Spiritualité*, vol. V, cols. 1368, 1449 ff.

39. *Oeuvres complètes de Bérulle*, ed. J. P. Migne (Paris: 1866), col. 161.

40. Parts I and II are edited by D. M. Rogers, *English Recusant Literature 1558–1640*, vol. 40, *William Fitch, 'The Rule of Perfection' (1609), James Tyrie, 'Refutation of John Knox' (1573)* (Yorkshire: Scolar press, 1970). The following account refers to the Scolar Press edition, and the page numbers are given in the text.

41. For the traditional scholastic component in Benet's education, see Gullick 'The Life', p. 57. Cuthbert, *The Capucins*, II, 404 ff. argues that the tendency of Capucin writers to interpret Bonaventure by way of St Thomas puts the traditional Franciscan spirit under inordinate strain.

42. For an account of the differences, see Brémond, *Histoire*, III, 111 ff.; 137 ff.

43. See Aldous Huxley, *Grey Eminence*, p. 74. The third part of the Rule was not translated in the early English editions. Huxley gives the most readily available summary with quotations. Page numbers to the following account of Huxley's theory on Benet are given in the text.

44. VII, 2–3, 5, trans. George Boas (New York: Bobbs Merrill, 1953), 43–5.

45. *Histoire*, II, 166–7.

46. Anthony Levi, *French Moralists*. The following brief account is abstracted from Fr Levi's study, and page numbers are given in the text.

47. See Gullick, 'The Life', p. 62. For a discussion of the medical views of the protagonists, see Jean Dagens, *Bérulle, et les Origines de la Restauration Catholique (1576–1611)* (Paris: Desclée de Brouwer, 1952), pp. 150–65.

48. See Gullick, 'The Life', p. 63 ff.

49. *The Mind's Road to God*, II, 1–2, trans. Boas, p. 14.

50. Ibid., II, 6, trans. Boas, p. 17.

51. Benet resorts frequently to emblematic techniques: the *Rule* is prefaced by an emblem, though it is not printed in the Scolar Press edition. It features a circular diagram with faces arranged in concentric circles. The commentary explains how at the centre is the sun representing the will of God and how the three rings of faces are souls living in the three degrees of the divine will. Outside the last circle are tools, which lie in shadow, though they are partly illuminated. They represent the works of men, and show how outward things are themselves in darkness though they have the capacity for being illuminated if referred to God. Throughout the text are emblematic descriptions, e.g. the soul glimpsing the spouse through the grates of a wall (139), the sacrifice of the soul on the altar of the heart (121), or the heart as a bed (93), and the elaborate treatment of the throne of Solomon according to the six degrees of spiritual ascent (89 ff.).

52. For an account of Zacharie's life and writings, see *Biographie Universelle* (Paris: L.-G. Michaud, 1828), vol. 52, pp. 28–9; *Dictionnaire de Théologie Catholique*, vol. 15², cols. 3675–6. The following account cites page numbers of the 1639 edition of the *Philosophie Chrestienne* in the text.

53. See Hildebrand d'Hooglede, 'Deux poètes', p. 160, for an account of the Capucin devotion to Mary Magdalene, and for details on the life and writing of Remi of Beauvais. Page numbers in the following account are cited in the text from *La Magdaleine* (Tournay: Charles Matin, 1617).

54. *Histoire*, I, 383.

55. See Francis Borgia Steck, *Franciscans and the Protestant Revolution in England* (Chicago: Franciscan Herald Press, 1920), p. 226.

56. Ibid., 229; Rev. Father Thaddeus, *The Franciscans in England, 1600–1850* (London and Leamington: Art and Book Company, 1898), pp. 105–14, lists a surprising number of English authors at work during this period compiling devotional materials.

57. Bérulle came with the Queen in 1625. The Grey Eminence had visited England in 1597, and continued to show deep interest in the English mission. Cyprien de Gamaches claims he was in correspondence with the Earl of Portland, and Fr Cuthbert describes his zeal for the conversion of England (*Capucins*, II, 339).

58. See Martin, *Works*, xxxii.

59. Ibid., xxi ff.

60. Richard Crashaw: *A Study in Style and Poetic Development* (Madison: University of Wisconsin Press, 1959), p. 137.

CHAPTER 5

1. The Cartesian spirit of an-historicism may also be important here. See Lucien Lévy-Bruhl, 'The Cartesian Spirit and History' in Raymond Klibansky and J. H. Paton, eds., *Philosophy and History. Essays Presented to Ernst Cassirer* (New York: Harper Torchbooks, 1963), p. 19 ff.

2. See Oscar Cullman *Christ and Time: The Primitive Christian Conception of Time and History*, trans. Floyd V. Filson (Philadelphia and London: SCM Press, 1951), and for a good survey, C. A. Patrides, *The Grand Design of God: The Literary Form of the Christian View of History* (London: Routledge and Kegan Paul, 1972).

3. For the Middle Ages see Norman Cohn, *The Pursuit of the Millennium* (London: Secker and Warburg, 1967), which describes the relationship between eschatology and revolutionary movements, and for the seventeenth and eighteenth centuries, Ernest Lee Tuveson, *Millennium and Utopia. A Study in the Background of the Idea of Progress* (New York: Harper Torchbooks, 1964). Tuveson's book was first published in 1949, and he suggests in a preface to the Harper Torchbook edition that 'Mr Cohn's book and mine in this sense complement each other, and should be read together.' (p.v.)

4. For the following account of Petrarch and his followers see Myron P. Gilmore, 'The Renaissance Conception of the Lessons of History' in *Facets of the Renaissance*, ed. W. H. Werkmeister (Los Angeles: University of California Press, 1959) pp. 73–86.

5. See also Theodor E. Mommsen, 'Petrarch's Conception of the "Dark

Ages"' in his *Medieval and Renaissance Studies*, ed. Eugene F. Rice. (New York: Cornell University Press, 1959), ch. VII.

6. Lloyd Berry argues that the *History* was written between 1632–8; 'Giles Fletcher the Elder, and Milton's *A Brief History of Muscovia*', *RES*, N.S., XI (1960), pp. 150–56.

7. See Patrides, *The Grand Design*, ch. 5 'Tradition in Renaissance England', p. 7 ff. for an account of the 'avalanche of universal chronicles'.

8. *The Works of John Milton* (New York: Columbia University Press, 1932), X, 140. Hereafter cited in the text. For a good bibliography on Milton as historian, see Patrides, *The Grand Design*, pp. 117–18.

9. See Ibid., p. 108.

10. See especially Roberta F. Brinkley, *Arthurian Legend in the Seventeenth Century* (Baltimore: Johns Hopkins Monographs in Literary History, 1932), pp. 126–41 for an account of Milton's revision of his plans; J. J. Parry, 'The Historical Arthur', *JEGP*, LVIII (1959), 365–79; Herschel Baker, *The Race of Time* (Toronto: University of Toronto Press, 1967).

11. *Works*, V, 309.

12. *The Reason of Church-government*, 2, 2 (*Works*, III, 246).

13. See *The Christian Doctrine*, I, 3 (*Works*, XIV, 73 ff.).

14. Written *c.* 1630.

15. For an account of Milton's Christology, see Barbara Kiefer Lewalski, *Milton's Brief Epic: The Genre, Meaning, and Art of 'Paradise Regained'* (Providence: Brown University Press, 1966), ch. VI, 'The Introduction and its Terms: The Problem of Christ's Nature', pp. 133–63.

16. See Barbara Lewalski, 'Time and History in *Paradise Regained*', in *The Prison and the Pinnacle: Papers to commemorate the tercentenary of 'Paradise Regained' and 'Samson Agonistes' 1671–1971*, ed. Balachandra Rajan (Toronto: University of Toronto Press: 1973). p. 51 ff. Lewalski makes the following contrast between Augustinian and Miltonic views of eternity.

17. *The Christian Doctrine*, I, 2 (*Works*, XIV, 45).

18. Ibid., I, 7 (*Works*, XV, 17–19).

19. See also, William Riley Parker, *Milton. A Biography*, 2 vols. (Oxford: Clarendon Press, 1968), I, 485.

20. John Owen, in a sermon before Commons, 19 April 1649. See Tuveson, *Millennium and Utopia*, p. 15 ff.

21. *Works*, IV, 338.

22. See William G. Madsen, *From Shadowy Types to Truth. Studies in Milton's Symbolism* (New Haven and London: Yale University Press, 1968), pp. 87 ff; 110 ff; Stanley Fish, *Surprised by Sin.*

23. Milton held mortalist opinions: see *The Christian Doctrine* I, 7 (*Works*, XV, 25), I, 13 (*Works*, XV, 223), I, 16 (*Works*, XV, 313): Parker, *Milton*, I, 496.

24. See Tuveson, *Millennium and Utopia*, p. 15 ff.

25. See especially J. G. A. Pocock, 'Time, History and Eschatology in the Thought of Thomas Hobbes', in *The Diversity of History: Essays in Honour of Herbert Butterfield*, ed. J. H. Elliott and H. G. Koenigsberger (London: Routledge and Kegan Paul, 1970), pp. 149–98. Michael Fixler, *Milton and the Kingdoms of God* (London: Faber and Faber, 1964), gives a good account of Milton's changing views on apocalyptic prophecies, from early

material hopes to the realisation in *Paradise Regained* that the kingdom of Christ comes first as a trial of faith.

26. *Millennium and Utopia.*
27. A. J. A. Waldock, '*Paradise Lost*', *and its Critics*, (Cambridge: Cambridge University Press, 1947), esp. ch. V, 'God and the Angels—and Dante', pp. 97–118.
28. *From Shadowy Types to Truth.*
29. See Ibid., p. 52; *The Christian Doctrine*, I, 6 (*Works*, XIV, 401).
30. See Barbara Kiefer Lewalski, *Milton's Brief Epic*, p. 104, and Gertrud Schiller, *Iconography of Christian Art*, trans. Janet Seligman (London: Lund Humphries, 1969), I, 145: 'At no period was the temptation a particularly prominent pictorial theme; indeed, it was strikingly rare, even among New Testament cycles.'
31. Elizabeth Marie Pope, *Paradise Regained: The Tradition and the Poem* (New York: Russell and Russell, 1962); Lewalski, *Milton's Brief Epic.* Other examinations of the structure have been less fruitful. Some examples are, A. S. P. Woodhouse, 'Theme and Pattern in *Paradise Regained*', *UTQ*, XXV (1956), 167–82; L. S. Cox, 'Food-word Imagery in *Paradise Regained*', *ELH*, XXVII (1961), 225–43; Roy Daniells, *Milton, Mannerism, and Baroque* (Toronto: University of Toronto Press, 1963), 196–208; Jackson Cope, *The Metaphoric Structure of 'Paradise Lost'* (Baltimore: The Johns Hopkins Press, 1962), ch. III, 'Time and Space as Miltonic Symbol', pp. 50–71; Laurie Zwicky, 'Kairos in *Paradise Regained*: The Divine Plan', *ELH*, XXXI (1964), 271–7; L. E. Orange, 'The Role of the Deadly Sins in Paradise Regained', *Southern Quarterly*, II (1964), 190–201; Stuart Curran, 'The Mental Pinnacle: *Paradise Regained* and the Romantic Four-Book Epic', in *Calm of Mind*, ed. Joseph Anthony Wittreich, Jr. (Cleveland: Case Western Reserve University Press, 1971), pp. 133–62; Lewalski, 'Time and History in *Paradise Regained*'.
32. Laurie Zwicky, 'Kairos in *Paradise Regained*: The Divine Plan'.
33. *Paradise Regained*, III, 440, ed. Merritt Y. Hughes, *John Milton: Complete Poems and Major Prose* (New York: Odyssey, 1957). All quotations from Milton's poems are from this edition, and are henceforth indicated in the text.
34. *The Christian Doctrine*, i, 9. Of the fallen angels Milton says: 'Their knowledge is great, but such as tends rather to aggravate than diminish their misery', *Works*, XVI, 111. For Milton's concern with time in *Christian Doctrine*, see Laurence Stapleton, 'Milton's Conception of Time in The Christian Doctrine', *Harvard Theological Review*, LVII (1964), 9–21.
35. Erwin Panofsky, *Studies in Iconology* (New York: Harper, 1962), p. 83.
36. Ibid., p. 73 ff.
37. All quotations from Shakespeare are from *The Complete Signet Classic* edition, and are indicated in the text.
38. See especially Sonnet VII: 'How soon hath time . . .' and 'On Time'. An even earlier Latin poem, *Naturam non pati senium*, contrasts an insatiable and self-devouring time (14–15) with Jupiter's providence (16).
39. For studies stressing the importance of time in *Paradise Lost*, see especially Laurence Stapleton, 'Perspectives of Time in *Paradise Lost*', *PQ*, XLV, (1966), 734–48; R. L. Colie, 'Time and Eternity: Paradox and Structure

in *Paradise Lost'*, *Journal of the Warburg and Courtauld Institutes*, XXIII (1960), 127–38.

40. See Edgar Wind, *Pagan Mysteries of the Renaissance* (Middlesex: Peregrine, 1967), p. 267. The following account derives from Wind's study.

41. Reproduced in Wind, *Pagan Mysteries*, plate 20.

42. See Wind, *Pagan Mysteries*, p. 265.

43. Ibid.

44. Ibid.

45. Ibid.

46. Ibid. See especially Albertus Magnus, *De Prudentia*, II, i–iv; Thomas Aquinas, *Summa theologica* I, ii, q. 57, art. 6, no. 4.

47. *Paradise Lost*, I, 720.

48. Pope, *Paradise Regained*, p. 57; Lewalski, *Milton's Brief Epic*, p. 193.

49. Demonic trinities were familiar during the Renaissance. See G. J. Hoogewerff, 'Vultus trifrons; emblema diabolica, imagine improba della SS. Trinita', *Rendicanti della pontificia accademia di archeologia*, XIX (1942–3). Milton's Satan-Sin-Death allegory in *Paradise Lost*, Bk II, is, significantly, a diabolic trinity. The relations of Sin, Death, and Satan to destructive time have already been indicated.

50. Vittore Carpaccio's 'The Courtesans' (Correr Museum, Venice) features a wolf with the prostitutes. *The Bestiary: A Book of Beasts*, ed. T. H. White (New York: Putnam's, 1960), p. 56: 'Wolves are known for their rapacity, and for this reason we call prostitutes wolves, because they devastate the possessions of their lovers.'

51. Macrobius, *The Saturnalia*, I 20: 'the likeness of a fawning dog indicates the issue of time to come, the object of our hopes, which are uncertain but flatter us', trans. Percival Vaughan Davies (New York: Columbia University Press, 1969), p. 139. See also *Bestiary*, p. 67: dogs indicate people who sin 'out of desire for some unknown thing.'

52. *Bestiary*, p. 7: the lion is ferocious, and is 'proud in the strength of his own nature.'

53. Trans. in D. W. Robertson, Jr., *A Preface to Chaucer* (New Jersey: Princeton University Press, 1969), p. 383–4.

54. See Pope, *Paradise Regained*, ch. V, 'The Triple Equation', pp. 51–69.

55. I, 2–4; I, 154–5; II, 133–5; IV, 178–80.

56. *Tetrachordon*, *Works*, IV, 150.

57. *The Christian Doctrine*, *Works*, XV, 361–3, 393.

58. *The Enchiridion on Faith, Hope, and Love*, trans. J. F. Shaw, ed. Henry Paolucci (Chicago: Henry Regnery, 1961), 3, 7.

59. *The Doctrine and Discipline of Divorce*, *Works*, III, 400.

60. *Confessions*, XI, 23, trans. Pusey, p. 265. All quotations from the *Confessions* are in this translation.

61. Ibid.

62. Ibid., XI, 26, p. 266.

63. *Logic*, I, 11. *Complete Works*, XI, 93.

64. See *Confessions*, X, *passim*, esp. p. 229. 'These three sorts of vices, the pleasure of the flesh, and pride, and curiosity, comprise all sins.'

65. *On Continence*, 19, trans. C. L. Cornish, in *The Nicene and Post Nicene Fathers* VI (Buffalo: The Christian-Literature Company, 1887), III, 386.

66. Ibid., 3–4, trans. Cornish, III, 380.
67. Ibid., 29, trans. Cornish, III, 392.
68. *Sermon* VII, 11, trans. in *A Library of Fathers of the Holy Catholic Church* XVI (Oxford: John Henry Parker, 1844).
69. *On The Trinity* XIV, 7, trans. Arthur West Haddan, in *The Nicene and Post Nicene Fathers* (Buffalo: The Christian Literature Company, 1887), III, 188.
70. Ibid., XIV, 8, trans. Hadden III, 189.
71. Ibid.
72. The best background study which encroaches on the Renaissance is Robertson, *A Preface to Chaucer*. See also N. J. C. Andreasen, *John Donne, Conservative Revolutionary* (New Jersey: Princeton University Press, 1967), for an application to Renaissance love poetry. For the drama see Roy Battenhouse, *Shakespearean Tragedy, Its Art and Its Christian Premises* (Bloomington: Indiana University Press, 1969).
73. Trans. J. J. Parry, *The Art of Courtly Love* (New York: Frederick Ungar, 1961), p. 28.
74. Robertson, *Preface*, p. 84.
75. *Enchiridion militis Christiani*, 33, trans, Himelick, p. 177. The martial imagery of the Christian soldier, and the stress on resistance to temptation throughout this book make an interesting parallel to *Paradise Regained*.
76. Ibid., p. 179.
77. Ibid., p. 180.
78. Ibid.
79. Ibid.
80. Ibid.
81. On *Paradise Regained* as an identity test, see esp. Lewalski, *Milton's Brief Epic*, pp. 133–63.
82. See Pope, *Paradise Regained*, ch. VII, 'The Temptation of the Tower', for interpretations centring on fear, violence, suicide, presumption, and identity. Lewalski, *Milton's Brief Epic*, pp. 309–12, sees a foreshadowing of the passion. J. M. Steadman *MP*, LIX (1961), 81–8, sees a temptation by adversity contrasting the temptations to prosperity. Dick Taylor, *UTQ*, XXIV (1955), 359–76, thinks Satan tempts Christ to take the storm as a portent.
83. *Works*, XVII, 203.
84. *Eikonoklastes*, *Works*, V, 151–3. Cf. *Christian Doctrine*, *Works*, XVII, 51.
85. *Eikonoklastes*, *Works*, V, 109–10.
86. *Works*, XVII, 209.
87. Cf. Nicholas Goran, *In quatuor Evang. Comm.*, 23. Nicholas comments on the three-fold sin, and locates pride in the irascible faculty. Cf. Milton, *Christian Doctrine*, *Works*, XVII, 209: 'The excess of anger is irascibility.'
88. *Sermon*, VII, 11, in *Library of Fathers*, XVI, 88.
89. *Sermon*, VII, 9, in *Library of Fathers*, XVI, 87.
90. *Sermon*, VII, 11, in *Library of Fathers*, XVI, 88.
91. Ibid.
92. Ibid.
93. The traditional interpretation: see Pope, *Paradise Regained*, p. 80 ff.
94. In Panofsky, *Studies in Iconology*, plate 35.

95. Ibid., p. 86. A further striking, though mediaeval, analogue is in the *Très riches heures de Jean de France*. See Robertson, *Preface*, plate 1. Christ, on the pinnacle, looks down upon a splendid castle representing worldly glory, and is tempted by the silhouetted figure of a winged, horned, and clawed devil. At the bottom of the picture are swans, a lion, and a treed monkey, which would represent lust, pride, and curiosity respectively. There is no specific indication of time, as in the tapestry, though the illumination is open to such an interpretation.

CHAPTER 6

1. See R. A. Wilmott, *Pictures of Christian Life* (London: 1841), p. 119 ff.
2. *An Essay Toward the Theory of the Ideal or Intelligible World*, 2 vols. (London: S. Manship, 1701–4), in the Preface to vol. II complains of the noise and hurry of the conditions under which the work was written.
3. Frederick J. Powicke, *A Dissertation on John Norris of Bemerton* (London: George Philip and Son, 1893), p. 32 quotes an anonymous assessment from *Chalmers Dictionary* which compares Norris favourably with Milton: 'the genius of Norris as a poet not at all inferior to that of his contemporaries; and that he displays specimens of genuine poetry, whose fire and sublimity are barely excelled by the 'Paradise Lost''.' Compare also the high opinion of A. B. Grosart in his edition of the poems: *The Poems of John Norris of Bemerton* (Blackburn, Lancs.: Fuller Worthies Library, printed for private circulation, 1871), p. 10 ff. For a list of editions, see Flora Isabel Mackinnon, *The Philosophy of John Norris*, Philosophical Monographs, vol. 1, no. 2 (Baltimore: Psychological Review Publications, 1910), p. 99 ff.
4. The main scholarly works on Norris are: John Hoyles, *The Waning of the Renaissance 1640–1740: Studies in the thought and Poetry of Henry More, John Norris and Isaac Watts* (The Hague: Martinus Nijhoff, 1971); George R. Wasserman, *A Critical Edition of the Collected Poems of John Norris of Bemerton*, Diss., Ph.D., Michigan (1957); Geoffrey Walton, *Metaphysical to Augustan: Studies in Tone and Sensibility in the 17th Century* (London: Bowes and Bowes, 1955); MacKinnon, *The Philosophy of John Norris*.
5. Letter, in *Works*, IX, 404.
6. The following account derives from the biographical sections in MacKinnon and Powiche, *supra*.
7. Wilmott, *Pictures of Christian Life*, p. 119.
8. See Powicke, *Dissertation*, from 'Phylades and Corinna', vol. III, p. 3.
9. Grosart, *Poems*; p. 116: 'A Pastoral on the Death of his sacred Majesty King Charles II'. All quotations from the poems are from this edition and are cited in the text.
10. See Powicke, *Dissertation*, p. 18, which quotes Clark, *Colleges at Oxford* (1891), p. 217.
11. Ibid.—the living was the favour of the Earl of Pembroke. For Locke's possible influence see Charlotte Johnston, 'Locke's *Examination of Malebranche* and John Norris', *JHI*, 19, 4 (1958), 551–8.

12. Cited by MacKinnon, *The Philosophy of John Norris*, pp. 12–13. 'The Charge of Schism continued. Being a Justification of the Author of Christian Blessedness for his charging the Separatists with Schism', in *Reason and Religion or the Grounds and Measures of Devotion*, p. 289. Norris's earlier essay in *Christian Blessedness, or Practical Discourses upon the Beatitudes* (1690), on the subject 'Blessed are the Peacemakers', had attacked the Separatists, and Norris continued the controversy also in *Two Treatises Concerning the Divine Light* (1692).

13. *Spiritual Counsel or the Father's Advice to his Children* (London: S. Manship, 1694), pp. 119–21.

14. Wasserman, *A Critical Edition*, p. 85, *et passim* deals with this intermediate position of Norris's style.

15. Also, the copying of Cowley's lines on Crashaw in Norris's 'Superstition' (*Poems*, 166–67) shows that Norris had read Cowley's ode and would probably know Crashaw's poems. See Wasserman's note.

16. As Hoyles points out, *The Waning of the Renaissance*, p. 124: 'he refines without extinguishing.'

17. Descartes is cited in *Poems*, 108, 'Annotations' to *The Elevation*, and line 15 of *The 148th Psalm Paraphrased* (*Poems*, 113), which, as Wasserman's note points out, is a compact summary of Norris's Cartesianism. Norris remained faithful to the ideal: see *Ideal World*, II, 167. See also MacKinnon, *The Philosophy*, p. 4.

18. See 'Plato's Two Cupid's' (*Poems*, 141), and 'Annotations' on 'The Passion of our Blessed Saviour, represented in a Pindarique Ode' (*Poems*, 46–54).

19. A combination of the lady, the bitter medicine, the initial failure of philosophy, the appeal to poetry leading to an attack on fortune and reconciliation in imprisonment reproduces the main line of argument of the *Consolation of Philosophy*.

20. There are many good accounts of Bérulle's life and works. The following biographical summary derives mainly from: Henri Brémond, *Histoire*, t, III, 'L'École Française'; Paul Cochois, *Bérulle et l'École Française* (Paris: Editions du Seuil, 1963); M. Houssaye, *M. de Bérulle et les carmélites de France, le Père de Bérulle et l'Oratoire, Le Cardinal de Bérulle et le cardinal de Richelieu*, 3 vols. (Paris: 1872–5); A. Molien, 'Bérulle', art., *D.S.* I, cols. 1539–81. An interesting biography prefaces the early edition of Bérulle's works by his disciple P. Bourgoing, *Les Oeuvres de l'emmentissime et révérendissime P. Cardinal de Bérulle* (Paris: 1644), reprinted with some emendations by Migne, *Oeuvres complètes de Bérulle* (Paris: 1866). The Migne edition is used in the following account, and references are cited in the text.

21. André Duval, *La Vie Admirable de Soeur Marie de l'Incarnation, Religieuse conuerse en l'Ordre de Nostre Dame du Mont Carmel, et fondatrice d'iceluy en Fràce, appellée au monde la DAMOISELLE ACARIE*, (Paris: 1621), I, chap. VI, fol. 133 ff.; chap. II, fol. 444 ff.; chap. XIII, fol. 672.

22. *Histoire*, III, 51.

23. See Molien, 'Bérulle', col. 1544: 'L'atmosphère spirituelle que respirait Bérulle semble donc avoir été saturée d'influences venues des Pays-bas.'

24. Bourgoing played down the Dionysian elements in Bérulle because of the quietist scare (Levi, *French Moralists*, p. 137), but Gibieuf (1591–1650)

energetically renews the emphasis, quoting Dionysius everywhere: *De la liberté de Dieu et des créatures* (1630). See Cochois, *Bérulle*, p. 153: 'pas une page . . . qui ne cite le Pseudo-Denys.' Bérulle's most important works are: *Bref discours de l'abnégation interieure* (1597); *Élévation à Jésus sur les principaux états et mystères* (1611–13); *Discours de l'état et des grandeurs de Jésus par l'union ineffable de la divinité avec l'humanité, et de la dépendance et servitude qui lui due et à sa très sainte Mère ensuite de cet état admirable* (1623); *Élévation à Jésus-Christ Notre-Seigneur sur la conduite de son esprit et de sa grâce vers sainte Madeleine* (1625); *Seconde partie des discours de l'Etat et des Grandeurs de Jésus, dans laquelle commence la vie de Jésus* (1629).

25. On this see Brémond, *Histoire*, III, 24 ff., 79 ff.; Molien, 'Bérulle', col. 1549.

26. See Bourgoing, *Oeuvres*, Preface, *passim*; cf. also Brémond, III, 153; Cochois, *Bérulle*, p. 23, describing a mystical insight which visited Bérulle in 1607, writes: 'On peut voir en cette grâce dont les conséquences ont été aussi importantes pour l'histoire du catholicisme français que l'a été pour notre philosophie la nuit d'illumination de Descartes (J. Dagens), la naissance de l'Ecole française.'

27. The main account of this relationship is by Etienne Gilson, *La Liberté Chez Descartes et la Théologie* (Paris: Libraire Félix Alcan, 1913). Brémond, *Histoire* (III, 41) disagrees that as much influence passed between the two men as Gilson believes, though he agrees there was some. The following account derives from Gilson, ch. V, 'La doctrine Cartesienne de la liberté divine et la théologie de l'Oratoire', pp. 157–210. See also Cochois, *Bérulle*, p. 102, and L. J. Beck, *The Metaphysics of Descartes. A Study of the Meditations* (Oxford: Clarendon Press, 1965), pp. 4–5 and 212, which concurs with Gilson's earlier suggestions.

28. See Gilson, *La Liberté*, p. 163: 'L'intimité qui exista entre de Bérulle et Descartes fut donc assez profonde pour que de l'un à l'autre une influence durable ait pu s'exercer.'

29. See *Meditations*, 4, ed. Wollaston, p. 147.

30. Ibid., pp. 136–7.

31. For a full account of this development, see Gilson, *La Liberté*, p. 178 ff.

32. See Molien, 'Bérulle', col. 1542, for Bérulle and the Franciscan tradition, extending through St Bernard.

33. See Pierre Blanchard, *L'Attention à Dieu Selon Malebranche* (Paris: Desclée De Brouwer, 1956), ch. IV, 'Malebranche Contemplatif Bérullien. L'Attention à Jésus-Christ', p. 201 ff.; Maurice Blondel, 'L'Anti-Cartesianisme de Malebranche', *Revue de Métaphysique et de Morale* (1916), pp. 1–26; Germain Breton, 'Les Origines de la philosophie de Malebranche', *Bulletin de littérature écclesiastique*, 4ᵉ serie, t. IV (1912), pp. 214–30. There are useful summaries of Malebranche's thought in English, but nothing on his spirituality. See R. W. Church, *A Study in the Philosophy of Malebranche* (London: 1931; reissued New York and London: Kennikat Press, 1970); Beatrice K. Rome, *The Philosophy of Malebranche. A Study of his Integration of Faith, Reason and Experimental Observation* (Chicago: Henry Regnery Co., 1963). Contains a useful bibliography.

34. *Dialogues on Metaphysics and on Religion*, trans. Morris Ginsberg, with a preface by G. Dawes Hicks (London: George Allen and Unwin, 1923),

p. 195. Further references are cited in the text.

35. Ibid., p. 69 ff.

36. Yet Malebranche does not go so far as Descartes in arguing God's liberty to arbitrate truth: see *Dialogues*, p. 223.

37. See especially Armand Cuvillier, *Essai sur la Mystique de Malebranche* (Paris: Librairie Philosophique, J. Vrin, 1954), pp. 32, 97, *et passim*.

38. Blanchard, *L'Attention à Dieu*, gives a discriminating account of the differences as well as the similarities, drawing attention to the reserve and lucidity of Malebranche as distinct from the 'imprécision regrettable' (p. 212) of Bérulle.

39. See *Meditation* 2, trans. Wollaston, p. 110 ff.; *Discourse* 4, trans. Wollaston, p. 60 ff.

40. *Dialogues*, p. 102.

41. The following summary derives mainly from *Dialogues on Metaphysics and on Religion*, a work which is a compact version of Malebranche's main ideas. The preface is also a useful introduction to Malebranche's thought.

42. See *Reason and Religion, or, the Grounds and Measures of Devotion* (1689, 2nd ed., 1693), pp. 185–6, on the idea that 'we see and know all things in *God*.' Norris says he had come upon this notion early, 'by the *Natural Parturiency* of my own mind', before he read other authors who confirmed him in it, e.g. Plotinus, Proclus, Ficino, Augustine, DuHamel, Aquinas, and Malebranche. The odd man in this predictable enough list is DuHamel, who, interestingly, was a Cartesian and also an Oratorian. This confirms the orientation of Norris towards Oratorian spirituality. Had he read DuHamel early in his career?

43. P. 156 ff. Subsequent references are cited in the text.

CHAPTER 7

1. See Richard A. Watson, *The Downfall of Cartesianism 1673–1712: A Study of Epistemological Issues in Late 17th Century Cartesianism* (The Hague: Martinus Nijhoff, 1966), p. 2 ff. *et passim*, for an account of the problems caused to Cartesian theory by the doctrines of substances and likeness principles.

2. Lady Masham to le Clerc, 12 Jan. 1705–6, quoted in H. R. Fox Bourne, *The Life of John Locke*, 2 vols. (London: Henry S. King and Co., 1876), I, 61–2: 'The first books, as Mr. Locke himself has told me, which gave him a relish of philosophical things, were those of Descartes.'

3. A support, Locke argues, 'cannot be nothing', First letter to Stillingfleet, *The Works of John Locke, A New Edition*, 10 vols. (London: Thomas Tegg, 1823), V, 29. For a discussion of substances and our inability to know them directly, see *An Essay Concerning Human Understanding*, II, 23, 'Of our Complex Ideas of Substances', ed. Alexander Campbell Fraser, 2 vols. (New York: Dover Publications, 1959), I, p. 390 ff., especially pp. 395, 405, 414. Hereafter cited as *Essay*, and with references to this edition given in the text.

4. *First Letter to Stillingfleet, Works,* IV, 53–6.
5. Many early attacks on the *Essay* sprang from this point. Since we don't know either the material or the spiritual substances, they may be alike. See *Essay,* IV, 3, 1, ff.
6. *De la recherche de la Vérité* (1674–5), 2, 1, 5.
7. See Ernest Lee Tuveson, *The Imagination as a Means of Grace: Locke and the Aesthetics of Romanticism* (Berkeley and Los Angeles: University of California Press, 1960), p. 21, *et passim.*
8. *Remarks upon some of Mr. Norris's Books, Wherein he asserts P. Malebranche's Opinion of our seeing all Things in God, Works,* X, 258. Hereafter referred to in the text as *Remarks.*
9. Ed. Gilbert D. McEwen (Los Angeles: The Augustan Reprint Society, no. 93, 1961), hereafter referred to in the text as *Reflections.*
10. *Works,* IX, 211 ff. Hereafter referred to in the text as *Examination.*

Index

239